DERAIL: WHY TRAINS CRASH

DERAIL: WHY TRAINS CRASH

NICHOLAS FAITH

First published in 2000 by Channel 4 Books
an imprint of Macmillan Publishers Ltd
25 Eccleston Place, London SW1W 9NF
Basingstoke and Oxford

www.macmillan.com

Associated companies throughout the world

ISBN 0 7522 7165 2

Text © Nicholas Faith, 2000

The right of Nicholas Faith to be identified as the author of this work has been
asserted by him in accordance with the Copyright, Designs and Patents Act 1988.

1 3 5 7 9 8 6 4 2

A CIP catalogue record for this book is available from the British Library.

Typeset by SX Composing DTP, Rayleigh, Essex
Printed and bound in Great Britain by Mackays of Chatham plc, Chatham, Kent
Plate section design by Anita Ruddell

darlow*smithson*

FILM & TELEVISION PRODUCTION

This book accompanies the television series 'Why Trains Crash'
made by Darlow Smithson for Channel 4.
Executive producer: David Darlow
Series Producer: Vyv Simson

The publisher has made every effort to ensure accuracy in the reporting of the facts
contained in this book.

Contents

Acknowledgements

Some of the people who helped me with this book can only be described as 'the usual suspects', who have performed the same invaluable role in my books on disasters in the air, on the seas and on the roads. Top of my Pops remain Katy Carrington of Channel 4 Books, who has patiently organized eight books for me; Daphne Slater, who has transcribed the interviews on which much of the books are based with awesome speed and accuracy; and Hazel Orme, copy-editor equally *extraordinaire*. At Darlow Smithson, the series producer, Vyv Simson, and his team – Niall McCormick, Deborah Coleman, Noddy Sahota, Christine Garabedian, Anna Whelpdale, Aaron Paul and Andy Webb were far more patient and helpful than I had any right to expect. And for this book Sam Arnold-Forster and Jerry Kuehl and Adele Kosviner provided me with unstinting hospitality which gave me the time and lack of disruption required for any book. Publishing details of books cited in the text are to be found in the Select Bibliography (page xxx).

Abbreviations and Glossary

ASW: Automatic Warning System
ATC: Automatic Train Control
ATP: Automatic Train Protection
Catenary: overhead structure feeding electric current to locomotives
CWR: Continuously Welded Rail
DMU: Diesel Multiple Unit
Drawbridge: lifting bridge hinged at one end
EMU: Electric Multiple Unit
Engineer: American word for engine driver
Fireboy: American Word for locomotive fireman
FRA: Federal Railway Administration
Ganger: overseer
Grade crossing: American term for level crossing
HST: High Speed Train
ICE: Inter City Express
KSI: Killed or Seriously Injured
MARC: Maryland Commuter Railroad
NTSB: National Transportation Safety Board
OHSA: Occupational Health and Safety Act
Pacific: type of locomotive
Shinkansen: Japanese high-speed railway
SPAD: Signal Passed At Danger
TGV: Train à Grande Vitesse
TSB: Transportation Safety Board (Canada)
TTC: Transport Technology Centre (Colorado)

Interviewees

Sheriff Joe Arpaio, investigator at Kingman crash
Gerald Dickens, descendant of Charles Dickens
Rick Downs, NTSB specialist in crashworthiness
Alan Earnshaw, railway historian
Russell Gober, NTSB investigator
Joacsim Gries, eyewitness to Eschede crash
Neal Halford, passenger in Amtrak sabotage crash
Stanley Hall, railway historian and writer
Ralph Harrington, lecturer on railway history
Markus Hecht, Professor of Engineering, Technical University, Berlin
Michael Jones-Lee, economist
Lynne Kirby, expert on trains and films
Joe Kolodrubsky, investigator with Transportation Safety Board of
    Canada
John Kopke, safety expert for MARC trains
Earren Kearns, eyewitness to Silver Spring accident
Arne Kühnel, chief designer, ADBM
Bob Lauby, NTSB investigator
George McDonald, international director of safety and health for the
    railroads, airlines and transit division, Transport Union
Bruce McGladry, NTSB investigator
Rev. John W. McKegney, priest at Armagh
John Malcolm, head of Greenock CID
Lawrence W. (Larry) Mann, lawyer specializing in US railroad legislation
Michael J. (Mike) Martino, NTSB crash investigator
Bill Misura, director of transportation, Ringling Bros Circus
Martin More-Ede, managing director, Circadian Technologies,

Cambridge, Massachusetts
Jim Murray, (Greenock) Railtrack spokesman
Masaki Ogata, head of safety, Japan Railways East, Tokyo
Norman Pattenden, rail historian, long-term BR official
Jean Poole, NTSB highway accident investigator
Erich Preuß, railway investigator
Peter Rayner, former BR manager
Robert Ray, driver on New York subway
John Reynolds, Federal Railway Administration (Hummelstown)
John Reynolds, executive, Canadian National Railroad (Hinton)
Dr Stephen Richards, University of Tennessee, expert on grade (level)
    crossings
Roger Ripley, FBI investigator, Kingman
Dirk Sarnes, PR for Ustra trains
Ian Scott, coroner at Thirsk
Kris Severson, scientist, Volpe Institute
Dr Ing. Jürgen Siegmann, head of railway studies at the Technical
    University, Berlin
Daniel H. (Dan) Stone, metallurgist at TTC
David Tyrell, scientist, Volpe Institute
Raf Vittone, ambulance driver, Benjamin Wallace circus
John Waugh, FBI investigator, Kingman
Roger Weatherup, local historian at Armagh
Bill Withuhn, railway historian, Washington DC

1
Death on the Rails

Accidents do not happen by accident.
Sir Herbert Walker, of the Southern Railway, after the Sevenoaks
disaster in 1927.

Derail: Why Trains Crash is an attempt to make sense of chaos, to describe and analyse important accidents over the past hundred and fifty years, to put the natural public concern about rail safety into its proper context and, above all, to answer some crucial questions: are railways as safe as they ought to be? What lessons have been learnt from past disasters? What has been done – and what steps remain to be taken – to increase rail safety? And can, or indeed should, we afford even more safety measures? Sadly, in Britain anyway, all these questions are especially relevant after the publicity engendered by recent disasters, especially the two most serious, which both took place on the approaches to Paddington, at Southall in 1997 and Ladbroke Grove in 1999.

Yet railways have always been exceptionally safe. Because this book is concerned exclusively with rail disasters, it may unwittingly give the impression that rail travel has been associated historically with tragedy. Far from it. Today, on average, only one passenger dies for every three billion miles travelled – 120,000 times round the world. This is nothing new: in Britain in 1861, an exceptionally bad year for accidents, an average of 3.5 million journeys were undertaken for every fatality. Attempts to show that travel by air is safer than by train are invidious because they compare not the number of passenger journeys but the distances travelled. By this misguided comparison a single transatlantic return journey counts the same as three months of commuting thirty miles daily to work. A more valid comparison shows that travel by bus is six times more dangerous than by train.

It does not help that rail accidents come in waves: a series of years in which there are few, if any, fatalities is succeeded by a group of troubles. This happened in the mid-1870s, both in Britain and the United States, in the second half of 1928, when there were five major accidents, and again in the six years after the end of the Second World War – though the later bunching could be attributed largely to wartime neglect.

Train travel has always been considered safer than the alternatives. In 1847 a train carrying the Queen of Belgium was involved in a crash. Offered the chance of continuing her journey by coach, the Queen declined. She was wise, observed Charles Francis Adams, since the chance of being involved in a train crash was a mere sixtieth of the likelihood of a mishap in a stage coach. Adams, writing in 1879, concluded, 'Viewing at once the speed, the certainty, and the safety with which the intricate monument of modern life is carried on, there is no more creditable monument to human care, human skill and human foresight than the statistics of railroad accidents . . . It is not, after all, the dangers but the safety of the modern railroad which should excite our special wonder.' He was echoing the words of John Bright, the British statesman: 'The safest place in which a man could put himself was inside a first-class railroad carriage of a train in full motion.' At the time first-class carriages were much more substantially built, with proper padding, but third-class passengers travelled in open wooden trucks. Those in the ill-fated train that crashed at Sonning on Christmas Eve 1841 (page 19) were in coaches without spring buffers. They were also open-sided, exposing the wretched occupants to the winter weather for the nine and a half hours it took for the train to travel from London to Bristol. 'Years ago,' Adams continued, 'it was officially announced in France that people were less safe in their own houses than while travelling on the railroads'; and in one year more people in Britain – ten – were killed by cricket balls than the eight passengers killed in train accidents.

Any author writing on this subject is confronted by a major paradox at the outset: the railway is by far the safest form of transport yet passengers assume that, unlike any other form of transport, it is *perfectly* safe. Railway travel seems regimented, organized and thus secure – to say that someone has gone 'off the rails' suggests that if we are 'on the rails' we are safe. For it's the solidity of the train, the fact that it runs on rails, the absence of seat belts, as worn on even the shortest journey in a car, and of the safety warnings that preface any flight that makes rail travel so comforting. The feeling is summed up in the gag '"The bad news," announced the conductor, "is that both engines have failed. The good news is that this is a train not a Boeing 737."'

Perhaps we expect too much: total safety, not only on but even before we get on to a train. Some people – especially lone women and the elderly – worry about dark stations and empty carriages, which is perfectly reasonable, but most people expect to be *totally* secure as soon as they step inside the railway system. But it is an environment in which we surrender control of our actions and thus increase the fascination. In the words of Ralph Harrington, from his paper 'The Railway Accident', even though other types of accident, industrial and natural, have claimed more lives,

It was the violence, destruction, terror and slaughter of the railway accident which dominated the headlines, commanded public attention and pervaded the contemporary imagination . . . It denied its victims any chance of controlling their own fate; it crystallized in a single traumatic event the helplessness of human beings in the hands of the technologies which they had created, but seemed unable to control; it was a highly public event which erupted directly into the rhythms and routines of daily life; it was no respecter of class or status; it was arbitrary, sudden, inhuman, and violent.

The sense of powerlessness experienced by railway passengers was a new phenomenon. Nineteenth-century travellers had to get used to putting their lives in the hands of the locomotive crew, of the signaller, of the railway professionals, and that took some adjusting to. You find this mentioned in many press reports of railway accidents, the feeling that you get in a train, all you can do is sit, you're completely powerless, you've no control over your motion, you've no control over when and how you will come to a stop and that feeling that you are powerless reinforces this idea that it has to be so safe that that anxiety can be banished.

Travellers expect trains not only to be safe but also on time – perhaps a subliminal revenge: the railway imposed 'railway time' on a hotch-potch of local times. 'The expectation of timekeeping on railways,' observes the rail historian Norman Pattenden, 'is very different with the customer from perhaps other forms of transport. How late is your bus in the morning? How late is your aircraft arriving at Heathrow? There appears to be a different ethos on timekeeping within the railway industry that doesn't exist elsewhere.

Perhaps in that respect people may be hypercritical.' Expectations become ever higher. 'As the pace of life has increased in recent years people find that time is valuable to them and that leads to pressure on railway staff to run trains to time. Contrary to what perhaps a lot of people think, there is a strong timekeeping ethos within railway staff because they don't like to be driving a late train, to be a guard on a late train, and we all know in the London commuter environment that tempers fray when trains are late or delayed, so the pressure is there and it's increased in recent years,' although, he adds, 'It's been happening for a long time.' In such an environment it is difficult for the driver, or anyone else, to remember the airline adage that it is 'better to be late in this world than early in the next'.

So on the railways we get annoyed at what in any other environment would be seen as minor irritations – overcrowding, dirt and lateness – and take out our frustration on what Alan Bennett so memorably described as 'a servant of the railway company'. As Charles Francis Adams pointed out, 'A railroad employee implicated in the occurrence of an accident lives under a stigma. And yet, from the tenor of public comment it might fairly be supposed that these officials are in the custom of plotting to bring disasters about, and take a fiendish delight in them.' The comment is as pertinent today as it was when it was made in 1879. Any major rail accident attracts an inordinate amount of publicity – partly because it is such a rare event. In Britain it is immediately followed by demands for expensive remedial measures as well as a frantic search for a scapegoat.

The first problem with the public's attitude to accidents, as Peter Semmens has pointed out, 'lies in the way we subconsciously set different standards for involuntary risks (travelling by public transport) and voluntary risks (our own skill in avoiding getting involved in road accidents)'. In a passage about level crossings that could apply to most safety situations railway historian Stanley Hall asks:

> Why should we demand a much higher standard of safety at a place
> where rail crosses road than we do at a place where road crosses
> road? There are many busy, dangerous crossroads which do not even
> have traffic lights, and even the busiest, most dangerous crossroads
> do not have barriers with a man to operate them [as in older types of
> level crossing] nor even half-barriers [as in the more modern
> crossings], nor have residents ever demanded that they be so
> equipped. So we ought not to apply double standards.

Of course, railways should be safer than any other form of transport. As Geoffrey Kitchenside writes, 'The very nature of trains – with flanged wheels running on rails – should ensure that they are guided in the right direction and do not veer into each other's path. Signals prevent crashes in all but the smallest percentage of cases, and the whole elaborate system is closely regulated. So they ought to be, and are, safer. Yet, absurdly we insist that they should be totally safe, free from any hazard whatsoever.'

It is because of this assumption of safety that the public is deeply shocked when, as is inevitable, there is a major rail disaster. On 8 August 1996 a driver passed a danger signal at Watford Junction and ran into an empty train, killing one passenger and injuring sixty-nine more. It was the first fatal crash on Britain's overcrowded rail system since one at Cowden in East Sussex, nearly two years earlier, in which two passengers had been killed. Both accidents – which in terms of fatalities had been far less serious than those that occur every weekend on Britain's roads – occasioned much breast-beating about rail safety and complaints about the allegedly increasing risks on Britain's railways.

Trains, locomotives, carriages, freight wagons, the tracks they run on, the signals that control them are all parts of an immensely complicated system so such tragedies result from many causes: brakes fail, signals are disregarded, drivers are inattentive, tired – or even drunk. On level crossings car drivers grow impatient at waiting for the train or their vehicles are simply too slow to leave the crossing. As Major Pringle, one of Britain's then small band of rail inspectors, observed in his report on an accident at Charfield near Bristol in 1928, when fifteen people were killed in a crash involving gas-lit wooden stock that burst into flames:

> Ten seconds later there would have been no obstruction. If the
> driver of the previous goods had told Button [the signalman] he
> needed water, the trains involved would have been cleared through.
> The existence of the bridge, the simultaneous movement of two
> trains in the opposite direction, the misty atmosphere and the early
> morning darkness combined to produce almost the worst conditions
> in which a collision at high speed would occur and rendered
> deplorable results inevitable.

In the middle of the nineteenth century the *Saturday Review* went further when it characterized railway operation as a sequence of close shaves with catastrophe: trains 'fly through junctions where the nodding pointsman has wakened with a start to turn the switches, and pass a siding where an ill-coupled train of coal wagons has lumbered off the line but a second before'.

Because of the multiplicity of factors that may be and often are involved, many, if not most, crashes can be classified in two or more ways. Almost every accident has multiple causations, is multi-faceted and I have picked out what seems to me the most significant.

It was L.T.C. Rolt who got to the heart of the matter when he wrote of the 'permanent fascination with train crashes, the contrast between trivial error and terrible consequence in which the drama of the railway accident lies. Is it not the essential stuff of all great tragedy?' Charles Francis Adams was making much the same point when he concluded that 'When a multitude of persons, travelling as almost every man now daily travels himself, meet death in such sudden and such awful shape, the event strikes the imagination . . . Even in the forms of sudden death on the rail, nature seems to take a grim delight in an infinitude of surprises.' He did not find it unnatural 'that people should think more of the few who are killed, of whom they hear so much, than of the myriads who are carried in safety and of whom they hear nothing.'

'Myriads' is a key word because rail travel is so much a part of everyday life, whether for business or pleasure. As the *Saturday Review* recorded after the horrific crash at Abergele in 1868, the impression on the public mind was profound, because of 'its nearness to us all', for 'we are all railway travellers, these trains and collisions, these stations and engines, and all the rest of its structure, are not only household words, but a part of our life'. In other words, in the midst of life, there is rarely death. As Lynne Kirby, an American expert on trains and films, points out, 'One reason that train wrecks continue to be so fascinating is that even if you forget about them, when they happen they're right here on earth in front of us, they're not far away, they're usually close to some town, they're easily covered by news, by cameras, and the train is still such a huge mechanical beast it's hard to ignore. It's still capable of huge amounts of destruction. Much as you're lulled to sleep when you're riding a train then shocked awake if there's an accident or an abrupt stop, I think Americans in general are shocked awake every time there's a train wreck in their midst.'

The almost voyeuristic element in our fascination is greatly increased when distinguished people are involved, for on the railways death is democratic. Typically, when Ascanio Schneider, normally the most dead-pan of chroniclers, wrote in *Railway Accidents of Great Britain and Europe* of an accident in 1924 at Bellinzona in Switzerland, he found it perfectly natural to note the presence on the express of the Italian ambassador to Denmark and a retired German cabinet minister. The fascination continues: the publicity attracted by the Southall collision in 1997 was boosted by the presence on the train of numerous journalists returning from a major political event in Cardiff. And even the puritanical Charles Francis Adams noted that the train involved in the Abergele crash was 'full of the wealthiest and classiest people'. The possessions recovered included 'diamonds of great size and singular brilliancy; rubies, opals, emeralds . . . of these the diamonds alone had successfully resisted the intense heat of the flame; the settings were nearly all destroyed.' Perhaps it was to be expected that, 'Among the thirty-three victims of the disaster the body of no single one retained any traces of individuality . . . The body of one passenger, Lord Farnham, was identified by the crest on his watch.'

This morbid interest is reflected in dozens of descriptions of the aftermath of rail crashes. To take one example, which is typical, yet surprising given that it took place in Switzerland, 'At the scene of the crash,' wrote one journalist, 'there was such a throng that one could scarcely get through the mass of humanity: on the meadows before the scene of the accident a whole collection of innumerable vehicles of all kinds had assembled. Numerous photographers take shots of the scene: already pictures of the scene of the disaster are sold here; the newspapers find rapid sales, and are read by groups in the streets, since people are eager to obtain complete lists of the dead and injured.' This is how the profoundly respectable *Schweizerisches Protestantenblatt* described the reaction of the stolid burghers of Basle to the collapse of a rail bridge in June 1891, which killed seventy-one of their fellow-citizens. On the road between Basle and the scene of the crash 'where the spectators and nosy-parkers make pilgrimages to and fro in whole crowds, and cabs, brakes, omnibuses, speed back and forth, travels many a silent vehicle, which is laden with coffins'. The ghoulish interest aroused by major rail crashes is clearly neither new nor whipped up by the media.

The press has always exploited public fascination with accidents and been routinely vilified for merely responding to public demand. 'There's no doubt,' writes Ralph Harrington, 'that railway accidents have always been over-represented in terms of the coverage they've received in the press, the amount of public concern that's been focused upon them.' The spotlight shone from the beginning.

'Victorian Britain was an industrial society, accidents were by no means unknown,' says Harrington. 'There were accidents in factories, accidents in coal mines and, of course, there were street accidents and various other "civil" accidents, the accidents of everyday life, but railway accidents were set apart because . . . they were not happening like a colliery accident in a hidden realm underground in which only colliers were involved, they were happening in the public sphere, affecting everyone who travelled by train. Look at where these accidents happened, in railway stations, on railway lines, in towns. They were highly visible, highly dramatic, large-scale, outside the disasters of war. Domestically, the biggest catastrophe you were likely to see was a railway accident in terms of destruction, in terms of injury, in terms of loss of life.'

Inevitably, as Harrington says, 'The press in Victorian Britain was like the press today: they liked a good story, they liked salacious details, and railway accidents were reported in great detail. Details of injuries were given, details of the dead, vignettes were recounted of people being rescued, of people uttering their last words, of children and women crying in pain. There's no doubt that the Victorian public were subjected in a sense to another form of melodrama in press coverage of accidents, and this again had an impact on the way people perceived the railway, its significance as a realm in which a new form of danger, an industrial danger, was brought into everyday lives.' It was also, like the press, democratic. As Harrington says, 'There was a new mass press commenting on the disasters that were happening on a large scale in a new mass form of transit. There was a convergence of cultural phenomena.'

But the fascination was not reflected only in the press. 'Strange as it may seem to us today, with our perception of safety on the railway,' says Norman Pattenden, 'after a derailment at Salisbury in 1906 a group of local photographers got together to produce postcards of the scene of the wreck. And Salisbury wasn't unique, I have seen other postcards produced of other crashes. To us today it just seems absolutely incredible that this was so but that was the way of things in 1906.' Salisbury also produced some appalling doggerel verse, and the ghoulish interest extended even to showbusiness in the deliberate staging of crashes. The vogue started unpromisingly in 1896 when W. G. Crush, the 'general passenger agent' of the Missouri, Kansas and Texas Railroad Co. set up a crash watched by 30,000 spectators assembled in a one-day tented town inevitably named Crush City. Although both engineers managed to jump off their locomotive in time (one even bowed to the crowd) two people were killed when the trains exploded.

But the tragedy did not daunt the king of the staged train crash, 'Head On' Joe Connolly, who wrecked 146 trains in his fifteen-year career, filling carriages with barrels of gasoline to create a fireball. He did not cause a single death among the crowds – up to 102,000 in one case – assembled to watch the fun. 'Trains crashing together was very much a spectator sport,' says Lynne Kirby, 'like a football match, and they would take place in these wide open spaces, large enough to get a good running start for the locomotives.'

'It was like a demolition derby,' says Bill Withuhn, an American railway historian. 'People were fascinated by these staged wrecks, and Scott Joplin's first popular hit was called "The Great Collision Crush" and was about these staged wrecks. It went on for several years until someone was killed by a piece of flying shrapnel, which put an end to it.' But not entirely: in 1931, twenty years after Head On Joe had retired, a final crash was arranged by the management of the Rutland, Toluca and Northern, a short line in Illinois that was about to go bankrupt. The railroad charged 25 cents a ticket to watch the collision, and paid back at least some of its creditors.'

The spectacles mounted by Connolly and his imitators proved natural fodder for a new art form: the cinema. Much of the drama, real and artificial, says Lynne Kirby 'was captured on film in the early cinema and then fed back to a paying public for the movies . . . Thomas Edison shot train wrecks not only as subjects in and of themselves as films, he also used some of that same head on locomotive crash footage in story-telling films. For example, in a film made in 1904, which is about a bank robbery where the robbers escape on a train and there's a crash, he uses exactly the same footage that was shot of a real crash staged at a county fair in 1904'.

In the following year, says Bill Withuhn, came Hales Tours, which was 'a marriage of the railroad and the cinema. You had train carriages in which people projected films of trains rushing headlong through space, the camera mounted on the front of a train, re-creating the sort of thrill rides of the roller-coaster and the amusement park, but simulating a real train such that people would rock the cars and, there would be whistle-blowing. The threat of a wreck was imminent in the experience of Hales Tours.'

Since then the train crash has formed the centrepiece of dozens of films, including some classics. Crashes were used for comic effect, as in *The Marx Brothers Go West,* which culminates in the brothers' systematic demolition of a train and, supremely, by Buster Keaton in the greatest of all silent comedies, *The General.* Of sound films, perhaps the most telling and appropriate of all crashes is that in *The Bridge over the River Kwai.* Even when trains are central to the action they, and railway stations, may provide atmosphere for romance (*North by North West* and, of course, *Brief Encounter*) or terror (*The Lady Vanishes* and *Strangers on a Train*).

But railway accidents do not breed only gawping hordes and unforgettable cinematic moments: they also bring progress, albeit in terms of what engineers call 'tombstone technology'. L.T.C. Rolt put it in a nutshell when he wrote, 'The railway disaster may represent the engineer's failure but never his defeat; always he has resolutely counter-attacked. From the terrible lessons learnt in the flaming wreck or the heap of shattered, telescoped coaches have come all those safety devices which combine to make the modern railway one of the most complex but at the same time most successful organizations which man has ever evolved.'

'The development of safety on the railways', says Stanley Hall, 'has been in learning the lessons of accidents and trying to work out some way of preventing them happening again, given the existing technology, given the money available, the need to do something and the justification for the expenditure, and given the effect that that might have on the ability to work trains at all.'

So, observes Charles Francis Adams, 'in the case of railroad disasters . . . the victims . . . do not lose their lives without great and immediate compensating benefits to mankind. After each new "horror", as it is called, the whole world travels with an appreciable increase of safety . . . The causes which led to the disaster are anxiously investigated by ingenious men, new appliances are invented, new precautions are imposed, a greater and more watchful care is inculcated.' His words, written in 1879, are as good a description as I can find of what this book is about.

2
In the Beginning

When we consider operational methods in the early days of railways
the remarkable thing is that there were not more serious accidents.

L.T.C. Rolt

Passenger rail travel began with an accident, and the person killed was no
ordinary man. He was William Huskisson, the most liberal member of the
Tory cabinet, who died on 15 September 1830 during the opening cere-
monies for the Liverpool–Manchester Railway. Huskisson was notoriously
clumsy, but that did not lessen the shock experienced by the enormous
crowd headed by the then Prime Minister, the Duke of Wellington.
Inevitably Huskisson's death scarred the celebrations. *The Times*'s corre-
spondent gives an excellent feel of the occasion: 'I had intended to give you
some faint description of this astounding work of art, of the crowds which
lined almost every inch of the road, of the flags and banners, and booths and
scaffoldings, and gorgeous tents, which have enlivened even the dullest
parts of our journey.' But then came the fatal accident, which happened,
ironically, just as Huskisson was going to shake hands with his political
enemy, the Duke of Wellington.

George Stephenson's locomotive, the *Rocket*, was on its way to be
refreshed at 'the watering place' so silently 'that it was almost upon the
group before they observed it'. Huskisson was unaware of its presence.
Worse, because he, like everyone else present on that momentous day, did
not realize that trains stayed on their tracks, he did not hug the side of the
carriage standing on the other track, which would have provided a safe
refuge. Instead, he hesitated: there was an embankment, 'an excavation of
some fourteen or fifteen feet' to one side, and he tumbled directly into the
path of *Rocket*.

George Stephenson himself drove the dying man on a spare engine to hospital in Manchester, covering the seventeen miles in a mere twenty-five minutes at the unthinkable speed of 40mph. But as *The Times*'s reporter observed, when the carriage passed, 'Mr Huskisson was laid at the bottom of it, pale and ghostly as death, and his wife was hanging over him in an agony of tears.' When he reached hospital Huskisson was given a massive dose of laudanum. He asked how long he had to live, and he was told six hours. Then this amazing man made his will, 'not forgetting to insert a dot over the i in his name and to insert another between the W and the H'.

His death introduced the theme of the inevitability of death when travelling by rail that recurred in much of what was written about the early railways. As the future Lord Chancellor, Lord Brougham, wrote in a letter, 'Poor Huskisson has been killed by a steam carriage. The folly of 700 people going fifteen miles an hour, in six carriages on a narrow road, exceeds belief. But they have paid a dear price.' The theme of the inevitability of crashes was taken up by the poet Thomas Love Peacock in 'Gryll Grange': when two 'long trains of strange machines on wheels' crash

> One is rolled
> Down a steep bank; one through a broken bridge
> Is dashed into a flood. Dead, dying, wounded,
> Are there as in a battlefield. Are these
> Your modern triumphs? Jove preserve me from them.

Not surprisingly, given the unprecedented nature of the 'railway experience', the speed, the reliance on mechanical rather than animal power, the idea of danger was always present in the minds of the earliest railway passengers. In his book *The Industrialization of Time and Space in the 19th Century*, Wolfgang Schivelbusch quotes a German author writing in 1845: there was a 'certain dampening of the spirits that never quite goes away despite all the pleasant aspects of train journeys', a sensation explained by the 'close possibility of an accident, and the inability to exercise any influence on the running of the cars'.

The anxiety unleashed by the possibility of an accident was accentuated by the fundamental difference between the nature of the rail accident and that of any previous experience. As Schivelbusch wrote,

> The pre-industrial era did not know any technological accidents,
> pre-industrial catastrophes were natural events, natural accidents.

They attacked the objects they destroyed from the outside, as storms, floods, thunderbolts and hailstones. After the Industrial Revolution destruction by technological accident came from the inside. The technical apparatuses destroyed themselves by means of their own power,

and as the power, and the speed, increased so did the effects of an accident. And in railway accidents there was no prior warning. In the words of nineteenth-century surgeon Eric Erichsen, 'In most ordinary accidents, as in a carriage accident from a runaway horse, the sufferer has a few minutes to prepare, is enabled to collect his energies in order to make an effort to save himself, and does not feel the utter hopelessness of his condition in his struggle for life and safety.' Hopelessness combined with helplessness: a victim had no control over events of which he was merely a hapless spectator. Such feelings are a feature of any type of mechanically induced accident, whether in the air or on the road, but they were felt first, and thus most strongly, by victims of the first accidents involving the first form of mechanically propelled travel: the railways.

Nevertheless, and surprisingly to observers of other forms of travel, accidents did not deter passengers: early rail users lived in an age resigned to levels of disaster unthinkable today, and nowhere more so than when travelling. In his novel *Mr Facey Romford's Hounds,* R.S. Surtees, an early railway enthusiast, wrote, 'People talk of the dangers of railways, but all horse owners know that there was no little danger attendant on the coaches. If a man had a vicious animal he always sold it to a coach proprietor.'

As Ralph Harrington observes of William Huskisson's death, it was 'a high-profile event for the railway and a high-profile accident. It certainly got extensive press coverage, but in a sense those who said, "This just shows how dangerous these railways are, and why they shouldn't be allowed to be in the public realm" were those who would have responded like that anyway. It confirmed the hostility people already had to the railway rather than making those who were undecided or who were previously enthusiastic hostile to it. There was a view that accidents can happen, but in any properly run system they will be minimized. The railway was such a great invention and people anticipated its transforming the world with such enthusiasm, that they didn't let the accident destroy that enthusiasm.'

Inevitably there were many accidents in the early days of railways, largely because of the casualness of operators, and of passengers who were used to the leisurely speed of coach travel and totally unaware of the power, speed and size of steam locomotives. Indeed what is surprising is that they got used so quickly to the whole idea of mechanical transport, despite its enormous difference in kind from previous experience. In *Railway Detectives* Stanley Hall points out some of the other dangerous features of early rail travel: 'Intoxication and trespass were a widespread problem, causing many deaths. Inebriated passengers often fell out of trains, or crossed the railway without taking care and were knocked down. Trespassers had not yet learnt that a railway train is a very effective killer.'

It took time for everyone involved to adjust to the sort of behaviour required to cope with the first mechanically propelled vehicle in the history of travel. As W.M. Acworth relates, in the early days, 'neither the companies' servants nor the public had yet learnt to treat railway trains with the necessary caution. Engine-drivers fancied that a collision between two engines was much the same thing as the interlocking of the wheels of two rival stage-coaches.' The same assumption, that trains were merely a rather faster form of stage-coach, also affected passengers, who 'tried to jump on and off trains moving at full speed with absolute recklessness. Again and again it is recorded, "injured, jumped out after his hat"; "fell off, riding on the side of a wagon"; "skull broken, riding on the top of a carriage, came in collision with a bridge"; "guard's head struck against a bridge, attempting to remove a passenger who had improperly seated himself outside"' – as passengers could on stage-coaches. 'Of the serious accidents reported to the Board of Trade,' wrote one authority, 'twenty-two happened to persons who jumped off when the carriages were going at speed, generally after their hats, and five persons were run over when lying either drunk or asleep upon the line.'

The railway companies were run by people unused to the extraordinary and unprecedented discipline required to run a railway compared not only with any previous transport system but also with any other industry. The result, wrote L.T.C. Rolt, was hair-raisingly slapdash: 'Engineers would commandeer a locomotive from the shed as light-heartedly as they would take a horse from a stable and drive themselves away, sometimes on the wrong road. If a train failed to appear at the expected time it was generally assumed that the engine had broken down and a relief was sent out to replace it.' Nevertheless, accidents resulted in surprisingly few casualties, partly because speeds were so low.

The companies' lack of experience also emerges in the often contra-dictory orders they gave to their 'servants'. In one accident, reported in *The Times* in February 1848, a passenger train stopped suddenly two miles from a station 'for no other apparent reason than to give time for a luggage train to come up and run into it'. During the twenty minutes between the halt and the accident the guard 'with creditable promptitude, began to execute what he believed to be his duty, according to the rules; and though they directed him undoubtedly to be in two places at a time, and perform three or four operations at once, he declined putting upon them their widest construction, but preferred limiting their sense by a reference to human capability'. As for the fireman, he was 'distinctly ordered to look out for-wards and backwards – in the former case with sharpness, and in the latter with frequency. How he is to accomplish this double duty of keeping his eyes vigilantly employed in two directions we are not aware.'

For it was not only the passengers who were still living in a coaching age – and not surprisingly, given that the stage-coach running on roads covered with 'macadam' was itself a relatively new phenomenon dating back only to the last years of the eighteenth century. 'The approach of railway companies in the very early days', says Stanley Hall, 'was based on what they'd always been used to on the roads. One train followed another, and if the train in front stopped, the driver of the second train also stopped because train speeds were low. That sufficed for a short period until train speeds increased, trains became more frequent and collisions became more fre-quent but generally at a very low speed. It was then necessary to try to devise in the existing technology of the time, which was very sparse indeed, some form of keeping trains apart, of stopping collisions at stations. In the very early days this took the form of a policeman at the stations. The policemen actually dated back to the very early days of railway construction. They were appointed by the local justices to keep order amongst the navvies who were building the railways and, of course, to look after the railway company's property. There were thousands of them. When the works were finished, the station was built, the track was put in and trains started to run, the constable was kept on to control train operations in the station. Signalmen eventually took over that duty. Interestingly enough, signalmen for many years – and still today in some quarters – were known as bobbies. That goes right back to the 1830s, 1840s, when bobbies, policemen, actually controlled the movement of trains.'

The chaos was compounded because, as Norman Pattenden says, 'In the early days of railways, timetables didn't exist as we know them today. Basically they just gave a departure time. Now we expect a train to arrive wherever at a particular time. Indeed fairly soon the timetables started to show arrival times but these were complicated by the fact that there wasn't a standard time in the country. Every town and village had its own local time. This was a particular problem on the Great Western line running east–west where there was a difference between London time and Bristol time of twelve to thirteen minutes. If you were going to catch a train from Bristol to London you had to remember that the railway was actually running on London time and adjust your clock or watch.' The confusion was not confined to lines running across 'time zones'. After one accident it was discovered that the down trains on the line from Birmingham to Gloucester used Birmingham time, while those in the other direction used Cheltenham time, which was between ten and fifteen minutes different. 'This all got very confusing', says Pattenden, 'and as a result there was a standardization of time. It was really because of the existence of railways and railway timetables that GMT, as we understand it now, came into being as a standard time throughout the country. That happened back in about the 1850s.

'When standard time was introduced, it impressed on people's minds the relevance of time, and railways published detailed timetables. This created the ethos of timekeeping, and led the railways to run to time, or try to run to time, and led to passengers' expectation that they would arrive at a certain point at the time printed on the timetable. This idea has dominated the railway industry ever since and you could say that in that respect the railways were their own worst enemy.' They had been responsible for introducing the prospect of punctuality 'to be beaten around the head with it when they failed to meet it'. As a result, he says, everyone who works now on the railway is ruled by the clock. 'I know this in my own private life in which I run to a very strict timetable much to my wife's annoyance, simply because it's what I've been used to over thirty-six years in the railway industry.'

In the United States in the early days the situation was far worse. Derailments were so common that a clause printed on the tickets obliged passengers to help to lift the train back on the track. This was partly because a journey of any distance took participants into the wilderness. Even in the relatively civilized north-east, says Bill Withuhn, 'very often you were in wilderness from the time you left. Not twenty minutes out of the station going between Philadelphia and New York City you would be in wilderness most of the way. So if there were difficulties along the way, sometimes the passengers themselves would have to help clean up the mess. Nowadays if you sit in certain seats in an airplane, near an exit, you have to help with the exit procedures. In the last century passengers were expected to help out because there was no quick disaster-response agency that could swoop in with helicopters. It might be hours before any help arrived.' Today help arrives sooner rather than later, and accidents occur far less frequently, but one aspect of rail crashes has not altered in the past 170 years: the shock they induce in those involved.

3
The Shock of the New

Just as the Victorian railway was a vast, dramatic and highly visible expression of technology triumphant, so the railway accident constituted a uniquely sensational and public demonstration of the price which that triumph demanded – violence, destruction, terror and trauma.

Ralph Harrington

It was not long before travellers involved in an accident started to note the difference from their pre-industrial mode of transport and thus their reaction to it. After an American traveller had been involved, without injury, in a minor accident in 1835 on the Manchester–Liverpool line, he continued to try to enjoy the sight of the trains from a bridge over the tracks as he had before the accident. However, 'As it approached the bridge on which I stood, I could not bear to look at it, and seemed inclined to run off, lest it should be carried away from under me; I shrank back involuntarily and refused to follow it with my eye to the goal . . . But still no accident occurred, except in my creative imagination.'

After another crash a newspaper described how its reporter saw 'a woman who had been in the first compartment of the car that followed right behind the locomotives; she had not received any injury, but had experienced a commotion so extreme when confronted by this horrible disaster that she did not remember anything of it at all'.

Very occasionally, the shock was beneficial, as can be seen from a letter to *The Times* in November 1869 from a gentleman who a few days before had been 'threatened with a violent attack of rheumatic fever' while on a visit to Manchester. In fact, he wrote:

My condition so alarmed me, and my dread of a sojourn in a

Manchester hotel bed for two or three months was so great, that I
resolved to make a bold sortie and, well wrapped up, start for
London on the 3.30pm Midland fast train. From the time of leaving
that station to the time of a collision my heart was going at express
speed; my weak body was in a profuse perspiration; flashes of pain
announced that the muscular fibres were under the tyrannical
control of rheumatism, and I was almost beside myself with
toothache . . . From the moment of the collision to the present hour
no ache, pain, sweat or tremor has troubled me in the slightest
degree, and instead of being, as I expected, and indeed intended, in
bed, drinking *tinct. aurantii*, or absorbing through my pores oil of
horse chestnut, I am conscientiously bound to be at my office bodily
sound. Don't print my name and address, or the Midland Company
may come down on me for compensation.

There had been many crashes in the dozen years that followed William
Huskisson's death, notably one on Christmas Eve 1841 at Sonning, which
stirred the British soul, but the disaster on the newly opened line between
Paris and Versailles, on 8 May 1842, was the first to startle the whole world
and made people realize that railways were not an unmixed blessing. It
introduced many of the themes, from the idea of metal fatigue in materials
and mechanically induced shock in people, to suspicion of the new
industrial giants represented by the railway companies, the ancestors of
today's multinational groups, which dominated the relationship between
railways and their public for decades to come.

In the Versailles crash fifty-two passengers died; most were burned to
death in their locked compartments. There were few railways in France at
the time, and already a prevalent intellectual antipathy to the impersonality,
the industrial implacability, of the new form of transport. (It was most
famously and frequently expressed by the poet Alfred de Vigny and is
echoed to this day in the French fear of globalization.) The nature of the
disaster – unforeseeable and incomprehensible, like many of its later equiva-
lents – provided ammunition to those opposed to railways, and brought
forth innumerable poems and prints. Despite the shock of the crash, within
little more than a decade France was well on the way to the construction of
one of the best rail systems in Europe. The crash echoed round the world:
'It is not easy now,' wrote Charles Francis Adams in the late 1870s, 'to

conceive the excitement and dismay which this catastrophe caused throughout France. The railroad was at once associated in the minds of an excitable people with novel forms of imminent death.'

For most of the world, Versailles was the first demonstration of the previously unimaginable consequences of a railway disaster. 'The breaking of a coach axle in the eighteenth century merely interrupted a slow and exceedingly bumpy trip on the highway', wrote Schivelbusch. In the case of the Versailles crash, 'The breaking of a locomotive axle . . . led to the first railroad catastrophe that caused a panic in Europe.' In 1844 the accident was perceived as a negative side of technological progress: 'The mass of the objects they set in motion, the velocity they engender, their very power, once halted or turned from its proper objective, is transformed into a terrible agent of destruction' (*Encyclopédie des chemins de fer et des machines a vapeur*, 1844). Steam power 'continually' puts man 'into a position best compared to that of a man who is walking along the edge of a precipice and cannot afford a single false step', what engineers term 'an unstable equilibrium, which can be upset by the least little effort'.

Versailles also marked the start of a gradual recognition of the many phenomena now associated with the terms 'trauma' and 'traumatized' and, more precisely, what is now known as post-traumatic stress disorder. The exploration of this phenomenon in the forty years following the disaster at Versailles marked an important episode in medico-psychological history.

At a personal level the effect of crashes can be shown by the example of two famous victims: Charles Dickens and Franklin Pierce. The latter was the successful Democratic Party candidate in the US Presidential election of November 1852. He had been a soldier, though more famous as a drinker – he had, they said, 'won many a bottle'. He was not an outstanding politician: he was a 'dark horse' candidate, a compromise choice on the forty-ninth ballot in an exhausted convention. However, between his election and the time he took office in the following March, he was involved in a rail crash in a year in which five fatal crashes, in quick succession, killed seventy-seven people. In the first, on 6 January 1853 at Andover, Massachusetts, a broken axle on an express out of Boston sent the train and carriages tumbling down a steep embankment. Franklin Pierce was travelling in it with his wife, Jane, and their only surviving child, twelve year-old Benny. At first it was reported that Pierce had been killed – it was as though Air Force One had fallen from the skies with the President on board.

In fact the President-elect and his wife were, physically, uninjured, but Benny was dead.

The loss of his son shattered Pierce. Ten years earlier, Benny's older brother Frank had died of typhus. Roy Franklin Nichols, Pierce's biographer, quotes a letter Pierce wrote at the time: 'We are commanded to set up no idol in our hearts and I am conscious that within the last two years particularly my prevailing feeling has been that we were living for our children. In all my labors, plans and exertions in them was the center of all my hopes, they were in all my thoughts. We should have lived for God and have left the dear ones to the care of Him who is alone able to take care of them and us . . . '

All Pierce's hopes since Frank's death had been pinned on Benny. As Nichols wrote:

> Pierce's great justification for assuming the burden of the Presidency had been the thought of building a heritage which might aid Benny's advance in life . . . His high honour had been purchased at the price of his son's life . . . it is difficult to express adequately the effect which the interpretation of the tragedy worked upon the President-elect. It became the fact of greatest importance in his life, troubling his conscience, unsettling him completely, and weakening his self-confidence for many months to come.

His wife collapsed and brooded over her loss for the rest of her days.

With such a profound psychological burden weighing on him it is not surprising that during his four years in office Pierce could do little to halt the deepening division in the country between the North and the slave-owning states in the South. Whether, in the absence of an accident, he might have surprised everyone by undergoing, like Harry Truman, a transformation in office, from a machine politician to a far-sighted visionary, is, however, unlikely. He was staunchly opposed to the abolition of slavery, and appointed Jefferson Davis, the future leader of the Confederacy, to his cabinet as Secretary for War. Indeed, probably the most profound effect of Benny's death was on public opinion. As Bill Withuhn says: 'The notion that someone so close to the Presidency, the highest office in the land, could be affected by this technology of course brought a number of people up pretty short.'

Thirteen years later Charles Dickens was involved in a crash that marks an important step in the recognition of the special problems associated with involvement in an accident. Dickens loved railways. He was living at Gads Hill Place in Kent and also in London. His descendant Gerald Dickens says he could 'make the journey between the two very easily, very swiftly and going off into the far-flung reaches of the country to do his research or off on his summer breaks into the Kent coast at Broadstairs. Dickens loved to live life as fast as he could, never wasted a second. To be able to get away from the horse-drawn carriages and off on these speeding express loco-motives was perfect for him.' He had even ridden on the footplate from London to Dover. More relevantly, he was also the first creative artist to be involved in an accident and provided the model for post-traumatic stress disorder.

'He had been travelling back from France where he'd been for a number of weeks,' says Gerald Dickens. 'He'd been finishing manuscripts for *Our Mutual Friend*, which would be his last completed novel, and he was travelling back to his publishers in London. He had come over from France to Folkestone on the ferry and caught the boat train to Charing Cross, and that was how he happened to be on that stretch of line at Staplehurst on the ninth of June 1865.'

The crash happened on a bridge that consisted of a series of cast-iron trough girders resting on brick supports to take the line across a muddy stream a mere ten feet below. John Benge, the foreman in charge of rebuilding the bridge, assumed that he had plenty of time to replace the last timber baulk in the hour and a quarter between two scheduled trains. So sure of this were he and his leading carpenter that their safety precautions were casual, indeed derisory.

'Unfortunately on the day concerned', says Stanley Hall, 'the detonators hadn't been used. It is said that the ganger in charge said, "Don't bother with detonators, the driver can't possibly miss you standing out there with your red flag." Unfortunately the man was just over five hundred yards away from the building works with his red flag.'

This was too close to avoid a crash when the boat train from Folkestone came along. The train was known as the 'tidal' because its timing varied with the tides. Unfortunately Benge had misread the timetable. He thought that the boat train would pass the viaduct at five twenty, but in fact it was due two hours earlier. (As if to guarantee disaster, the carpenter, who had also been issued with a copy of the timetable, had lost it.) The train approached the broken viaduct at its top speed of 50mph. 'When the train hit the gap over this muddy pool, and it was quite a short gap,' says Stanley Hall, 'the engine and the tender actually leapt over it, dragging the first coach with them but then couplings snapped'. L.T.C. Rolt continues the story: 'The first coach came to rest hanging at a perilous angle supported by the van coupling, but the next five fell through the gap into the muddy bed of the stream where they lay in a confusion of splintered wreckage, one standing on its end and another on its roof. Ten passengers in these coaches died and another forty-nine were injured.'

Dickens had been in the lucky first carriage, 'the only one', as he wrote to a friend, 'that did not go over into the stream. It was caught upon the turn by some of the ruin of the bridge, and hung suspended and balanced in an apparently impossible manner . . . Suddenly we were off the rail.' Of his two companions, he said, 'The old lady cried out, "My God", and the young one screamed.' Dickens reassured them as the carriage came to a halt. He then climbed out of the window of the locked compartment 'without the least notion what had happened'.

Nevertheless he kept his composure. Seeing the two guards running up and down the train 'quite wildly', he called out, 'Look at me. Do stop an instant and look at me, and tell me whether you don't know me.' One of them answered, 'We know you very well, Mr Dickens' – in the days before illustrated papers, his must have been one of the handful of faces familiar to most in the country, especially since he had started to give readings of his novels. Dickens then told him, 'For God's sake, give me your key, and send one of those labourers here, and I'll empty this carriage.'

He clambered down into the river and found some of the wounded. 'All he had with him', says Gerald Dickens, 'was his hip flask with brandy and his top hat. He filled his top hat with water from the river and just went round dousing people's heads, cooling them, giving them a drink of water, maybe giving them some brandy from his hip flask. Of the first two people he came across, one man was horribly injured with a cut right across his forehead, and as Dickens held him in his arms, he said, "I am gone," and died there and then. Dickens then helped a lady who was sitting next to a tree. He gave her a drink of water, but when he came back she was dead as well. He met a young man who was desperate to find his wife. They found her dead. All he could do was comfort the husband. There was nothing to be done from a first-aid view, if you like, it was too serious, but he could comfort, he could cool, he could calm, he could talk, and his self-control, by all accounts, was quite remarkable through all of it.'

In a letter Charles Dickens described the horror: 'No imagination can conceive the ruin of the carriages, or the extraordinary weights under which the people were lying, or the complications into which they were twisted up among iron and wood, and mud and water.' Dickens concluded with a couple of sentences that have since become the first classic definition of post-traumatic stress disorder. 'I have a – I don't know what to call it – constitutional (I suppose) presence of mind, and was not in the least flustered at the time. I instantly remembered that I had the MS of a number [of his magazine *Household Words*] and clambered back into the carriage for it. But in writing these scanty words of recollection I feel the shake and am obliged to stop.' Dickens' narrow escape was, says Gerald Dickens, 'quite a remarkable story and, yes, they wanted to know the exact circumstances. Detailed etchings were made of the accident showing Dickens moving among the wounded, tending them, rather romantically portrayed.' But while for the British public Dickens' accident was a nine days' wonder, for the novelist, says Gerald Dickens, 'it was a far more serious experience that haunted him till his death'.

We can chart the longer-term effects of the crash through his letters, over a dozen of which were written (or dictated because of the shakiness of his hand – 'I can't sign my flourish being nervously shaken') soon after the crash. On 21 June, twelve days after the accident, Dickens was writing, 'I feel curiously weak – weak as if I were recovering from a long illness. I begin to feel it more in my head. I sleep well and eat well, but I write half a dozen notes and turn faint and sick' – this from a man accustomed to a truly prodigious work rate. 'I am getting right, tho' still low in pulse and very nervous. Driving into Rochester yesterday I felt more shaken than I have since the accident.' At the same time he noted, 'I cannot bear railway travelling yet. A perfect conviction, against the senses, that the carriage is down on one side (and generally that is the left, and not the side on which the carriage in the accident really went over) comes upon me with anything like speed, and is inexpressibly distressing.'

Early the next year he was still brooding, with all the imagination of a great novelist, upon the incident: 'Is it not curiously significant of the action of a great railway accident on the nerves of human creatures that my watch (a chronometer) got so flustered in my pocket on that Staplehurst occasion, that it has never since been itself to the extent of two or three minutes? I reasoned myself out of an inability to travel by express, but I can't reason the watch out of this absurd behaviour.'

He never got over the accident. 'The railways shake me,' he wrote in early 1867, 'as witness my present handwriting. Since the Staplehurst experience, I feel them so much.' And in May 1868, nearly three years after the accident, when the Irish Mail crashed at Abergele, he reflected:

The Irish catastrophe naturally revives the dreadful things I saw that day [for] my escape in the Staplehurst accident of three years ago is not to be obliterated from my nervous system. To this hour, I have sudden vague rushes of terror, even when riding in a hansom cab, which are perfectly unreasonable but quite insurmountable. I used to make nothing of driving a pair of horses habitually through the most crowded parts of London. I cannot now drive, with comfort to myself, on the country roads here; and I doubt if I can ride at all in the saddle. My reading secretary and companion knows so well when one of these momentary seizures comes upon me in a railway carriage that he instantly produces a dram of brandy, which rallies the blood to the heart and generally prevails.

'Almost exactly a year after the accident,' says Gerald Dickens, 'he wrote a short story called "The Signalman" . . . It deals with a stretch of railway line that is haunted. The poor signalman in his signal box spends all of his time there alone and he's haunted by a figure of death near the signal light and a whole series of catastrophes happen on this stretch of line. There are accidents, people die on the train, they have fits, and eventually the signalman himself is cut down by the train. The atmosphere of that piece is dark. The walls of the railway cutting are incredibly deep, not a gleam of sunlight gets down into there. Everything is black and dark and it's almost as if the memory of the horror of the rail accident is hovering over this whole railway line.' However, after a carriage of a train on which he was travelling caught fire he managed to exorcize to some extent the horrors of railway travel by writing a riotously funny piece entitled simply 'Mugby Junction', which formed a whole issue – mostly penned by Dickens himself – of his magazine, *All The Year Round*.

But the shakes continued. As Gerald Dickens says, 'His son Henry and his daughter Mary both recorded that they watched him on a train and as soon as it went across the points he would grab hold of his chair and look straight at the floor. He would sweat, he would tremble, and when he went to America on a reading tour some two years after the railway accident, his tour was based around railroad travel. The journeys were the only opportunities he had to relax and he couldn't. He just spent the whole time in abject terror and it exhausted him . . . He had suffered a number of spasms, maybe mini-strokes, and he had a lot of trouble with the left-hand side of his body – always had done, I think that the fear of rail travel after that added to those problems.'

But there is another dimension to the incident, alluded to only indirectly in the letters, that the 'two ladies' who shared his compartment were Ellen (Nelly) Ternan and her mother. Their presence naturally coloured his attitude to the crash. Charles had separated from his wife for love of Ternan, a young actress. Dickens had a lifelong love of the theatre, says Gerald Dickens, 'and the two just hit it off. They began a long, happy relationship. Dickens and the Ternans were travelling back from France together. Ellen and her mother had been in France with him throughout the early summer of 1865 and, with his position in society, he just couldn't afford for that to come out. Victorian society wouldn't have accepted it, especially as his image was of the hearth-and-family man. Ellen and Charles kept their relationship secret all the way through, right up to the end of his life. She and her mother were very quickly spirited away from the scene of the accident. Ellen broke her arm, and a young lady presented herself at a hospital a few days after with a broken arm but wouldn't leave her name. She said she wanted to protect her relatives; she didn't want them to be concerned about her. The arm was duly bandaged and away she went.'

According to Clare Tomalin, Dickens was 'absolutely intent on covering up the fact that he had not been travelling alone. He made sure the name of his injured companion was given to no one and he categorically refused to give evidence at the inquest.' As for Nelly Ternan, 'One report mentions a young woman who refused to give her name, ostensibly for fear of alarming her relatives. It is not at all clear how Nelly was got from the scene of the crash to a hospital or doctor; it must have been a nightmare for all three of them.'

But Dickens did expose himself: he wrote to the station master at Charing Cross three days after the accident about the jewellery Nelly had lost, his gifts to her in the eight years of birthdays and Christmases they had known each other: 'A lady who was with me in the terrible accident on

Friday lost, in the struggle of being got out of the carriage, a gold watch-chain with a smaller gold watch-chain attached, a bundle of charms, and a gold seal engraved "Ellen". I promised the lady to make her loss known at headquarters, in case these trinkets should be found.'

Staplehurst not only had a purely personal psychological effect on Dickens: he suffered 'socio-psychological' repercussions too. As Tomalin says, the crash 'put Dickens into a panic' so far as his relationship with Nelly Ternan was concerned.

> [It] brutally threatened Dickens' privacy and brutally brought home
> to Nelly the humiliations of her position; for whatever physical
> injuries she received, his fear of exposure and his inability to give her
> hope and comfort openly when she most needed it must have been
> painful too. It made very clear to Nelly and her sisters that, whether
> she was guilty or whether she was innocent, she was obliged to live
> her life somewhere in the gap between what could be said and what
> really happened. The gap was a wide one in mid-nineteenth-century
> England, but that did not make it any more comfortable.

Dickens' last words on the subject came, appropriately enough, in the form of a 'postscript in lieu of preface' to *Our Mutual Friend*: 'I remember with devout thankfulness that I can never be nearer parting company with my readers for ever, than I was then, until there shall be written against my life the two words with which I have this day closed this book: The End.' By a most astonishing coincidence Dickens died, aged fifty-eight on 9 June 1870, the fifth anniversary of the crash at Staplehurst.

Dickens had confined his direct comments about the accident to the discretion of his letters but it was at precisely the time he was suffering from the trauma associated with the crash that doctors started to tackle seriously the peculiar nature of the injuries suffered by victims like him. 'It can be argued,' writes Ralph Harrington, 'that systematic medical theorization about psychological trauma in the modern West commenced with the responses of mid-Victorian medical practitioners to the so-called "railway spine" condition,' thirty years before Freud and Breuer considered the matter in their *Studies in Hysteria*.

At first doctors treated sufferers of shock resulting from railway accidents as for a physical problem, 'railway spine', the result of the jolt to the spinal column caused by the accident. The need to distinguish between the physical and the psychological consequences of an accident became even more important once the railway companies had become legally liable for the health and safety of their passengers. Already in 1849 they had founded the Railway Passengers Assurance Company, though they did not make any effort to sell its services.

In 1864 Lord Campbell's Act (the Act was named after its proposer) made it possible for the relatives of victims to sue the railway companies – which they did enthusiastically and successfully. Inevitably the subject of railway-induced injuries became of considerable public interest if only because their effects were so vague and long-lasting. For the next twenty years medical and legal experts had to decide whether a victim's claim was medically sound or based on imaginary disability, and the companies were notoriously reluctant to pay up. In 1867, for example, the South-Eastern Railway tried to impose a limit of £100 on compensation payments. As it was, said the company, 'We have to pay large sums of money to people of a low class of life, and there is a desire on the part of solicitors and others to connive at attempts to extort large sums of money from the railways.'

As the *Lancet*, Britain's most respected medical journal, put it in a ground-breaking series of articles in 1862, 'The difficulties proverbially attached to the exposure of the tricks of military malingerers are as nothing compared with the task of determining the reality of some of the injuries to health, physical or mental, which those interested in recovering "substantial" damages assign to railway collisions' (quoted in 'The Influence of Railway Travelling on Public Health'). The prevalence and difficulty of such cases put doctors in awkward situations, possibly, as Harrington notes, 'as paid stooges of the railways'.

The *Lancet* shrewdly pinpointed the symptoms as 'functional', meaning, in Ralph Harrington's words, 'that the injury was thought to be located in the nervous apparatus controlling the proper function of the affected organs, rather than in the substance of the organs themselves' – a first step in distinguishing between physical and mental explanations of the victims' suffering, which was reinforced by the writer's emphasis on the unique degree of violence associated with railway crashes.

The year after Dickens' accident brought three publications on railway accidents and injuries resulting from them: a series of articles by Thomas Buzzard in the *Lancet*, 'On Cases of Injury from Railway Accidents', and two books, one by another medical author, William Camps, *Railway*

Accidents or Collisions: Their Effects, Immediate and Remote, upon the Brain and Spinal Cord and Other Portions of the Nervous System, and the other, the most significant, by John Erichsen, *On Railway and Other Injuries of the Nervous System.* All three agreed that a railway accident had effects on the nervous system 'quite beyond those of any ordinary injury' as wrote Camps, a shock so severe that it might 'shatter the whole constitution' during a life that might 'be reasonably expected to be curtailed in its duration', even though the external physical injuries were 'apparently slight to the visual perception of the medical man'.

Erichsen, whose book was widely reviewed, went further. He echoed Dickens' experiences in remarking that after an accident the victim

> congratulates himself upon his escape from the imminent peril to which he has been exposed. He becomes unusually calm and self-possessed, assists his less-fortunate fellow-sufferers, occupies himself perhaps actively in this way for several hours, and then proceeds on his journey. When he reaches his home, the effects of the injury that he has sustained begin to manifest themselves. A revulsion takes place. He bursts into tears, becomes unusually talkative, and is excited. He cannot sleep, or, if he does, he wakes up suddenly with a vague sense of alarm.

Wolfgang Schivelbusch quotes Erichsen's list of other symptoms induced by railway shock: 'fatigue, headaches, difficulty in concentration, digestive problems, forgetfulness, stammering, reduction of sexual potency, cold sweats, states of anxiety, etc'. Erichsen also noted that 'Sleep is disturbed, restless and broken; dreams much, the dreams are distressing and horrible.' Buzzard mentioned that one female patient had complained 'that she saw the engine coming in at the window'.

Nevertheless, in the first edition of his book, published in1866, Erichsen refused to distinguish between the physical and the psychological injuries suffered in crashes. Although he also admitted that 'in no ordinary accident can the shock be so great as in those that occur on railways' and that they 'may be peculiar in their severity', they were not, he emphasized, 'different in their nature from injuries received in the other accidents of civil life'. As Harrington concludes, 'An existing disorder, well-known to medical science, had been made more frequent and more serious by the appearance of railways'.

However, in his second, much expanded edition, published nine years later, *On Concussion of the Spine, Nervous Shock and Other Obscure Injuries of the Nervous System in their Clinical and Medico-Legal Aspects*, Erichsen had changed his position: 'A serious accident may give rise to two distinct forms of nervous shock . . . The first is mental or moral, and the second purely physical. These forms of "shock" may be developed separately, or they may co-exist. It is most important . . . to distinguish between these two, and if co-existing to assign to each other its proper importance.'

'His acceptance,' Harrington observes, 'of the role played by a purely psychological influence, in the form of fright, as a causative agent in the traumatization of railway accident victims reflected a significant reorientation of his medical thought.'

In 1883 a railway company surgeon, Herbert Page, went further: he recorded the notion that the jarring of the spine caused the nervous symptoms. In Harrington's words, he had concluded that 'The emotion of fear alone was sufficient to inflict severe shock on the nervous system, and he saw the psychological effects of involvement in a railway accident as quite capable of inducing nervous illness and collapse.'

Foreign 'alienists', as early psychiatrists were described, took up the themes first explored by a generation of British surgeons. The great Charcot acknowledged the importance of Page's contribution, and indeed the empirical work of British surgeons had clearly anticipated the idea of what we now term post-traumatic stress disorder. Freud's own early writings on hysteria and trauma were prompted by the debates on railway accidents to which he had been exposed in Paris and Berlin in the 1880s.

By the mid-1880s Hermann Oppenheim came up with the idea of 'traumatic neurosis'. Subsequently, as Schivelbusch remarks, 'The literature on the subject grew by leaps and bounds, introducing competing and partially overlapping terms such as "traumatic neurosis", "fright neurosis", "hysterical neurosis", "libidinal neurosis" and [with the First World War providing new realities] "war neurosis" ' – or shell-shock, the result of one of the few physical experiences worse than a train crash.

Originally legal dogma asserted that only physical injuries counted as a basis for compensation, but by the mid-1880s this had been replaced by the new idea of 'traumatic neurosis' not connected with physical injuries. Yet in 1899 one textbook declared, 'Damages resulting from mere sudden terror or mental shock could not be considered the natural consequence of the negligence complained of.' Recognition, when it came, was grudging. As late as 1963 another textbook asserted, 'Nervous shock is a form of personal injury for which damages may or may not be recoverable according to the circumstances of a particular case.'

In Harrington's words, 'The traumas of rapid industrialization, of human independence surrendered to the vast powers of the machine, of uncontrollable speed, of sudden, shattering catastrophe, found expression through the neuroses of the railway age. Conceptualizations of "railway spine" had begun with shaken spines; they had ended with splintered minds.'

4

The Road to Armagh

A muddle of railways in all directions possible and impossible, no public scheme, no general public supervision, enormous waste of money, no fixable responsibility.

Charles Dickens, letter, 10 December 1865

The effect of the Versailles crash was not only psychological – and mechanical – it was also what might be termed politico-industrial. The effect in Britain can be judged from a letter written to the *Morning Chronicle* by the Reverend Sydney Smith. Because Smith was so witty, people then – and now – tended to underestimate the good sense of what he wrote. He was an early supporter of railways. 'Railroad travelling is a delightful improvement of human life. Man is become a bird,' he had written to a friend. But after Versailles he started to fight against the Great Western Railway, which, like all railway companies at the time, was thought of as a monopoly run by directors intent on exploiting the public and concerned only with their own profits (*plus ça change . . .*).

'In all other positions of life there is egress where there is ingress. Man is universally the master of his own body, except he chooses to go from Paddington to Bridgwater: there only the Habeas Corpus is refused.' For the first time, Smith made the distinction between the reasonable care the traveller should take and the responsibility of the company carrying him or her. 'There can,' said Smith, 'be no other dependence for the safety of the public than the care which every human being is inclined to take of his own life and limbs. Everything beyond this is the mere lazy tyranny of monopoly, which makes no distinction between human beings and brown paper parcels.'

Smith poured scorn on the proposed solution, to lock only one side of the carriages. 'If the wheel comes off on the right, the open door is uppermost and everyone is saved. If, from any sudden avalanche on the road, the carriage is prostrated to the left, the locked door is uppermost, all escape is impossible, and the railroad martyrdom begins . . . [The company leaves] me to escape the best way I can.' And after what he assumes will be a fire, he will be lucky to get out 'only half-roasted, or merely browned, certainly not done enough for the Great Western Directors still anxious to lock all their carriages' – for the GWR locked both the doors on all its passenger carriages.

Taking locked carriages as his theme Smith was the first writer to grasp the sequence of events involved in railway safety. Travel by rail, indeed, was splendid:

> everything is near, everything is immediate – time, distance and delay are abolished. But, though charming and fascinating as all this is, we must not shut our eyes to the price we shall pay for it. There will be every three or four years some dreadful massacre – whole trains will be hurled down a precipice, and 200 or 300 persons will be killed on the spot. There will be every now and then a great combustion of human bodies, as there has been at Paris; then all the newspapers up in arms – a thousand regulations, forgotten as soon as the directors dare – loud screams of the velocity whistle – monopoly locks and bolts as before.
>
> We have been, up to this point, very careless of our railway regulations. The first person of rank who is killed will put everything in order, and produce a code of the most careful rules.

Smith – who should have been, but never was, a bishop – imagines the death, inevitably by fire, of a bishop. A 'burnt bishop' should 'remember that, however painful gradual concoction by fire may be, his death will produce unspeakable benefit to the public . . . From that moment, the bad effects of the monopoly are destroyed; no more fatal deference to the directors; no despotic incarceration, no barbarous inattention to the anatomy and physiology of the human body . . . We shall the find it possible "voyager libre sans mourir".' It was the first description of the phenomenon known as 'tombstone technology' that a major disaster – at sea or in the air as much as on the rails – must occur before the introduction of safety regulations that are often elementary, long overdue, or both. Indeed, the history of railway safety seems to go like this: disaster, huge media coverage, investigation, public debate, safety fix. It is a course of events that finds distinct echoes in Britain today.

Yet, despite accidents like the one at Versailles, the introduction of even the most elementary safety measures in the nineteenth century was dangerously slow, largely because of their cost – a current theme in arguments over train-control systems today. Indeed, it was nearly half a century after Versailles, and a far worse disaster at Armagh in Northern Ireland in 1889, before Britain's hundreds of railway companies were finally forced to conform to safety procedures, most of which had been available for decades and which, to be fair, had already been adopted by the more safety-conscious companies.

For, as Bill Withuhn points out, referring to the United States, train crashes are always news. Unsurprisingly, 'It didn't take long for publishers, editors, writers to figure out what sold newspapers, and certainly sensation always did. An engraver would come up with a picture of the scene showing people gathered, the horrible injuries, the fires that usually swept through the wooden coaches when they crashed.'

'These accidents slowly brought the public to a point at which it demanded change for its own safety, and the government was finally able to persuade the railroads that this met their profit interests too. But it was a long road from the first railway wrecks in the 1830s until the first safety legislation in the 1890s, and it really only came about when the railways saw it in their own self-interest, but I think journalists, photographers, and the engravers working in the pre-photo age all helped.'

The same phenomenon could be seen in Britain. 'The first consumer journalism is a very interesting way of looking at press coverage of railway accidents,' notes Ralph Harrington. 'There's no doubt in many journals and newspapers that there was an agenda at work hostile to the railway companies. The view was that these companies were badly run, they were penny-pinching, they were unwilling to spend the money necessary to make themselves as safe as they ought to be. All the papers took up this cry: they all criticized the companies on these grounds. In a sense there was a consumer agenda going on here: the middle classes were travelling by train, felt vulnerable, read about accidents in the papers and wanted something done. The newspapers acted as an articulate spokesman, a channel for those opinions through which those who were responsible for the state of the railways, the directors, the managers and of course, Parliament, which regulated them, had to hear public opinion.'

The same applies today. As Bruce McGladry of the NTSB points out, his organization 'has no regulatory authority. We make recommendations to organizations on how to correct problems. But those organizations in general can choose to respond or not respond, follow our recommendation or not follow our recommendation. We do manage to entice people to get things done and to adhere to our recommendations in a couple of ways – one is to do a very thorough investigation and prove our points, another is to make sure that the information we've gathered and the recommendations we develop make it into the public arena so that it isn't just the recommendation of the NTSB but of a larger body politic that's aware of the issues that led to a particular accident and the potential solutions. The NTSB produces reports, and those reports get to the general public through press coverage. The press has a valuable service to perform in getting that information out to everyone. If everyone is knowledgeable about safety issues, problems and solutions, then many more people are interested in finding a way to increase safety measures.'

The original pressure for regulation built up throughout the second half of the nineteenth century, but the problems multiplied as trains became heavier, faster and more frequent. As Ascanio Schneider writes, 'In the first decades of British railway history the concentration had been more on traction technology and speed of travel' than on safety. The shape of demands on the system to come was first apparent in February 1845 in an event that permanently increased the strain on every element in the railway system. That month the Great Western announced a regular service of trains that would cover the 200 miles between Exeter and London in a mere five hours, averaging an unheard-of 40mph.

In the United States the situation hardly differed from the British experience. As Bill Withuhn says, 'The trains were faster and heavier, there were more accidents each decade and public pressure to improve safety was rising. However, the legal tradition in the United States was that the government had no presumptive interest in this and people rode at their own risk. Thus there was much agitation but little progress. One accident in particular focused attention on railway safety: that at Ashtabula, when a New York Central train actually collapsed a bridge. The train landed in the river below amid splinters of wood and flying metal. Pot-belly stoves set the wreckage on fire, which killed more people than were drowned. Spectacular accidents like this one finally forced some action but not until the 1880s and only when the railroads decided it was in their economic best interest.'

In the United States, increased safety, says Withuhn, 'usually only occurred when the railroad corporations realized that it was, in fact, an avenue to better profits, less loss, more reliability, in particular faster speeds. The law that enforced safe couplings and safe air brakes didn't come in till 1893 and this was at a time when railroad tonnages and speeds were increasing in leaps and bounds. In fact these better couplings and the air brakes allowed the trains to be run economically, so I think the railroad barons decided, "Well, what the heck? Let's call it safety and we'll be able to run heavier and faster trains".'

In Britain the foundations of the road to safety were laid in 1840, two years before the Versailles crash, when the Board of Trade had been given its first powers to supervise the railways. Above all, its officials could inspect railway lines before they were opened. Two years later the authority was extended to prevent the opening of any line they judged to be dangerous, without right of appeal by the railway company.

But the more general problem of control over the railway remained. In Britain the railway companies were competitive, they were also independent and independent-minded, in a society that disliked any form of state interference. Moreover, as the biggest enterprises of their age, indeed the most substantial ever seen in Britain, they were powerful politically as well as financially, and for a generation they were notably unwilling to take any guidance, let alone instruction, from those they regarded as mere clerks. The combination of haughtiness and disdain was by no means confined to the many disreputable railways constructed and managed by shady operators. Geniuses like Isambard Kingdom Brunel, and the directors of the London & North Western Railway, the biggest concern of its kind and a pioneer in railway management, were affronted by the idea that any outside opinion should be explored. As late as 1872 Richard Moon, the chairman of the London & North Western, told shareholders that 'he believed the Board of Trade were as responsible for railway accidents as the railway companies were. It was a divided management, with all the responsibility on one side only [i.e. the companies were responsible for paying up]. The Board of Trade insisted on signals and other works, which involved a large expenditure by the companies.'

Naturally, such attitudes bred opposition. In 1862 the eminently respectable *Saturday Review* claimed that railway accidents were hardly accidents at all, but 'might be more correctly described as pre-arranged homicide', given the 'system of mingled recklessness and parsimony' which it accused the railways of operating.

But the1840 Railways Act also produced the Railway Inspectorate, first suggested in a letter written by George Stephenson. For more than 140 years the Inspectorate, until recently recruited from retired officers of the Royal Engineers, did its job with skill and persistence, without fear or favour. In recent years they have been shuttled from the Board of Trade, their original home, to the Ministry of Transport, to an umbrella Department of the Environment, then to the Department of Transport, and in the late 1980s to the Health and Safety Executive, a move that, as we shall see, has not been without its critics.

Their motto, says L.T.C. Rolt, was 'supervision without interference'. Under the Act they were not given the precise power to investigate but did so anyway. They set an internationally recognized standard as the first and most effective band of 'railway detectives'. That the government did not provide them with specific powers, writes Stanley Hall, was sensible: it 'felt that such powers would take the responsibility for managing railways out of the hands of the directors and place it fairly and squarely upon the Board of Trade, a very undesirable development (such views are still relevant today).' They lived up to what Hall described after a crash near Purley, south of London, in 1989 as their principal *raison d'être*. In a letter to *The Times* of 21 September 1989, he wrote, 'The prime objective in accident investigation must be to discover in what way the system was flawed, so that it can be put right. Systems must provide for the possibility of human error because people make mistakes, however unwittingly.' In this they succeeded admirably.

When investigating accidents, wrote Peter Rayner, in *On and Off the Rails*, 'There is no substitute for experience, which is exactly what the Inspectorate could offer. Accident investigation is not just about calculus and facts, it is also about talking on the site of the accident with other persons with other skills. The relationship between the vehicles derailed and the track, between what the driver said he was doing and what others think he was doing, all are mixed.'

The Railway Inspectorate was internationally respected. As the American writer Charles Francis Adams pointed out in 1879, the great advantage of the British system was that every accident was investigated by the same group of people, whereas in the US, 'The same man never investigates two accidents, and, for the one investigation he does make, he is competent only in his own esteem.'

The Inspectorate's position, however, was delicate. 'There were many railway companies in the nineteenth century,' says Stanley Hall, 'and they tended to take different views on investment in safety depending on the feelings of the general manager or the chairman of the board. Generally speaking, they spent as much as they needed to in order to keep Parliament and the general public satisfied, and in order not to deter passengers from travelling because it was so dangerous, but they didn't spend more than they needed to to keep the public satisfied.'

Yet despite the lightness of their touch the inspectors were bitterly opposed through most of the nineteenth century – and not just by the chairmen of the railway companies, the 'fat cats' of their day. Daniel Gooch, Brunel's distinguished successor on the Great Western Railway, objected to 'minute and irresponsible interference'. Nor were the inspectors an entirely united body. Their chief for much of the period, Captain Tyler, was for persuasion rather than legislation while a senior colleague, Colonel Yolland, favoured more direct supervision. Both faced an issue that has haunted the safety community to this day: just how far automation of safety procedures should go. In the words of Sir Richard Moon, 'These mechanical appliances were all inducements to inattention on the part of signalmen and drivers' – which to him meant any improvement to the signalling.

Another major advantage of the British system was that the inspectors' reports provided all the information required to improve safety standards, a degree of openness not found elsewhere. At the opposite end of the spectrum was Soviet Russia, where in 1931 it was ruled that breaches of discipline were to be punished by imprisonment. Even before this edict the Russians had not been forthcoming: Peter Semmens writes simply of one accident at Omsk in 1923 that 'An express train was derailed' – killing 82 people and injuring 150 more. The French were little better: all Semmens can record of a crash in 1939, when 35 were killed, was that 'A collision took place.' And details of the worst crash in French railway history, that at Modane in 1917 did not emerge until over fifty years later. Even the Americans, now apostles of openness, eschewed candour. Until well into the twentieth century their annual railway safety reports did not disclose the location of individual accidents or the name of the railway company involved.

In Britain, however, the inspectors never pulled their punches. Typically,

Captain Tyler (quoted in Jack Simmons, *The Victorian Railway*) reported of an accident near Coventry in 1872 that

> The passenger lines near the site have been left for a series of years without any means of protection either by a stationary signalman, or by safety-points . . . Is the Board of Trade responsible, on the one hand, for such an accident – occurring from the want of apparatus which it consistently recommends the company to adopt? Is not the Board of Trade justified, on the other hand, in insisting, as far as it has the power to do so, on the application of appliances necessary for safety, even though they 'involve a large expenditure on the companies'.

For nearly half a century the inspectors fought an uphill battle. Nevertheless, as Jack Simmons writes, over time the experience of generations of inspectors came

> to form a substantial body of experience. As new safety precautions were devised and perfected, they felt justified in recommending those they believed in. They also had things to say about locomotives, about the materials used in making their boilers and axles and tyres, about the suitability of particular types of engines for the duties to which they were assigned. They persistently criticized the working of engines tender-first as a source of danger. Several of them disapproved of the use of tank engines to haul fast trains and said so, with growing insistence, from 1866 to 1912.

Proof, indeed, of the length of the battles faced by the Inspectorate. These were on a wide front, but as time went on they were concerned, above all, with two principal causes of accidents: the signalling, and its links with points and rails, and brakes – or lack of them.

As Stanley Hall says, 'In the early days of railways when there was no means of communication between stations there had to be a way of letting trains follow each other keeping a safe interval between them. The interval that was adopted was the only one available: a time interval. Trains were allowed to follow each other at stated intervals, which varied with different railway companies but, generally speaking, if five minutes had elapsed after a train had gone, a second train would be allowed to go after the driver had been cautioned that the train in front of him was only five minutes away. If the train in front broke down, it was the guard's duty to jump off, run back along the line waving a red flag or a red lamp at night and place fog signal detonators on the line to explode and warn the driver of the second train. It wasn't a very safe system but it was all that was available in the early days.'

Hall adds that the 'exploding fog signals, which were invented in 1840 by William Cooper, are still in use today. They consist of a little metal disc, two inches in diameter, filled with gunpowder, about half an inch thick, with some little percussion caps inside. They're fitted on top of the rail head and held on by lead straps. When the train comes along its first wheel compresses this disc, the percussion caps ignite the gunpowder and there is a loud bang. That alerts the driver to something amiss ahead. He knows from his rulebook that as soon as he discharges a detonator he must brake, so it's a good safeguard.'

Hall's 'early days' lasted a long time. As late as 1879, Charles Francis Adams wrote of how on one main line 'The interval between two closely following trains was signalled to the engineer [driver] of the second train by a station master's holding up to him as he passed a number of fingers corresponding to the number of minutes since the first train had gone by. For the rest the examination revealed . . . a queer collection of dials, sunglasses, green flags, colored lanterns and hand-targets.'

However, the electric telegraph provided operators with the means to allow signalmen to communicate with each other. By the 1840s it could not only signal left or right on the receiving instrument but could also employ Morse code to send precise information. But it was sixty years before the time-interval system was completely replaced with the so-called 'block' system, which divided the track into sections, or blocks, and ensured that no train could to move into a block if it was still occupied by another. (The name derives from the lump of wood used in early days to block the operating handle of the telegraphic instrument.)

The emerging block system was backed up by increasingly sophisticated signals. Originally these had been hand-held flags; they were superseded by mechanical rectangular boards or discs turned by levers at the foot of the post, which evolved into the familiar semaphore signals that indicated the state of the track by the angle of the arm: horizontal for danger, 45 degrees for caution, down for clear or red, green and white where colour signals are being used.

The companies often made it difficult for themselves – and, above all, for their often illiterate employees – by issuing instructions that might be thought hilarious had they not been so vital to safety. One such was issued by the London North & Western Railway and quoted by Jack Simmons:

> The fan or arm of the auxiliary signal at Cheddington, Leighton, Roade, Blisworth, and Weedon are repainting [sic] to a yellow colour which will be more discernible than green, the ground colour is obliged to be nearly red, the signal will, however, continue to be shown for the assistance of the drivers, although it is not intended they should stop thereat but come on as heretofore as far as the stationary post, when the policeman will tell them why the train has been stopped.

'When the electric telegraph was invented,' says Stanley Hall, 'it was used at first between stations for enquiring of the whereabouts of trains, but fairly quickly a system was developed whereby the electric telegraph was used between stations or between signal boxes for a signalman to say to his fellow at the box further back that a train had arrived safely, the section between the two of them was now clear and it was safe for the signalman [in the signal box] one back to send another train. That became known as the space interval because there was always a space of a section between trains, and that is a system that is still in use on traditional branch lines today.'

The next advance was to connect the signals with the track and, more particularly, with the points. 'In the absence of interlocking between the signal levers and the point levers,' says Hall, 'it was perfectly possible for the signalman to give a signal towards the left-hand route, which was clear, whilst his points were set towards the right-hand route on which a train was standing. That obviously was dangerous and it caused quite a lot of accidents in the nineteenth century before the use of interlocking frames in signal boxes.' But from the 1860s on, the points and signals were grouped together in a single frame and were interlocked by mechanical bars and locking bolts. This ensured that if the points were set for a particular line only the signal levers for that line could be pulled to give clearance to a train. This prevented signals allowing trains to pass on points set for other tracks, because they would automatically follow the way the points were set.

But even this apparently sensible system gave rise to opposition – and not only because it was expensive. According to L.T.C. Rolt, 'John Chester Craven, that most formidable martinet among locomotive superintendents', objected that 'by transferring much responsibility from the engine drivers' block working would 'augment rather than diminish the risk of accident'. Indeed, the argument that ever-increasing automation may reduce safety by lulling drivers and signalmen into a false sense of security has intensified over the years.

If communication between driver and signalman and between guard and driver were essential, so was the ability of driver and guard to communicate with passengers. In the mid-1850s the inspectors reckoned that an average of half a dozen accidents took place each year that might have been prevented had there been some means of communication between driver and passengers (the Americans already had a bell-cord system).* Progress here, as in so many other aspects of rail safety, was patchy, but in a Regulatory Act passed in 1868 the railway companies were forced to introduce some means of communication between driver and passengers on any train that ran for twenty miles without stopping, but this proved difficult to enforce.

However, problems of communication were as nothing compared with those posed by the need to stop not just the locomotive, but the whole train. For half a century endless experiments were conducted to devise a suitable braking system. The inspectors wanted it to be continuous – so that it would act on the whole train – and to be used as a matter of routine, not just in an emergency. It would have to be instantaneous and would be applied automatically if, as often happened, one part of the train became detached from the body. It also had to be 'fail-safe', meaning that its functioning required no positive action by the driver. Stanley Hall makes an analogy with a car driver who 'puts his brake on by pressing on the brake pedal. That is not a fail-safe system. The fail-safe system would be if he had to keep the brake pedal depressed all the time to keep the brakes off and had to release his foot to put the brake on.'

Originally, trains had only handbrakes on the engine although they could also be stopped by throwing the engine into reverse. 'In the very early days,' says Roger Weatherup, a local historian at Armagh, 'they used the kind of brakes fitted on horse-drawn vehicles, but soon realized that they just did not

---

* An amusing case that stemmed from lack of communication was described by a clergyman in a letter to *The Times* in which a young man 'disrobed' in front of himself and a young lady. The young man then proceeded 'to indulge in antics which were even more indecent than they were extraordinary'.

work. Several different methods were tried. There was no standardization – different companies used different systems.'

'As trains got heavier and went faster,' says Stanley Hall, 'this became a much more important issue. In 1875 the Railway Inspectorate arranged for trials to be held at Newark. About ten of the railway companies entered and they all showed off their own systems, which they thought were best, so the trials were inconclusive because none of the companies was prepared to budge and adopt somebody else's system . . . It just happened that two years earlier the American engineer George Westinghouse had invented his foolproof air-brake system in America, but none of the railway companies at that time were prepared to adopt it. Several did in later years and it was made compulsory by the 1889 Regulation of Railways Act.'

In fact, two types of brakes had been developed that depended on air pressure. They worked either by sucking air out of the system to create a vacuum or by pumping air into a reservoir so that the compressed air would operate the brakes. In the early versions of the 'sucking' type the vacuum relied on the engine ejector using steam to suck the air out of the brake pipe so that the resulting vacuum pulled a piston on the cylinder on each carriage. But this system relied on a continuous supply of steam from the engine, which was obviously cut off in a crash.

Westinghouse solved the problem by providing individual reservoirs in each carriage. His system was fail-safe, and it worked even if the individual carriages were uncoupled. He took out his first patents in 1869 and soon attracted the support of the Pennsylvania Railroad, the biggest and most far-sighted of US railway companies. In Westinghouse's design the train pipe and the reservoirs in each coach were charged with compressed air to hold the brakes off. If the driver applies the brakes or the pipe breaks, air is let out of the pipe and a valve on each coach sends compressed air from the reservoir to the brake cylinder to apply the brakes. This ensured that the braking system no longer depended on a supply of steam from the engine.

The advantages of the Westinghouse brakes had become clear as early as the mid-1870s. In 1876 a Pullman car in the middle of a Midland Railway express came off the rails. The automatic brakes prevented a serious accident, even though the train was travelling at a full 60mph. A few months later the locomotive of a similar express without these brakes from the North Eastern Railway came off the tracks at 25mph. Three carriages were completely destroyed, and three passengers were killed. Charles Francis

Adams compares two accidents in the United States, one that occurred in 1854, the other eighteen years later. In the latter incident, the train was equipped with two safety improvements, the Miller platform and Westinghouse brakes. In the first accident, a train approaching Detroit at 20mph ran into a gravel train doing 15mph. The two leading carriages, carrying emigrants,* telescoped and were crushed with the loss of forty-seven lives and sixty injured. In the second crash, in which an express was travelling at 40mph, the carriages were thrown all over the place but there was no telescoping and the passengers suffered only a few minor bruises.

All these problems, particularly those of control, were inevitably heightened on single-track railways. The worst crash on a single-track line in Britain occurred on 10 September 1874 – at a time when two-fifths of all the rail mileage in Britain took place on single-track lines – at Thorpe between Norwich and Great Yarmouth. The mail train from Norwich had to wait at Blundell because the evening express from Yarmouth was expected. It was late so the inspector wrote a telegraph despatch permitting the mail to come through, but did not sign it, clearly intending that it should not be sent. The express arrived and the inspector allowed it to come through. In the meantime, though, the telegraph operator had decided after a brief period to send the still unsigned message that allowed the mail train to proceed. The crash was inevitable and sudden. Fortunately there were a number of empty carriages between the locomotive and those containing passengers, but both engine drivers were killed, along with seventeen passengers. Four died later of their injuries.

As a result a famous engineer, Edward Tyer, devised the tablet system, in which a token is given to the train driver. Only when this had been slotted into an electric interlocking device at the other end of the single-track line was another train allowed to pass. This, also called the staff system depending on an electric, metal staff or key, was peculiarly British. It is a tribute to the safety of Tyer's system that there were no fatal accidents on a single-track line in Britain between 1921, at Abermule, and 1994, at Cowden.

'Non-regulatory' progress, like the Tyer key, was more common in the United States. Of particular importance was the Miller platform and buffer.

---

* Emigrant trains, slow and disregarded, were always vulnerable. After a crash in 1864, of a train on its way to Montreal on the Grand Trunk Railway, over a hundred died. Many of them, wrote Charles Francis Adams, 'lay heaped upon one another like sacks, dressed in the traditional blue clothing of the German people'.

This enabled the cars to meet exactly when strained, which forced the heavy spring buffers and floor timbers to compress together thus forming a strong mass. Previously, the looseness of the couplings had caused the train to break up. Even so, the meaner railroad companies protested that loose coupling led to desirable flexibility.

On many railways accidents were waiting to happen. As Charles Francis Adams points out, 'In August 1871, the Eastern Railroad was run as if it were a line of stage-coaches in the days before the telegraph.' All its weaknesses were revealed when two trains collided near Revere, north of Boston, Massachusetts, one summer Saturday, at a time when holidays had increased the usual traffic of passengers and trains by more than half. The death toll of fifty-nine precipitated a classic case of 'tombstone technology' in the introduction of the Westinghouse brakes and Miller platforms.

Progress in Britain was slower, although that same year another Regulatory Act gave the Railway Inspectorate the power to summon railway officials and inspect all relevant documents. At the same time, public pressure for higher standards of rail safety was rising. 'Everybody had to travel by train because there was no other means of getting around the country,' says Stanley Hall. 'People began to take more interest in rail accidents and, of course, to demand higher standards, often through their MPs. Several parliamentary commissions were appointed in the 1860s and 1870s to examine railway safety. It had become a major issue.' Gradually, the inspectors' policy of patient pressure for improvements had a considerable effect. By 1872 the block system had been fitted to 44 per cent of all lines in Britain, rising to nearly 75 per cent by the end of the decade – such progress due mainly to the insistence of management in the face of opposition from often penny-pinching directors that the extra money was spent.

Nevertheless reform stuttered along until 1889 and the terrible accident at Armagh in Northern Ireland, which proved the most influential on the safety of train travel in British railway history. It involved a Sunday school special excursion with 940 people on board, two-thirds of whom were children. Excursion trains tended to be overcrowded, used old stock and under-powered engines, and employed drivers who were often not familiar with the route, giving rise to a number of accidents. For example, in 1851 nine thousand passengers travelling to the Chester Cup, a famous horse-racing event, piled into six trains, two of which were involved in a crash in Sutton tunnel. Six people were killed and it was only the presence of mind of the guard of the fifth train, who sprinted back to warn the sixth train with his lamp, that prevented an even greater disaster. (Afterwards the Railway Inspectorate urged that block signalling be mandatory in such circumstances.)

Of Armagh, says local priest the Reverend John W. McKegney, 'The annual excursion was something that everyone looked forward to. It was a big day out, children would be excused school for it. It was a bright sunny day, a band led children and adults from the Methodist church down to the railway station. For many of the children it was the only time they ever got to the seaside. They looked forward to it for months . . . Children of all denominations, with their parents, would take the opportunity of going away for the day to Warrenpoint.'

'When the train was assembled in Dundalk,' says Roger Weatherup, 'it was supposed to include thirteen carriages but because of the numbers the driver was sent round by Portadown to pick up an extra carriage. In fourteen coaches there were 941 people.' So the train was overloaded – it had an extra carriage and the extra passengers. In addition, says Roger Weatherup, 'A number of unauthorized people managed to get on board. The train was probably too heavy for the engine.'

The engine, says John McKegney, 'was designed to take fast, light passenger trains. The excursion train needed a powerful goods engine. As they had the light passenger engine they would really have needed another engine to help push the train up the steep hill towards Warrenpoint . . . But the driver was sure he could do it with a small engine, even though he was annoyed that he'd been sent it.'

They got started 'with comparatively little delay', says Roger Weatherup, 'They locked all the carriage doors to make sure that the children wouldn't get lost on the way up . . . and they got almost to the top of that long climb out of Armagh. Less than a mile would have taken them over the brow of the hill and they'd have been on the downward run towards Newry. However, just before the train got to the top of the hill the engine stalled and the train had to stop. Once you stop a steam train, particularly on a slope, it is difficult to start again. The driver and the supervisor decided that the only thing to do was to split the train in two, take one half on into the siding at Hamiltonsban station, which was at the top of the hill, then come back for the other half. To do that they had to disconnect the rear carriages from the ones in front.'

This exposed a major defect in the braking system, which was an example, says Stanley Hall, of 'Smith's simple vacuum system' and 'consisted of a pipe running all the way down from the engine under each carriage to the guard's van. The driver created a vacuum in this pipe to put the brake on by means of a steam valve on his engine. Under each coach this pipe was connected to cylinders that acted upon cast-iron brake blocks to grip each side of the wheels. The problem with this system, which was quite good at putting the brake on, was that if the brake pipe was divided for any reason, air rushed into the system and destroyed the vacuum, thus rendering the brake useless. It wasn't a fail-safe system. At Armagh, as soon as they'd uncoupled between the fifth and sixth coaches, air rushed into the system and rendered the brakes useless. The train was therefore held only by the brake on the engine and the brake in the guard's van at the back.'

'As a precaution,' says John McKegney, 'the supervisor had stones placed behind the wheels but when the driver started off again, he slipped back slightly and the front carriages hit the rear ones, just hard enough to start them sliding. The guard's brake was not working properly and once the train started there was no way they could stop it and it ran straight back down that long hill. That was what caused the disaster – the fact that once the brake was disconnected from the front of the train, the rear carriages had no effective braking system.'

Ten carriages, with six hundred passengers on board, had been left standing on the hill, restrained only by stones beneath the wheels to prevent them running away. This precaution was not as ridiculous as it sounds, as Roger Weatherup explains: 'It's a common method, inherited, of course, from the days of horse transport when you put a cog or a block behind a wheel to stop it slipping back till you got the forward motion on again. Later it was very often done with early motor cars but obviously it was totally insufficient to hold the train.'

As the stones started to shift, the carriages moved down the hill at 40mph – and collided with another train puffing up the hill. The second train had been allowed to proceed because the line was being operated on the time-interval system and the stationmaster had thought that the ten minutes that had passed since the departure of the Sunday school special was a sufficient safety margin. Roger Weatherup adds, 'The rear portion of the train started downhill slowly and the guard tried to wedge it with more stones, which was futile.'

'At first,' says John McKegney, 'they thought they could catch it but as it built up momentum and as the gradient increased, the train gathered speed and it might have been doing fifty or sixty miles an hour by the time it hit the goods engine coming up the hill.'

'Some of those who realized what was happening' says Roger Weatherup, 'were able to climb out of the windows and jump or actually in some cases passed the children out but once it got up a fair speed there was no chance of that and the unfortunates inside simply had to hope for the best. They could do nothing as it went hurtling back towards Armagh down that long high straight outside the station. The driver of the next train, Hood, could do nothing because all he saw were these carriages descending on him. He applied his brakes but he could do nothing to prevent the crash. The wooden carriages hurtled straight into the front of his engine, overturned it, and were smashed into smithereens on impact. The people who were in the carriages were thrown out on both sides, and luggage and bodies went down the embankment.'

It did not help, as John McKegney points out, that 'the carriages were built of wood, not much stronger than a garden shed, really. They were designed from the old horse-drawn carriages of the previous railway era, so when the coaches crashed into the locomotive, it just sheared the bodies off and that's where most of the casualties were caused. The old pictures show matchwood all over the place.' Eighty people died, many of whom were children, and a further 262 were injured in by far the worst accident in the then near sixty-year history of Britain's railways.

Armagh had provided so dramatic a demonstration of the inadequacies of the existing system – brake overloading, the mistaken reliance on the time-interval signalling system – that, as Stanley Hall says, 'The impact on public opinion, especially with lots of children killed, was enormous. The public was outraged and Parliament was outraged, as was the Railway Inspectorate because for many years they'd been pressing the railway companies to improve their safety systems but had had no legal powers to enforce their recommendations. Immediately they applied to Parliament for legal powers of enforcement. The accident happened on the twelfth of June, and an Act was rushed through Parliament to this effect. It received the Royal Assent only two months later. This, the Regulation of Railways Act, was the only piece of legislation concerned with railway safety passed in the nineteenth century and, indeed, for the bulk of the twentieth century as well.'

Its most important provision was the compulsory use of interlocking combined with the absolute block system, which meant that a train could not enter a section of track until the previous train had left and the signalman had given an indication to this effect. A second Act ensured that trains had automatic brakes so that if ever a train split it would automatically come to a halt and runaways could be avoided. As Hall says, all three measures had been 'inscribed in the hearts of the railway inspecting officers throughout the previous forty years. Now, the railway companies weren't expected to adopt these safeguards overnight, but they were given time limits within which they should modernize their systems. In fact most railway companies had already done so, it was merely the laggards who, usually because they didn't have enough money to do so, had failed to modernize.' After Armagh, wrote Ascanio Schneider, 'The fundamental safety principles still valid in railway operation today were established. This accident put an end to a period in Great Britain which, with its impetuous development, had often led to an experimental chaos in the fundamentals of safe railway operation.'

Yet, to this day, some railways outside Europe have not learnt the lessons of Armagh. In 1981 more than 130 people were killed at Beni Helouane in Algeria when a train stalled on a steep section of track. A second locomotive was called for but in the meantime the original locomotive was uncoupled, leaving the carriages not properly secured. They ran back down the slope to crash into the freight train whose locomotive had gone to the rescue of the passenger train.

Eighteen years later, at least seven people were killed and over two hundred injured when two commuter trains collided just south of Manila in the Philippines. The accident happened when three carriages from one of the trains uncoupled from the engine while the train was on a hill. The carriages rolled backwards on the track and hit another oncoming passenger train.

At Armagh itself, as Roger Weatherup says, the tragedy 'lived on for a long time. It was commemorated in ballads, and there are memorial plaques and gravestones in the churchyards around Armagh. It was a traumatic event. Nothing like it had happened in Armagh history before, and really nothing as serious happened for many years afterwards. It entered the folklore and remained there certainly as long as trains came to Armagh, which they did until 1957.'

John McKegney says, 'I had the experience of talking to a very elderly man who had been on the trip the previous year but wasn't allowed to go that day. He had the grim experience of seeing his own friends lying on a hillside when he came back from school that afternoon as a six-year-old boy.' 'A century later,' says Roger Weatherup, 'the accident was the subject of special exhibitions and special memorial services.' Ten years before the centenary, Warrenpoint, the little seaside resort that had been the train's destination, was the scene of another tragedy when an IRA bomb exploded killing Earl Mountbatten and members of his family.

5

Tombstone Technology

Long-term development and research, indeed faith in the long-term future, are all needed for a project of this nature but are very difficult to achieve in all the many upheavals, both internal and external, that have plagued BR in the last thirty years.

Stanley Hall, writing in 1987

After Armagh, wrote L.T.C. Rolt, 'the work of the railway inspectors changed'. Previously they 'were almost wholly concerned to eliminate the causes of accidents by urging the installation of improved protection devices'. Their success in ensuring that these devices became legally required ensured that they became 'more and more concerned to mitigate *the effects* [his italics] of accidents', which inevitably became more serious as trains grew heavier and travelled faster.

'The changes imposed following the Armagh disaster,' says Hall, led to the introduction of further refinements, especially when mechanical interlocking was replaced by electrically powered systems. 'The improvements in signalling – putting in a proper signalling system and interlocking – made railway travel a lot safer because they guarded against the signalman making an error. Electrically operated controls were placed on the operation of the signals and telegraph instruments which became known as block instruments. So signal boxes became safer and safer until we had this major change to what we have today: large power signal boxes controlling many miles of track from a central location through killer light signals.'

It seems that the inspectors acquired more confidence and started to look for more general causes of accidents, and tried to influence railway procedures systematically, rather than just after crashes. But their influence remained limited, because until 1923 Britain still had hundreds of railway companies. That year they were all merged into four groups. At the time, according to Stanley Hall, the Inspectorate had three major concerns, none of which was ambitious, let alone revolutionary. They wished 'to do more to help the driver in his obedience of signals, especially during fog and darkness; to do more, by the increased use of technical equipment, to prevent errors by signalmen; to insist on stronger coaches and the elimination of gas lighting.' But they had problems even with this modest agenda – if only because each of the new giant railway companies was better able to stand up for itself against the authorities than their smaller predecessors. This situation contrasts with other countries like France, which had only a handful of companies, all strictly controlled by the State.

The most significant progress was made in providing new signalling systems to replace the traditional semaphore signals on the busiest lines. The most advanced were the so-called four-aspect colour signals. Green meant 'all clear' and red was for danger; a double yellow light gave a preliminary warning, and a single yellow indicated that the driver should slow down. Sensibly, white was avoided, since it was used in street-lights and might be misleading in built-up areas. But progress was slow and even after the Second World War many busy lines relied on old-fashioned signals and the Sykes lock-and-block system of control. This, wrote Peter Semmens, involved

> the use of plungers, which interlocked the instruments controlling
> the block with the signalling. The starting signal in one box was
> freed only when the signalman in the one ahead had accepted a train
> by pressing his plunger. Once it had been pulled, this lever could not
> be replaced until the train had actuated a needle on the track in
> advance of a signal. In this way a cyclic system was set up, physically
> linking the movements of the trains with the block instruments and
> the signal levers.

Obviously there had to be some form of release for use in exceptional circumstances so each box contained a release key to be employed – in theory anyway – only under stringently defined conditions. This, however, meant that the system could not be described as absolutely safe because of the danger involved in human intervention. This gap was demonstrated in a crash at South Croydon, south of London, in 1947. It was foggy and a signalman thought that the instruments had failed. He used the release key, which allowed a train to crash into another, killing thirty-two people on a busy suburban line on which colour light signals had not been installed.

But one company had shown the way forward even before the First World War. This was the Great Western Railway – 'God's Wonderful Railway', as it was proudly called by its employees (and by many passengers) – the only company to have been left intact after the 1923 amalgamation. Its automatic warning system was the result of a crash in 1900 when a Paddington–Falmouth express ran into the back of a passenger train standing in Slough station. By 1906 the GWR had already installed an experimental warning apparatus based on an earlier design, known as Kempe and Rowell's patent, which was primarily designed to avoid the need for specialized fog-signalmen. As part of the general drive to harness electricity for signalling, the GWR experimented with means of warning the driver rather than the signalman. The GWR version involved what Stanley Hall describes as 'a fixed ramp between the rails which made contact with a spring-loaded shoe on the locomotive. When the Distant signal was "Clear" an electric current passed through the ramp and rang a bell on the locomotive. When the Distant signal was at "Caution" no current passed and the raising of the spring-loaded shoe broke an electrical circuit and sounded an alarm. It was thus fail-safe; a fundamental principle of all signalling and safety equipment.' The experiment was so successful that the GWR immediately extended the use of the equipment to all its main lines, and by 1908 it had already been applied to the main line from Paddington to Reading. In the forty-six years from 1912 to 1957, 31 per cent of the deaths resulting from railway accidents that occurred in other railway companies would have been avoided by an automatic warning system (AWS).* The GWR's only major crash in that period – at Norton Fitzwarren west of Taunton in December 1940 – had nothing to do with the failings of the AWS but resulted from failure to install rigid safety couplings exacerbated by the driver's problems.

The upheavals involved in creating the three other groups, often from dozens of different companies, each with its own culture, customs and practices, inevitably brought to an abrupt halt any experiments previously conducted by their constituent companies. In the succeeding quarter of a

---

* It was also, misleadingly, described as automatic train control or automatic train protection (ATC or ATP), terms applied to later systems that forced, rather than encouraged, the driver to slow down or stop.

century there were few trials even of the GWR's or other systems, and this despite the recommendations of two high-powered committees set up in the 1920s and a terrible accident that might have been avoided by the GWR's system. This occurred in October 1928 at Charfield, between Bristol and Gloucester, when an express crashed at full speed into a goods train. Fifteen people lost their lives in a blaze that intensified when a train of wooden wagons on the other line caught fire. Not surprisingly the committee then sitting came down firmly in favour of the GWR system, and advised that locomotives should be designed to provide the crew with a clear view of the track ahead. By then, though, the depression was taking hold, and while the new railway groupings were bigger than their predecessors, with the rise of the motor car and lorry, they were not necessarily more profitable – contrary to received opinion, lack of investment in Britain's rail system did not start with nationalization. Under the circumstances, neither the committees' recommendations, nor the Charfield crash, nor repeated warnings by the Railway Inspectorate that the GWR system would save more lives, had any noticeable effect. Typically, the London Midland and Scottish, biggest of the four, conducted a few perfunctory trials but put its faith in colour-light distant signals – used more widely by the Southern Railway. These were, indeed, much more easily visible in fog but they did not provide an audible warning for the driver in the cab.

Confusion may result, with serious consequences, when signals are not reinforced by an automatic control or warning system. In 1927 there was a near miss involving an express at Northallerton in north Yorkshire. The driver, writes Ascanio Schneider, 'omitted to keep a proper look-out for his own home signal, which was to the left above his track'. But 'the collection of light and semaphore signals lying in a straight line in front of the London express, could, at night and from a distance, present an optically confusing picture. In particular the colour of the double signals, blending with one another and only becoming disentangled on close approach, demanded undivided attention for almost every second.' A year later the driver of a 'mixed' train, which carried passengers as well as parcels, was confused by the meaning of a signal on a side line that did not, as the driver assumed, allow him to proceed on to the main line; to do so, he needed another signal, the confusingly named 'Up Home, Duplicate to Main', which in the event stood at danger. His train collided with an excursion train from Scarborough, killing twenty-five and seriously injuring forty-five.

Behind the resistance to the installation of any form of automatic warning system was the recrudescence of an older thought pattern that, as Stanley Hall put it, 'Nothing should be done that might in any way distract the driver from his primary duty of observing and obeying signals, and that any mechanical or other aids might eventually and unwittingly lead to a reduction in his overall level of concentration. It was a view that was to prevail in some quarters for another half century and more.'

Outside Britain progress was faster. After the First World War, the French installed a warning system that relied on contact between metal brushes under the locomotive and a ramp (or 'crocodile', as it was nicknamed) between the rails. The contact provided the warning signal, so it was not fail-safe like the system installed by the GWR, and its inadequacies certainly played a role in a terrible accident at Pomponne in eastern France just before Christmas 1933, the worst in peacetime in twentieth-century western Europe, killing two hundred and injuring five hundred more. In Switzerland the introduction of automatic train control was speeded up after an accident in 1932 when a driver ran over a block signal in the smoke-filled Gutsch tunnel, just outside Lucerne.

Yet in Britain the magic of 'tombstone technology' also worked – albeit less comprehensively than on the continent. After a crash at Bourne End in Buckinghamshire, in September 1945, which killed forty-three people, caused by the failure of a driver to slow down for a diversion, the inspecting officer pointed to possible confusion over the signals that were showing and the ambivalence was cleared up.

After Bourne End the railways replied to the Inspectorate's demand for the installation of an automatic warning system by claiming that 'Apart from the question of finance, the installation of AWS . . . would occupy a considerable time and employ a large number of skilled men. The supply of such staff is strictly limited, and its employment on this installation would therefore necessarily delay the execution of other work such as the modernization of signalling, the extension of track-circuiting and other similar works.' This argument had some justification, for throughout the post-war period the railways could not pay competitive wages for skilled staff, like signalling engineers – a failure that had fatal consequences at Clapham in 1988. But the result was further tragic accidents, including that at Harrow and Wealdstone in October 1952, with the loss of 112 lives, far and away the worst disaster in peacetime in the history of Britain's railways, and that at St John's, Lewisham, in December 1957, with the loss of ninety lives (see pages 82–83), might all have been avoided through AWS.

With nationalization the Western Region of British Railways, the former GWR, had inherited 1400 route miles with non-standard equipment. Attempts to install a standard system country-wide was further complicated by the fact that on the Southern Region (formerly the Southern Railway) any such system had to cope with third-rail electrification and high-density operation. Nevertheless, between 1954 and 1962 British Railways installed 1232 miles of its own type of AWS – effectively a form of the system installed by the former GWR. Despite the proven effectiveness of AWS systems, and even though Britain lagged behind Europe, British Railways could never persuade the Ministry of Transport – ever the motorist's friend – to accelerate investment in safety expenditure. Eleven years later the figure was 3795 route miles including 700 miles on the old GWR modified to the BR system. This was little more than half the target mileage, and in the 1970s there was a natural concern about the delay in installing AWS throughout the BR system, especially because of the arrival of newer, faster trains, and by the end of 1985 6313 route miles had been equipped with AWS. This investment, together with large-scale resignalling schemes, enormously improved BR's safety record.

But the old rivalries had left a bitter legacy. After the Harrow disaster the blame was laid on the refusal of the former LMS to adopt the system employed on the Great Western. As a railway magazine put it at the time: 'The answer, as many believe, is to be found in the obstinate refusal to accept something that another company has conceived.' The Southern Region was also recalcitrant for the same reasons that had led it to ignore pre-war recommendations to install AWS. Its trains, increasingly, were multiple units in which the driver, seated right at the front of the train, had an unrivalled view of what was happening, and the company preferred to go in for multiple-light signalling equipment. Also it took until 1963 to overcome the difficulties inherent in installing the electric warning system on a line where there was third-rail electrification. The lack of progress was dramatically demonstrated on 19 December 1978 (that Christmas curse again) when an EMU on the London–Brighton line standing at a signal was run into by a similar train, killing three people, including the driver of the second train. If signals had been provided with AWS there would not have been an accident. In the following three years three more avoidable accidents, fortunately none fatal, proved the point.

Even with AWS the colour-light signalling, especially on the ever-more crowded routes like those on which the Southern was operating, created its own problems, even with the four-colour system involving two yellow signals. The audio signal was the same for double and single yellow signals. Inevitably drivers of commuter trains habitually ignored the first double yellow to maintain their punctuality record. They knew that their trains could brake more speedily than the time scale built into the AWS system, which had been designed to accommodate the slowest braking freight trains (this problem could be resolved by employing two different sounds for single and double yellows).

Given the tightness and short-sightedness of the financial controls exercised by the Treasury through the Ministry of Transport, long-term progress was always a struggle. In 1981 Peter Rayner, then a senior railway manager, had a row over the replacement of a major signal box. With the technology then available, 'It was feasible', he wrote in *On and Off the Rails*, 'to make a quantum leap forward at quite reasonable expense.' But 'lack of government backing, short-term objectives and political pressures' all ensured that the cheapest alternative was chosen. 'It confirmed my view once more', he continued, with understandable bitterness, 'that the cheap solution, covered with public relations hype, was the BR Board's way and the government's way.'

The limitations of AWS, which is what might be called a self-regulating safety system depending on the driver (as opposed to ATP where the train stops automatically), have been shown in a number of cases where familiarity with the warning signal bred an apparent contempt for its significance – for instance, in October 1984 an electric EMU from Euston to Bletchley ran past a danger signal and collided with a freight train, which was just leaving the sidings at Euston. Nevertheless the figures show the progress made over the decades. In the first seven years of the 1930s there were thirteen accidents, which might have been prevented by AWS, with the loss of sixty-three lives; in the following fifteen years there were fifteen accidents, with 241 lives lost. But in the decade 1976–85 there were only two such accidents, killing three passengers and three railway workers.

However, the most percipient observers were not entirely convinced by the apparent progress. As Stanley Hall wrote: 'The spread of AWS and power signalling with multiple-aspect colour-light signals and continuous track circuiting has certainly reduced the number of serious collisions caused either by signalmen's errors or by drivers passing signals at danger. Indeed, of the twenty-nine fatal accidents on BR in the twenty-one-year period 1969–89, signalmen were involved in only three, a remarkable change from the situation of earlier days. But still much needs to be done to help the driver.'

Of course, AWS is 'advisory' as opposed to the more modern type of ATC, which is 'automatic' or something between. Stanley Hall calls this alternative a 'monitoring system' through which the train's speed is continuously monitored and the external control intervenes only when it is travelling too fast for the conditions:

> The basic requirement of a monitoring system is that it should continuously detect the state of the signals ahead by interrogating equipment laid in the 'four foot' (the space between the two rails) so that when the train came within braking distance of a red signal or speed restriction the appropriate speed calculated from the braking curve could be displayed on the driver's instrument panel. If the driver did not keep his speed below the level indicated, the brakes would automatically be applied. Such a system leaves the actual driving of the train to the driver, so that he still feels – indeed, is – responsible, and will thus remain alert, while still providing that essential element, a fail-safe system.
>
> In case this proposal should be thought to be too revolutionary [Hall adds bitterly, in a passage that sums up admirably all that has afflicted Britain's railway system over the past half-century], it might be mentioned that the French and Italian railways have had something similar for twenty years or more [to 1987]. Even BR were experimenting with the idea, but it was killed by the lack of a settled and established political, organizational and economic framework . . . There is little doubt that if during those thirty years BR had enjoyed the same happy, progressive and supportive relationship with, and generous treatment from, its political masters as its continental railway colleagues have had from theirs, we too would have a more effective train protection system by now.

He ends with a warning of the long-term nature of any serious investment programme 'five–ten years for development, design and proving, and a further five to ten years for installation on high-speed routes'.

Hall might also have been thinking of Holland where ATC had been installed in the 1970s on major tracks. In January 1962 an EMU on the main line between Rotterdam and Amsterdam collided with an express that had missed a distant warning signal. Ninety-three people were killed and hundreds injured in the country's worst-ever rail accident. As a result the Dutch authorities started work on an AWS system, which also provided control over the driver's actions and ensured that he could not pass a signal at danger. But even this was not enough. In 1976 the danger of fast and slow working on mixed tracks, a problem that continues to haunt railwaymen, was shown dramatically when an EMU passed a danger signal and hit the Rhine Express. This had switched tracks to avoid a stopping train, which piled into the crash with the loss of twenty-four lives. This disaster ensured that today virtually all lines in Holland have ATP. (Even this advanced system does not work perfectly – for example, where temporary speed limits are concerned.)

Modern ATC, says Hall, is 'a foolproof method of ensuring that drivers don't go past red signals. It's a computer-driven system and when a train is approaching a red signal a message is received on the locomotive's computer from trackside equipment. The computer calculates the rate of braking necessary to stop at the signal. It then compares the computer-generated rate of braking with the actual rate of braking shown on the engine speedometer. If it discovers that the speedometer is straying outside the braking curve it reminds the driver that something is going wrong. If the driver doesn't immediately respond, the brakes are engaged to ensure that the train stops at the red signal. It is a very safe system. You might almost call it foolproof, although one hesitates to call anything foolproof, but it is a very good system.' In Britain the problem of deciding whether or not to introduce this 'very good system' came to the fore in the aftermath of privatization of the railways and the two major accidents, at Southall in 1997 and on the approaches to Paddington Station, two years later.

In no other country in western Europe would a line as important as that from Paddington to the West Country have been left unelectrified, which greatly increased the death toll. The disaster claimed thirty-one lives, and many of the victims burned to death because of the flammability of the diesel used in both trains. It was a reminder that fire remains a major hazard in railway operation. The Paddington disaster echoed a tragedy that took place on 20 August 1868 at Abergele involving some wagons and the Irish

59

Mail on its way from London to Holyhead. The wagons had been loaded with barrels of petroleum and thirty-three people were burned alive. A survivor, the Marquess of Hamilton, remarked grimly that 'Probably this is the only very disastrous railway accident in which there have been no wounded, with the exception of one individual. It has been death in a most dreadful form or an entire escape.'

Even more recently diesel played a disastrous role in the crash between an Amtrak train and a local commuter train at Silver Spring in Maryland. John Kopke reckons that 'Without the fuel in that incident, we may have had three deaths instead of eleven because three of the deaths were from trauma and eight were from fire. It was like a lightning strike. It is not the norm for a railway accident to actually introduce four to five hundred gallons of diesel fuel into a car that's basically fire and flame resistant.' Since then some locomotives 'incorporate the tank into the structure of the locomotive . . . I believe ultimately we'll have some sort of containment within the tank that will preclude the fuel escaping and perhaps some of the technology that might have been used in the aircraft in the Second World War and in some of the submarines might be employed, as to where they can take a bullet strike and not leak.'

Dangerous loads, like that at Abergele, remain dangerous, as a number of horrific accidents have proved over the years. Two accidents, both in April 1930, but otherwise different from each other, showed the many possible causes of fire: in Japan seventeen people were killed when dynamite in the locomotive coal – probably the result of a blasting misfire at the colliery – exploded. The explosion wrecked not only the locomotive and several coaches but also set off a forest fire that burned all night. A few days later, forty-five people were killed in a railway fire near Moscow when methylated spirits was spilled into a coach and accidentally set alight by a dropped match. Four years later there was a spectacular accident in San Salvador when more than 250 people were killed, and around a thousand injured when seven tons of dynamite exploded on a train and set fire to a nearby warehouse full of petrol. The high death toll included those whose nearby houses caught fire. As recently as 1985 over a hundred were killed when three wagons containing 120 tons of industrial explosive blew up at Arazamas, 250 miles east of Moscow.

At the time of Abergele, and indeed for most of the first century of railway history, most carriages were made of wood, and in the United States the only heating provided for passengers was from stoves. This resulted in a class of what Charles Francis Adams called 'stove accidents'. In one case the flames rushed 'through the car so swiftly as if the wood had been a lot of hay'. But not only was the fuel used in the stoves flammable, so was the gas used to light the carriages.

A major accident at Aisgill on the Settle–Carlisle line on Christmas Eve 1910 – one express crashed into the rear of another, killing fourteen people when the pipe of a high-pressure gas cylinder allowed gas to escape – induced the Midland Railway to abandon gas lighting in its carriages. On other companies' trains, it was still in use even after the reorganization of 1923. As late as 1928 – and despite a long campaign by the Inspectorate – three-quarters of the carriages on the normally safety-conscious Great Western Railway were still lit by gas, and even the Southern Railway had converted only two-thirds of its carriages to electricity, largely as a fortunate by-product of its programme of electrification.

Tragedies caused by gas lighting were not confined to Britain. In the first nine months of 1921 France's railways underwent forty-three accidents, killing 140 people and injuring 542. On 5 October the disaster trail culminated in an accident in the Batignolles tunnel just outside St Lazare station in Paris. Twenty-eight people (possibly more) were burned to death. The railway companies were ordered to abolish gas lighting. Three years later, on the descent from the St Gotthard Pass near Bellinzona in Switzerland, on a line without interlocking, the points man in charge of setting the points forgot the existence of a goods line. In the resulting crash the gas-lit leading carriage of the Milan–Dortmund express became a fireball and fifteen died. The Swiss promptly banned all gas-lit coaches.

But the replacement of gas lighting on trains did not remove the danger posed by gas, albeit indirectly. As late as 1975, at Nuneaton in Warwickshire, a 20mph limit advance warning board was still lit by gas lamps. The gas was running low, the light was dim and the driver of a sleeping-car train missed it. He ploughed through the station at 80mph. Luckily 'only' six people died. And even the elimination of gas does not remove the possibility of fire: in 1978 twelve people died in a sleeping-car train near Taunton in Somerset when some laundry had been left too close to a heater.

In theory, and indeed virtually always in practice, electricity removed many of the elements that, historically, have transformed rail crashes into disasters, from exploding boilers to the dangers inherent in the use of coal or diesel as fuel. But it brought with it its own drawbacks. As always advances in locomotive technology without accompanying changes throughout the system can be disastrous. This was demonstrated by the investigation into a crash that took place in 1906, a bad year in the United States with 321 passengers killed. That crash marked the start of scientific investigation into rail crashes after twenty-three people were killed when an express derailed in the Bronx in New York. The investigators performed detailed work on the forces imposed on the track by both steam and the newly introduced electric locomotives. They concluded that additional spikes were needed to pin down the sleepers safely: electric locomotives were operating in pairs because of the additional strains imposed by the increased weight and speed resulting from electrification.

One of the worst disasters resulting from the introduction of electrification came in 1903 on the newly opened Métropolitain subway system in Paris. The power line between two engine cars arced and started to emit smoke. As the train was being shunted to its destination fire broke out in one of the wooden carriages, but many of the passengers would not leave the train for fear of having to pay another fare – some even started to belabour the staff trying to herd them to safety. When the fire caused the lights to fail there was a stampede and eighty-four people died, most from carbon monoxide poisoning. In August 1914 one of the earliest petrol-electric railcars * in the United States was involved in an accident. Forty-seven people were killed when it burst into flames after crashing at a fair speed. The fact that such railcars were much lighter than their locomotive-hauled predecessors cast a shadow over allowing such cars to run on the same tracks as orthodox trains.

The problems were inevitably greater in trains that operated on two distinct electrical systems, if only because of the complexities of the equipment. In March 1961 five deaths resulted from a short-circuit when an electric train equipped to cope with both direct and alternating current caught fire in the Bonassola tunnel on the spectacular line along the Italian coast east of Genoa. Ironically, five passengers died of suffocation because they had remained calmly seated while their panicking fellows escaped from the deadly carbon monoxide fumes.

Possibly the single most important lesson in the history of railway disasters is that the failure of a single element in a system can be fatal,

* They were nicknamed 'Doodlebugs', a name also applied to the V1 rockets that bombed London in the summer of 1944.

especially when the strain imposed is increased. Possibly the greatest, most rapidly increasing strain is on the crucial interface between the wheel and the track. This apparently fragile link has proved capable of containing strains of up to 300mph on the same principles as those which pertained when George Stephenson first set forth. However, too great a strain imposed on the crucial point at which the wheel meets the track may prove especially fatal. And that strain may produce even worse results if it is combined with an inadequate, discontinuous braking system, in which the driver has no means of activating the brakes on individual wagons.

Between the First and Second World Wars, most railways in western Europe installed continuous brakes linking every wagon on freight trains, in conformity with the provisions of the Treaty of Versailles. In Britain – apart from a handful of particularly fast freight trains, used for mail or for perishable goods like fish and milk – most freight trains were not fitted with continuous brakes, and relied on the braking power of the locomotive, which slowed them down and made rail transport even less competitive with road transport. The reason for this that the majority of the wagons were owned by independent private companies and it would have been unthinkable for the government to interfere with their operations. This made matters worse: most of the wagons were owned by coal companies, who needed thousands of cheap, short wheelbase wagons designed to cope with the sharp curves at the collieries.

The fundamental problem, says Alan Earnshaw, a railway historian, is that at a time 'when we were putting a man on the Moon we had wagons that were designed in the Victorian era'. As he points out, 'Freight was always going to be slightly slower than passenger traffic but the whole concept was to move away from this ten-foot-wheelbase wagon that had originated in the Victorian era to trains that could travel at express speeds' – by freight standards anyway – 'fifty, sixty miles an hour, whereas an express passenger train could be doing, and eventually did, over a hundred miles an hour.'

Such was the high level of discipline among the employees of the railway companies that the great difference in speed between freight and passenger and freight trains sharing the same tracks resulted in few accidents. However in July 1967 one such accident showed the danger inherent in any attempt to speed up freight trains. A train of twenty-six new-style cement wagons travelling at 45mph – which was then considered fast – derailed on to an embankment near Thirsk in north Yorkshire. One of the wagons fell into the path of an express from King's Cross to Edinburgh, which was travelling at 80mph when the driver saw the wagon and hit the brakes. It was still travelling at 50mph when it ploughed into the derailed wagon. The left-hand side of the locomotive was crushed and derailed taking the first seven of the thirteen coaches with it. Seven passengers were killed and forty-five severely injured. The locomotive, a prototype of the famously powerful English Electric Deltic diesel-electric type, was damaged beyond repair.

'The driver of the express had not noticed anything untoward', says Ian Scott, the Thirsk coroner, until 'he noticed that one of the signals, which he should have been able to see further up the track, appeared to be slightly obscured by mist. He immediately took action by starting to brake. He then saw the cement wagon, which was partly blocking his path, and he was between the devil and the deep blue sea. Had he really braked hard then the passenger train could have jack-knifed. So he just braked as hard as he could and when he realized that there was going to be a collision he switched his engine off so that there would not be a risk of a severe fire. He thought very quickly, and had he not done what he did, it might have been a much more severe accident.'

Scott points out that, in his statement, 'the guard of the cement train had remarked on "the side to side movement of the cement trains in general". For that reason he said that he had kept a complete watch out of his little window in the guard's van. He had seen nothing untoward until at the point of crash. The cement trains had a tendency to "hunt", or move from side to side, as they went up the track and, of course, when it goes round a bend this tendency helps to stabilize the wheels but this was a particularly long straight and this is what he was worried about.' The subsequent inquiry discovered that 'The cement trains had a bad record for breaking springs [so] every cement train which was travelling up laden from the south to the north was inspected at least four times.'

Alan Earnshaw says that these wagons 'were not owned by British Railways. They were generally owned and operated by the Cement Market-ing Board and the cement companies. The development of cement wagons had started in 1948. Obviously you can't carry cement in open wagons because even if it's in bags it is exposed to the elements and goes rock hard. They had converted grain carriers to take cement and found that if they loaded them from the top then discharged from the bottom by an air compressor, cement could be transported in a perfectly dry state.' Unfortunately cement is 'a very heavy material and it compacts during travel. If that compaction is level and equal the train will ride perfectly smoothly, but that wasn't happening in most cases. Various experiments were tried with a variety of specialist containers until we came to the Cemflow. With the Cemflow we thought that we'd got a solution to the problem' – and not only that of carrying cement. These wagons, says Alan Earnshaw, 'had taken us into a new era, the era of the block train, complete loads going from a single generating point to a single destination, they weren't altered at any time during their journey whereas previously trains had been made up. At every station they called at, a wagon would be taken off and a new one added on.'

They found then that 'the cement, being an abrasive powder, was getting into the joints, into the axle bearings, into a whole variety of places and causing wear during movement. As the cement settled in the tanks it was causing a very uneven ride. These wagons had two axles, four wheels, and the load imposed on each axle quite often differed dramatically and the load on each wheel within an axle would differ, so the wagon couldn't ride evenly. When the wagon was in a train it would tend to snake about and zigzag along the tracks, not perceptibly so but one driver described it very much like the tail wagging the dog. For, as the train travelled along the track, the wheels were moving slightly from side to side, and the effect was exacerbated if there was any discrepancy in the track at all', as there was on the line at Thirsk. 'After the wagons were inspected after the accident, though nothing was clearly visible beforehand, one of the wheels was worn by something under a tenth of an inch. This was apparently enough, what with the small discrepancies on the track, to hit one side, bounce back to the other, be thrown back and then cause an accident.'

So, says Alan Earnshaw, 'You get a situation where the train is really becoming unstable, and it was eventually discovered, much later than the inquiry itself, that wagons of this type were sometimes travelling along with the couplings maintaining tension but some of the wheels not making full contact with the rail. They were gliding along on top of the rail. Now, that was fine as long as the train was in tension and the track was in good state . . . and although there had been minor problems with the Cemflow trains, nothing really came to light until Thirsk.' The track there was slightly uneven and that, combined with the wheels floating along the top of the track, derailed the train.

As Ian Scott notes, such wagons 'had been used very successfully for many years on the continent and had achieved high mileages without any problem', so why did the problem in Britain culminate in the Thirsk crash? Afterwards, says Earnshaw, 'the people who were designing wagons for special traffic began to look in more detail at the new concept of longer wheelbases, bogey wagons rather than rigid under-frames and making trains that could run at speeds of fifty, sixty, seventy miles an hour to carry freight speedily to its destination. Specifically Thirsk started a debate. In the short term Cemflow wagons were limited to thirty-five miles an hour but that wasn't the answer. In Britain of the 1960s and early 1970s industry wanted to get its goods quickly from A to B without any delay, in other words within a day. Thirsk started a debate about how the way ahead would go, what traffic could be carried in block trains, what maintenance would have to be undertaken to privately owned wagons, what inspection schedules would be needed'. But with increased speeds came an increased number of derailments. The peak came in 1969, which saw 383, and a reduction was only achieved as less freight was carried on the rails.

Thirsk, and dozens of other crashes, show the dangers inherent in trying to run modern trains at modern speeds using systems and tracks devised a hundred or more years ago (most of the main lines in England were built before 1852).

The result wrote L. Kutas in a letter to *Modern Railways* of December 1999, 'is a proliferation of signalling and communication systems to provide an operational environment for twentieth-century trains [not to mention those running in the twenty-first century!] on nineteenth-century track. Many of these additions were conceived and executed pretty poorly' – hence the increased strain on drivers and the need for greater and more reliable automatic control systems.

The situation is worsened when fast and slow trains have to share tracks or have to switch between them. The failure to ensure a strict separation of tracks, between fast and slow, was a major factor in the Harrow disaster in 1952 when a local train was switched to a main line. This remains the worst accident in Britain in peacetime, in terms not only of lives lost – 112 – but in the amount of wreckage, which formed a pile of a size never seen before or since. The Harrow crash occurred as one train crossed the track of another, inevitably a danger point – as was shown again by an accident at Watford Junction in August 1996 in which one passenger was killed when a stock train crossing from the slow to the fast line collided with a commuter train. It takes years and costs millions of pounds to iron out even the simplest such junction and much more to replace them with flyovers. In the United States Amtrak has a bad record of safety for passengers partly because most of its trains run along tracks owned by freight railroads, which have adapted their tracks to the needs of immensely heavy but relatively slow freight trains and which have to retain hundreds of level crossings, especially on lines with little traffic.

Many accidents now occur when fast trains and slow trains get in the way of each other, as happened at Southall in 1997. Under these circumstances, if the installation of separate tracks is impossible, a halfway solution is to ensure that the traditionally slower commuter trains can match the speed of the expresses. (This is what is happening as the West Coast main line north of Euston is modernized, with the operators of the commuter services from Euston to Northampton ordering trains capable of 140mph, a previously unthinkable speed for a commuter train).

It is important not to use such crashes as arguments against speed in itself, for with trains, as with motor traffic on motorways, fast travel can be the safest, provided that the vehicles are running on separate tracks. Typically Eurostar trains can travel at up to 300kph in France as part of a TGV system that has not witnessed a single accident in nearly twenty years of intensive operation. The key to the excellent safety record of such tracks – not only in France but also in Japan where there has not been a single accident since the Bullet Train was first introduced in 1964 – is that they are dedicated to one type of traffic. There are no crossings, fewer points, no level crossings, longer rails, smoother ride, special materials and a radio-controlled signalling system because the drivers are travelling too fast to see line-side signals.

Inevitably, the installation of new track is of no use without accom-panying advances in control systems. For their fast, tilting Pendolino trains the Italians rely on track-side beacons that can detect the speed of the train and, if it is going too fast, automatically apply the brakes. But a crash near Piacenza in 1997 that left eight dead and twenty-nine wounded resulted from a beacon having been wrongly set: it should have allowed trains through at 62mph but it did not stop the train involved in the crash from going through at 100mph. Railways are a system of many parts and any flaw in any part may cause a fatal accident.

6
What About the Workers?

Deaths were expected, and the navvies increased the ever-present hazard by their own recklessness.

Terry Coleman, *The Railway Navvies*

Historically, the people who have been most at danger on the railways have been those building them or working on them. Deaths among railway workers, which occur regularly even today among those maintaining or replacing the rails, sleepers and rail bed never make the headlines or gain the attention given to injuries among the passengers for whose safety they are ultimately responsible. Indeed, virtually the only time they are noticed by the public or the press is when a driver or a signalman is held responsible, often unfairly, for a crash.

But the inherent danger of working on a system involving powerful machines operating at ever-greater speeds existed even before construction started. In the 1850s, and despite the best efforts of troops commanded by the future General Sherman, dozens of surveyors picking out the best routes through the Rocky Mountains were ambushed by the local Indians and killed. The first recorded death of a 'navigator' (a worker who dug canals, the predecessors of Britain's railways, hence 'navvy') – at least one building a railway rather than a canal – predates the opening of the Liverpool and Manchester Railway in 1830. In the words of the *Liverpool Mercury* of 10 August 1827, 'The poor fellow was in the act of undermining a heavy load of clay, fourteen or fifteen feet high' – while helping to excavate a cutting at Edgehill on the outskirts of Liverpool – 'when the mass fell upon him, and literally crushed the bowels out of his body.'

His was only the first of many thousands of deaths incurred in the building of the world's railways. When Isambard Kingdom Brunel, a most humane engineer, was shown a list of 131 navvies severely injured over a nine-month period during the building of the Great Western Railway, he commented simply: 'I think it is a small list . . . considering the very heavy works and the immense amount of powder used . . . I am afraid it does not show the whole extent of accidents incurred in that district.' And the young were not spared: adolescent lads were run over by the wagons they guided to the top of the embankment. In Britain there was no compensation, although when the navvies went to work in France they found such a system already in place.

It did not help that navvies were careless of their own lives. In *The Railway Navvies* Terry Coleman records how 'one navvy on the Great Western line was twice reproved by his ganger for earthing under too great a fall of dirt, undercutting into the face of the soil. He carried on: it was quicker that way. A quarter of an hour later the overlap fell in and killed him. "He was a good workman," said the ganger, "and a nice sort of chap."' He was not alone. On another site, according to Coleman, 'The men had taken to riding on a rickety temporary tramway, which was designed to take wagons of soil from a cutting to an embankment. One man was killed when a truck was derailed, but this did not deter others, and a few days later a gang of navvies riding down to their dinner were thrown off and buried beneath the derailed trucks and their load of earth.'

In New England, Henry Thoreau lamented that 'Every sleeper marks the death of an Irishman who died that the road might be built' – although this, it has to be said, was partly because the Irish were especially keen on the most dangerous jobs, such as working the horses when building cuttings or embankments. And on the Central Pacific line in California the death rate was artificially increased by the Irish habit of exploding their dynamite when they were digging down from the surface while their Chinese rivals were still working in the cuttings beneath.

The biggest disasters, however, were associated with shoddy construction, a recurring theme in the story of railways the world over. When a partially built viaduct collapsed at Ashton-under-Lyme in 1845, leaving fifteen dead, it was found that the interior was filled with mere rubble instead of solid brick or stone. Although the jury at the inquest spoke of negligence the formal verdict was 'accidental death'.

Tunnels provided the highest casualty rate. In the early 1990s, and even with the most modern equipment and the most stringent safety precautions five workers died while building the Channel Tunnel between Britain and

France. A hundred and fifty years ago the toll was inevitably grimmer: thirty-two navvies lost their lives when blasting the Woodhead tunnel through the Pennines. As the reformer Edwin Chadwick wrote in an offical report at the time, 'Thirty-two killed out of such a body of labourers, and one hundred and forty wounded, besides the sick' – the workings were so damp that most navvies had a chronic cough – 'nearly equal the proportionate casualties of a campaign or a severe battle. The losses in this one work may be stated as more than 3 per cent killed, and 14 per cent wounded'. It was a higher proportion, he pointed out, than the deaths incurred among Wellington's soldiers in four of his battles with Spain during the Peninsular War. Nevertheless, the railway contractors were furious with Pomfret, the gallant surgeon who provided the figures on behalf of the navvies, for then, as now, whistle-blowers were not popular.

Twenty-four workers died in a single accident in the Simplon tunnel that runs through Mont Blanc between France and Italy, and at least the same number every year during the fifteen long, painful years it took to build the tunnel beneath the St Gotthard Pass between Italy and Switzerland during the 1860s and 1870s. According to Gosta Sandstrom in *The History of Tunnelling*, the tragedies were due to

> accidental explosions from unignited cartridges, rock falls, train accidents, burst pipes, etc. More serious, however, were the diseases induced by the wretched working conditions. Rock dust, explosive fumes, exhalations from men and animals, temperatures that at times rose to 122°F caused numerous ailments and an untold number of men died from 'miner's anaemia'. A man became incapable of working after three or four months; if he persisted, he died or became incapacitated for life. The toll among animals was just as bad, about thirty horses and mules dying each month.

As Sandstrom points out, disease was an even bigger killer than accidents, and not only in the tunnels. Epidemics of cholera or dysentery were inevitable in the primitive camps in which the men were huddled together at a time when the most elementary notions of hygiene were unknown or ignored. During the building of the Chinese Eastern Railway across Manchuria in the 1900s bubonic plague claimed the lives of 1400 navvies. Worse, throughout the building of the railway across the Isthmus of Panama, half a century earlier, one worker in five died every month from tropical diseases.

It was not only workers who succumbed. Most of the greatest railway engineers died young, from prolonged overwork – a succession of twenty-hour days and seven-day weeks – the wear and tear of constant travel on primitive, bumpy roads, when they were often frozen or soaked to the skin. The death rate among the contractors and even the bankers was also high, thanks to the stress involved in any major railway construction project. The contractor, Louis Favre, who was responsible for the St Gotthard tunnel, died in 1879, 'broken', wrote Sandstrom, 'by the combination of evil forces – seven years of incessant struggles with the mountain, during which he had spent days on end submerged in water up to his waist personally supervising the work, the shocks and frustrations, his long persecution by the railway management, and, lately, his deteriorating economic conditions'. Favre had been a rich man when he took on the contract, but he died bankrupt. His second-in-command died shortly before him, and Alfred Escher, the banker whose vision had seen the project through endless obstacles, died seven months before the tunnel finally opened.

Even when railway construction had been completed the workers continued to suffer and employment on the railways was among the most dangerous of all occupations. Railway workers, especially outside Britain, came from previously agricultural communities. They were unused to the pace of industrial life and found it appallingly difficult to adapt to working in what would now be considered normal industrial jobs. The problem has recurred on a smaller scale in Britain since privatization, which has involved the widespread use, in particular on maintenance contracts, of sub-contractors whose employees lack the instinctive sense of danger on the tracks bred into the bones of railway workers. At the end of the twentieth century, the situation was quickly recognized and resolved – but a hundred and fifty years ago life was cheap and horrific injuries were taken for granted.

In the early days of railways it did not help that virtually every railway worker faced a combination of inconceivably long hours and working conditions that were either uncomfortable or dangerous or both. Sixteen-hour days, seven-day weeks were the norm for the first fifty years of the railways' existence and the results might be fatal to both workers and passengers. 'Signalmen were dazed by want of sleep,' wrote the *Lancet* in 1862. Nevertheless in 1880, the London and North Western Railway, biggest and best-managed of Britain's railway companies, withdrew a proposal to allow signalmen two Sundays in three off duty and forced their employees to work two twelve-hour Sundays out of three, with a shift of a mere eight hours on the third.

And it was not only the drivers and signalmen who suffered. The fogmen were called out at any hour to place detonators. As Frank McKenna wrote in *The Railway Workers 1840–1970*:

> The fogman posted in the reeking air at the base of the signal post, was blinded by fog and choked by the fumes of his 'fog devil'. This was a coke-burning brazier, whose heat kept the signal wires from icing up. On shift, the fogman often had to cross running lines to do his duty; many were knocked down and mutilated by trains. A moment's delay could lead to appalling consequences. Fogmen often stood by their posts for sixteen unfed and frozen hours.

In 1873 a parliamentary inquiry reported that a guard who died in an accident 'had been nineteen hours on duty and was over-fatigued, and omitted to apply his brake. The driver of the pilot engine was stated to have been confused by drink, after having been on duty for thirty-two hours. He was employed altogether for forty hours. The fireman had been asleep on the engine and was unfit for duty.' Eight years later a sixty-year-old signalman who was on duty at the time of another accident 'had been on duty for nearly thirteen consecutive hours, while his daily work on weekdays, exclusive of the time he may have taken in walking to and from his home, would average over fifteen-and-a-half hours'. The inspector who reported on the case was firm if restrained in concluding that: 'It is hardly too much to say it is a scandal that such an amount of work as is implied by these hours should be expected from any man upon whose vigilance depends the safety of the public, and who by a momentary act of forgetfulness may, as in this case, cause a fatal catastrophe.'

Until recently, one major danger came from what McKenna calls 'lodging-house men, men who had effectively two homes, the second at wherever they were sent to stay overnight regularly on long journeys. They were involved in two of the worst crashes in post-war British railway history, at Bourne End in 1945 and five years later at Harrow and Wealdstone. Guards who worked at night on the relatively primitive goods trains common in Britain at least until the 1960s had an especially hard time of it: 'Throughout the night hours,' wrote McKenna, 'his body was buffeted and banged by every wrinkle in the rail, his ears were tuned to the early screech or groan of tortured axles, and his eyes grew red and strained looking for the ugly glow of an axle tree running red and hot.'

Nevertheless, the 'servants of the railway company'* displayed an astonishing loyalty to their employers. After the second crash in two years on the Manchester, Sheffield and Lincolnshire railway had killed twenty-five passengers on a races special, the employees offered to forgo a day's wages to defray the cost of the accident. (The company graciously declined.) The loyalty of their workers was also useful to railway companies in the United States who did not want to invest in safety devices. In 1879 Charles Francis Adams pointed to 'that singular relying of the corporation on the individuality and intelligence of its employees . . . one of the most striking characteristics of American railroad management, without a full appreciation of which it is impossible to understand its using or failing to use certain appliances.' In Britain it was thought that personal comfort might lead to carelessness so drivers and firemen were refused shelter in the form of a proper cab on the engine.†

Apart from the general stresses and strains of railway employment, there were more specific causes of many accidents. For example, the engines' boilers had to withstand mechanical strain too great for the iron of which they were constructed. According to Stuart Legg, in *The Railway Book*, in one early accident a driver 'was blown up with his boiler. His arms and legs were hurled in different directions, and one of the former actually went through the window of a private house and fell upon a breakfast-table round which the family were sitting at the time.'

But the major source of injuries was the primitive methods used to link passenger carriages to freight wagons. As David Tyrell, a scientist at the Volpe Institute, explains, 'The initial impetus to move from the chain-type drawbar linkage arrangement to an automatic coupler was because people were getting killed in coupling the wagons together. With an automatic coupler somebody did not have to stand between the cars to couple them. People were getting killed because it's hard to control the train motion accurately and if somebody's standing between the cars there's the potential for them to be crushed.'

---

* As they were called most recently in 1961 by Alan Bennett in the revue *Beyond The Fringe*. Bennett was mocking older forms of diction but ones that might have been heard in some sections of British society at least until 1939.
† The same applied to tractor-drivers a century later.

Until new types of coupling came into common use in the early 1900s carriages and wagons alike were coupled by hand, where the main casualty was a worker's fingers. In the nineteenth century, in the United States at least, when yardmasters engaged casual brakemen and switchmen they asked the applicants to hold up their hands. Only those with one or more fingers missing were hired. It was considered a sure sign that they were experienced in the work.

The best source of descriptions of the appalling accidents suffered as a matter of course by American railroad workers in the middle of the nineteenth century is *The General Manager's Story*, by Herbert Hamblen, a veteran railwayman. On his first day at work he met an old fellow who

> had only one eye, and a terrible scar ran diagonally across his face from eyebrow to chin. This had crushed and distorted his nose, drawn one corner of this eye down, and the opposite corner of his eye up, thereby showing a couple of filthy, tobacco-stained husks, and giving him the most repulsive appearance of any human being that I ever saw . . . His overalls were black with dirt, and so shiny with grease that when the sun shone on him he glistened like a crow. His left arm was cut off just below the elbow, and finished off with a three-pronged iron hook, in which he carried a great iron pail filled with coloured cotton waste soaked in oil.

The atmosphere was such that one worker 'believed that accidents were largely due to the recklessness of the men themselves . . . he hoped to escape the almost universal fate by being careful. Poor fellow! He was blown from the top of his train a few months afterwards and found by the section gang, frozen stiff.' Another victim of what Hamblen – who ended as a boss himself without any pity for the workers he left behind – calls 'the insatiate maw of the railway' had been impaled on the drawhead of a rail car. 'He was a poor man with the usual poor man's blessing, a large family, so we made up a purse to bury him.'

That this picture is no exaggeration is clear from the account of an everyday accident reported in the *Evening Republican Tribune* of Trenton, Missouri, on 24 July 1905 and reprinted ninety years later by a journalist whose great-uncle had been fireman on the train involved. In those days the brakeman of freight trains had to mount the top of the guard's van when passing through stations to keep a proper lookout. Twenty-two-year-old

James Murphy was doing his duty when this particular train derailed and tipped over on to its right side: 'somewhere in that crash, James Murphy's life was crushed out . . . Nearby two tanks of naphtha oil burst open as a result of the impact and burst into flames, forming a funeral pile for the poor brakeman.' But the most extraordinary aspect of what must have been a routine occurrence was the laconic paragraph later in the story that 'It is a co-incident, worthy of mention, that about a year ago at the same town' another brakeman lost his life. There was only one difference between the two accidents: 'His train going east, however, while this one was coming west.'

None the less, so far as British railways are concerned, the story over the past century and a quarter has been relatively happy – and can probably be replicated in most industrialized countries. In the 1860s up to eight hundred railway workers were killed in the course of duty every year, around ten times the numbers killed in train accidents. Indeed, according to a survey conducted in 1865 the risk of accidents was fifty times greater for railway workers than for passengers. By the end of the 1880s annual fatalities were well below five hundred and had reduced to around four hundred by the outbreak of war in 1914. This number was halved in the 1920s, and in the first twenty years after nationalization in 1948 dropped to fifty or fewer. The reasons were obvious: railwaymen were better trained, they no longer had to work with manual or mechanical equipment, or with steam locomotives, while the rails themselves lasted longer and needed less regular maintenance. Nevertheless, when railwaymen were injured they still received only minimal compensation. As late as1956 a fireman received only £1400 when a leg had to be amputated after a collision, and another the same amount for losing his eyesight when a whistle chain broke.

But the best evidence I came across of the tardiness of progress came from George McDonald, an American union official, who says: 'Before 1970 between two and five workers per year were killed in the New York City subway system, either run over by trains or electrocuted. In 1970 the federal OHSA came into play and where we weren't bound by it we adopted its standards. Then there were between one and three members per year killed. In 1985 the New York City Transit, New York state came under federal regulations and today we have about one person killed every five years. I don't think we've had a fatality in the last two years. There was one in the early nineties. We have a total of about 150 transport-union workers that were killed on the job and we have a plaque upstairs as a memorial to them.'

Perhaps it would help passengers to reflect on the dangers faced by the men who built and worked on the railways in the past if such plaques, like war memorials, were erected throughout the world's railway systems.

7

War and Other Disasters

So the train mov'd slowly along the Bridge of Tay,
Until it was about midway,
Then the central girders with a crash gave way,
And down went the train and passengers into the Tay.
          William McGonagall, 'The Tay Bridge Disaster', 1879

In wartime and in periods of bad weather the usual strains and stresses to which railways are subject are multiplied a hundredfold. The result was vividly expressed by Martin Peterson, a former fighter pilot, who had survived a train crash. During the Second World War, he says, 'My job flying Typhoons [the fastest pre-jet fighter-bomber ever built] was as a train-buster. We attacked numerous trains, and I was officially credited with twenty-six trains destroyed. As I was groping my way down the side of the train that morning after the accident, I thought, "Now you know what it was like for the crew and people on those trains that you thought nothing of destroying during the war." '

Eighty years before the Second World War the vulnerability of trains to destruction was already a major feature of strategic thinking. It was General Sherman, during the American Civil War, who pointed out that while 'they can't stop the Tennessee river and each boat can make its own game' any 'railroad running through a country where every house is a nest of secret, bitter enemies' would inevitably suffer, 'bridges and water tanks burned, trains fired into, tracks torn up . . . engines run off and badly damaged'. He made sure to destroy all the railway lines during his famous march through Georgia so that they could not be used by Confederate troops.

Fifteen years later the triumphant advance of German armies that had swept through France in 1870 might have been brought to a grinding halt when the French blew up a viaduct at Fontenoy-sur-Moselle. Luckily for the Germans, though, the saboteurs were a month too late to stop their advance. In the Boer War sabotage by the Boers' Irish Brigade of the single railway line on which the British troops depended was far more effective.

But the vulnerability of railways to attack by saboteurs in wartime as well as by aircraft was best shown in the Second World War. Bombing raids on the marshalling yards at Hamm in the Rhineland were a regular feature of news bulletins while sabotage reached its peak in France in 1943–44, thanks to railway workers loyal to the Allied cause – a loyalty celebrated in a famous film, *La Bataille du Rail*, and ensuring that they were treated as war heroes for a generation or more. However, the damage was relatively insignificant to the progress of the war as road transport provided a more flexible alternative transport system, even for the largest armies.

The effects of war on railways were not restricted to bombing: during both world wars the accident rate rose catastrophically as rail systems – and those operating them – were stretched to the limit and beyond. Attempts were made to cover up the crashes to guard against a loss of morale, and when, as usually happened, they became public knowledge even the worst did not have nearly as great an impact as in peacetime, if only because there was so much worse slaughter going on elsewhere. These disasters did not affect only front-line countries. In the USA, which was in theory less affected than other combatant countries, collisions and crashes in the year to the end of June 1942, after the United States had been at war for only seven months, numbered over 9500, which was 3000 more than for the previous twelve months.

In wartime, old rolling stock had to be brought out of retirement and it caused the deaths of 196 people in Germany on 22 December 1939. This was the last of a series of seven accidents in the first winter of the war, most of which had been caused by the use of old rolling stock when the German railways were not under any particular strain. (British schoolboys joked 'Travel by train and see the next world.')

The single worst accidents in the history of both French and British railways, in terms of lives lost, both occurred during the First World War. Far and away the worst accident in the 170-year history of Britain's railways occurred at Quentinshill, north of Carlisle, on the main line from London to Glasgow on 22 May 1915, mainly because of the pressure imposed on the system by wartime conditions. It occurred after a relief signalman turned up just after his 6am clock-in time and was too occupied in rewriting the register to cover his lateness to cope with the number of trains passing through. One was a special troop train running to Liverpool. Next came a northbound local train sent ahead of two late-running northbound overnight expresses. Due to confusion in the signal box the troop train was allowed through on the same line as the local train, which was standing at the station. As Geoffrey Kitchenside describes the accident, in *Great Train Disasters*:

> The troop train did not stand a chance. It was travelling fast
> downhill from the Beattock summit . . . Its engine hit the engine of
> the local train head-on and many of its twenty-one coaches – largely
> old gas-lit six-wheelers, packed with soldiers – became a pile of
> wreckage compressed to less than a quarter of its original length.
> The railwaymen in the signal box looked on aghast as tragedy
> unfolded, then suddenly realized the signals were at 'clear' for the
> first of the overnight expresses from London, fast approaching and
> only about a quarter of a mile away. Although they tried to warn it,
> the two engines hauling the heavy express had hardly slowed when
> they ploughed into the debris of the first collision. White-hot coal
> was flung from the firebox and, with gas escaping from the ruptured
> pipes of the lighting of the old coaches, an inferno soon broke out.
> The whole pile burst into flame: the blaze did not die down for
> twenty-four hours.

No one knows precisely how many people died – it was at least two hundred, certainly, with more injured – because the military records were destroyed in the blaze. As it was wartime the signalmen were gaoled for manslaughter.

Two years later, in December 1917, the French experienced their worst-ever crash, which was far more directly related to wartime conditions than Quentinshill had been. The crash at St-Michel-de-Maurienne, near Modane, just north of the Mont Cenis tunnel through the Alps, killed 543 soldiers going on leave. The driver refused at first to take a grossly over-loaded train down a steep gradient but he was forced to do so by the officers in charge of the train. The brakes grew red hot and sparks set fire to the wooden carriages. The locomotive and the leading carriage derailed and the remaining carriages piled up behind them. Fortunately a signalman had seen the runaway train and prevented an ambulance train from piling into the wreckage. (Such was the French obsession with secrecy that the crash did not become public knowledge until 1970.) This was by no means the only major crash in wartime France: several British soldiers were killed in one while travelling in trucks labelled '*hommes 36–40, chevaux 8*', which became infamous when used to transport Jews and other victims of the Holocaust to their final destination.

The consequences of wartime disruption did not end in 1945, if only because it takes so long to bring a war-torn system back to normal. In 1946 Britain's railways were hit by a spate of accidents, starting with a serious collision at Lichfield on New Year's Day when twenty passengers were killed. In October 1947 there were two accidents in the space of three days, resulting in sixty deaths – 121 were killed that year, the second highest annual death toll in railway history. And the problems continued. There were over 1200 accidents yearly between 1948 and 1953, half as many again as had taken place in the five years before war broke out in 1939, although fewer train miles were being run. As the then chief inspector, Sir Alan Munt, remarked, an accident at South Croydon in 1947 'would not have occurred if colour-light signalling and track circuiting had been in use, and it was proposed to commence to equip the line between Battersea Park and Coulsdon in 1940 but the war had postponed the work'.

Railways have always been susceptible to nature's often devastating whims in the form of snow, ice, storms and floods. The problems have been accentuated in that, from their earliest days, railways have always tackled the most fearsome natural obstacles – indeed, it was one of their major advantages that they could find routes across, through or round even the biggest mountain chains. Moreover, early railways tended to follow river courses, often the only way through a mountain range. And train companies have always prided themselves on maintaining a service even in the most severe weather.

Probably the first naturally caused disaster came when in 1841 an early goods train travelling west from Paddington ran into a landslip precipitated by abnormally heavy rain near Sonning. The crash had one unexpected effect: it instilled a largely unjustified fear in intending travellers of boarding the leading carriage of any train. Among the British public it caused a sensation, not only because a rail crash was a novel event but also because it occurred on Christmas Eve. From then on – as you will notice in this book – the Christmas season witnessed far more than its fair share of crashes.

Some related to the foul weather normal for that time of year, while others stemmed from more trains being run, which brought back older, less safe locomotives and carriages into service, overcrowding, tension and over-tiredness in drivers and other railwaymen.

Bad weather has not only caused many accidents, it has also impeded rescue efforts. Typical was an accident at Elliot Junction on 29 December 1906 – yet another Christmas-season horror story. There had been severe snowstorms on the east coast of Scotland and the driver of a northbound freight train was stuck in one. He decided to move south on to another line and propel the train south, and neither the block system nor the time interval system was working. The driver's manoeuvre ended in disaster when an express, with its locomotive running tender first thus restricting the driver's view, collided with the local train. The rescue was a shambles: it took four hours for the information to reach head office in Edinburgh less than forty miles away and even then no rescue equipment was available. The driver of the express admitted that he had accepted a drink from passengers 'to keep the cold out'. He was convicted of culpable homicide.

Typically, a blizzard which intensified the effects of a major crash on a single-line railway on Christmas Eve 1938, killing ninety-three people and injured 147 at Etulia in Romania. The crash was caused by a misunder-standing between three station masters, but the prevailing weather con-ditions not only created chaos but delayed the despatch of rescue trains for several hours and prevented news of the tragedy reaching Bucharest until late in the afternoon of Christmas Day.

With storms come avalanches, a feature of some winters in the Alps, which have sometimes proved fatal despite the network of anti-avalanche sheds erected by the Swiss railways. Probably the worst came in late April 1917 after an avalanche-ridden winter when a guard and nine passengers lost their lives – some because they had jumped out of the train at the last minute when they would have had a better chance of survival had they stayed put.

The most pervasively dangerous natural phenomenon is fog, which obscures vital visual signals and man-induced poor visibility, in smoke-filled tunnels, has been another dangerous hazard.* Even when fog is not the only

* In one instance forty-three people were killed when an empty stock train ran into an excursion train in fog. As most of the railway staff were arrested, the Baltimore and Ohio Railroad Company said it couldn't make its own investigations because all the witnesses it wanted to call were in prison.

cause of an accident – and most crashes have multiple fathers – it is at least a major contributory factor, by adding to the strain on drivers and signal-men alike. In Germany in November 1900, a notoriously foggy month, the driver of an express train near Mühlheim-am-Main failed to notice a signal until the last minute. He backed his train to behind the signal and a local train collided with it. Twelve lives were lost. In December 1966, twenty-nine people died in a crash in Spain when the driver of a heavy freight train, failing to see a signal in thick fog, crashed into and virtually destroyed a diesel multiple unit.

The worst single peacetime accident in French railway history, was due to dense fog. It happened on 23 December 1933 at Pomponne, east of Paris on the main line to Strasbourg. An express train from Paris to Nancy composed of old-fashioned wooden carriages, which had been delayed by the fog, crashed into a local train – even though there were detonators on the line – killing over two hundred and injuring another five hundred. The driver and fireman of the express, who were arrested afterwards, claimed with every justification that the fog had prevented them from seeing the local train and the signals and it had muffled the sound of the detonators. Neither had they received any signal from the so-called 'crocodile' which provided a back-up acoustic warning for main-line signals. The capacity of fog to muffle sound was also largely responsible for a crash in Italy in 1960 when the driver failed to see a signal and did not hear the warning detonators.

In Britain perhaps the most famous crash in which fog played a major role – not only in the crash itself but in creating the tensions due to delayed trains that exacerbated the situation – was also the second worst accident on Britain's railway system in peacetime. It took place at St John's, Lewisham, in south-east London in early December 1957. The fog was a real 'pea-souper', a regular feature of London's winters until the Clean Air Act passed in the previous year started to have an effect. Ninety people were killed and 109 seriously injured when an express train from Charing Cross to Ramsgate ran first through a double yellow and then a single yellow signal at full speed. It collided with a stationary DMU, which had its brakes on, increasing the severity of the crash. The front carriage crushed the rear of the locomotive's tender. As Peter Semmens tells the story, 'Both were forced sideways, dislodging the centre pillar of the bridge above . . . Two of its girders subsided on the train below, completing the destruction of the front coach and badly crushing the second and the front half of the third. Throughout the area visibility had been bad during the afternoon and was particularly bad in the area where the accident occurred, with the two vital distant signals barely visible.'

Most of the worst disasters inflicted by nature occur when severe conditions affect bridges, which are often flimsy and thus the weak spot on many systems. Even today in India bridges and embankments are regularly washed away by the monsoon rains. The greatest challenge to the engineers of the early railways lay in building bridges, often of a size previously unknown. Their genius is shown in that many of these, as well as their viaducts and embankments are still in use today. But before the arrival of computers, which can calculate with minute accuracy the strength required for a given structure, even the most gifted engineers could go wrong. It was a combination of increasingly heavy trains and a storm that undid the work of the famous nineteenth-century French engineer, Gustave Eiffel. In 1874–75 he had built a bridge just outside Basle, in Switzerland, over the river Birs. In 1881 severe autumn storms weakened the masonry and ironwork of the bridge, which had to be replaced. As heavier trains started to run over it, the cross-members were strengthened but not the main bearers. On the afternoon of 14 June 1891 an exceptionally long train destined for a nearby music festival caused the bridge to collapse, killing seventy-one passengers and injuring 171 more. The investigators found a whole litany of problems. The original design – and the iron used in its construction – had not been suficiently strong, and had been weakened in 1881, but the patching up had not tackled the root of the problem.

The combined forces of bridge failure and severe weather was dramatically demonstrated in the famous crash on the Ashtabula bridge near Lake Erie in 1876. The bridge, an iron truss with a 150-foot span, ran high above a ravine, and on the day of the accident the train had to force its way through a snowdrift to get to the bridge. When it began to cross, with most of the carriages still on the bank, the engineer heard a sudden cracking sound. Fearing that the bridge was falling he opened the throttle, the locomotive sprang forward and the bridge collapsed. The leading locomotive was safe across but the other engine and the carriages plunged into the ravine. As the carriages fell on each other the heating stoves set fire to the train – even though the ravine was waist-deep in snow.

Another famous American disaster, known to railway history as the

Johnstown Flood, came in 1889 when the banks of the Conemaugh river overflowed and water swept away the main line of the Pennsylvania Railroad, which followed its banks for forty miles. The engineer managed to haul his locomotive out of the advancing flood. Most of those in the part of the train carrying local passengers escaped to higher ground, but twenty-six of the long-distance passengers in another part of the train were drowned.

Most famous of all, though, was the collapse of the Tay Bridge between Edinburgh and Dundee on 29 December 1879, drowning the crew and seventy-five passengers in a disaster comparable in its impact to the one that thirty years later accounted for twenty times as many souls on the *Titanic*. The disaster not only ruined the career of the designer, Thomas Bouch, and led to major changes in the design of bridges, it also inspired in the Scotsman William McGonagall one of the worst poems ever penned about railways:

> Beautiful Railway Bridge of the Silv'ry Tay!
> Alas! I am very sorry to say
> That ninety lives have been taken away,
> On the last Sabbath day of 1879
> Which will be remember'd for a very long time.

However, despite the poem's evident failings, it makes good sense, albeit expressed with what might charitably be described as the poet's typical clumsiness:

> I must now conclude my lay
> By telling the world fearlessly without the least dismay,
> That your central girders would not have given way,
> At least many sensible men do say,
> Had they been supported on each side with buttresses,
> At least many sensible men confesses,
> For the stronger we our houses do build,
> The less chance we have of being killed.

He had a point. The North British railway company had asked Thomas Bouch to design a bridge to shorten the journey north from Edinburgh and thus compete with the alternative west-coast route north from Glasgow that avoided the estuaries of both the Forth and the Tay. As Schneider and Mase put it, in *Railway Accidents of Great Britain and Europe*, Bouch was 'above all an extremely ambitious man with many aesthetically daring ideas, but not prepared to take seriously the responsibility for their practical execution . . . his delight in unorthodox ideas tempted him into a carelessness which was completely foreign to contemporary railway builders in Great Britain.' Long before the Tay Bridge he had 'designed a very elegant high-level viaduct over a Pennine Valley . . . The railway company there was suspicious and had the project checked over by no less a person than Robert Stephenson, who had the piers and other load-bearing parts strengthened.'

After it had been discovered that the foundations would not, as had been hoped, rest on solid rock, the design of the Tay Bridge – by far the longest in the world when it was opened in 1878 – was changed from the original slender lattice-like structure to an apparently sturdier form based on heavy girders. Bouch laid stone columns on top of the brick foundations, but after tests had been made before it was opened to traffic, the inspecting officer, Major General Hutchinson, recommended a speed limit of 25mph on the bridge and asked for 'an opportunity of observing the effects of a high wind when a train of carriages is running over the bridge'.

The bridge foundered under the stress of no ordinary 'high wind': the signalman delivering the token used on single-track lines that allowed the train to pass on the single track had to crawl back to his cabin on all fours. But perhaps the most startling evidence as to the force of the storm came six weeks later, in the middle of February 1880, when fishermen on the western coast of Norway, four hundred miles across the North Sea, spotted what at first they took to be a sea monster. When they finally hauled it on to the beach they found that it was a railway wagon. According to the local paper, *Morganbledet*, 'The wheels were off, the windows smashed, and one door hanging on its hinges. By the name on it, "Edinburgh and Glasgow Railway", it was at once surmised that it must have been one of the wagons separated from the train which met with the disaster on the Tay Bridge.'

Even the most scrupulous precautions may be of little use when nature makes its mind up to be really beastly. In June 1938 forty-seven people were killed following the collapse of a bridge across the evocatively named Custer Creek, a tributary of the Yellowstone River. The bridge had been designed to withstand the flash floods to which the creek was subject and had been inspected only a couple of hours before its collapse. However, in the mean-time a cloudburst caused a twenty-foot wall of water to sweep down the river, taking with it one of the piers. The locomotive and the first coaches got across safely but two sleeping cars fell into the water – the force of the water was such that bodies were recovered from the river fifty miles away.

Bridges, and the accidents associated with them, come in all shapes and sizes. Drawbridges are still as dangerous as they were back in 1906 when fifty-seven were killed when an electric excursion train fell into the Elizabeth River in New Jersey. The accident led to better warnings on such bridges but many still exist in the United States. Disasters have also been caused by the failure of nearby bridges. In June 1914 the collapse of an old road bridge on the new Highland Railway in Scotland formed a dam that was bound to fail from the weight of water descending from the Grampians during a terrific summer storm. The dam was breached in front of a train from Glasgow to Inverness. And as recently as October 1987 four people were killed when a diesel train plunged into the river Towy in mid-Wales on the line between Llanelli and Craven Arms. It had been running slowly but in the dark the crew could not see that the bridge had collapsed into the swollen river that had undermined its foundations. Six years later forty-two passengers and five members of the crew were drowned when an Amtrak express running from Miami to Los Angeles fell into the Mobile River, a tributary of the Mississippi, after the pilot of a tugboat had bumped into a column of a bridge after losing his way in thick fog and straying up the wrong creek. (His radar didn't help: he thought the bridge was another tugboat.)

Nevertheless, modern technology can mitigate the effects of disasters caused by the vagaries of nature. Such was the case in a crash that occurred in August 1997 at Kingman in the Arizona desert. It involved a daily Amtrak express, the South West Chief, from Los Angeles to Chicago, one of the most famous trains in the US dating back to the Superchief once beloved of Hollywood's stars and producers.

The train was crossing the Arizona desert at around 90mph with 281 passengers on board. A bridge across a narrow gully had been washed away in a flash flood, leaving only unsupported tracks. According to David Tyrell, 'It's essentially a level, straight track so everything should be very smooth. A flash rainstorm caused the support for a small bridge to wash away and the train derailed. It tore up a fair amount of track but all the cars stayed

(Left) The accident on 8 October 1952 at the London suburban station of Harrow and Wealdstone not only claimed more lives (122) than any other in British railway history in peacetime, it was also notable for creating the biggest pile of wreckage ever seen on British railway tracks. (Hulton-Deutsch Collection/Corbis)

(Right) One of the deadliest fires in railway history. After two trains had collided on 20 August 1868 at Abergele in Wales, on the line between Chester and Holyhead, all the thirty-two passengers in the front coaches were burnt to death in the intensity of the fire which was fed by paraffin being carried in the freight train involved. (Mary Evans Picture Library)

(Left) The dreadful crash at St Foy-La-Gironde, west of Bordeaux, on 8 September 1997 resulted from the collision of a passenger train with a petrol tanker. It killed twelve people and was one of the worst seen on French railways since the war. (PA News)

The crash of an express train into a freight train at Southall in west London on 17 September 1997 killed seven people. It provided a stark reminder of the many lapses in safety resulting from the privatisation of what, for over 150 years, had been one of the world's safest railway lines. (PA News)

After the crash at Ladbroke Grove on the approaches to Paddington station in October 1999, firemen had to search every train carriage in the fear – happily unfounded – that they contained more bodies to add to the toll of thirty-one dead. (PA News)

(Right) Salisbury, 1 July 1906. This crash, due to a boat train travelling from Plymouth to London speeding through a station, killed twenty-eight people, mostly rich Americans. (Mary Evans Picture Library)

(Left) The vulnerability of wooden rolling stock became appallingly clear in 1912 when a train crashed after running far too fast through Shrewsbury station, killing eighteen people.
(Mary Evans Picture Library)

(Right) Saved by modern rolling stock. Fortunately, none of the passengers were killed when an Amtrak train derailed near Kingman in Arizona on 9 August 1997 because the carriages were strong enough not to buckle. (PA News)

The aftermath of one of the most influential crashes in British railway history at Armagh in Northern Ireland on 12 June 1889 when eighty people were killed, many of them children on an outing to the seaside. Within two months Parliament had imposed an unprecedented series of regulations on all the country's hundreds of railway companies. (Mary Evans Picture Library)

The most influential crash of all: at Meudon on 8 May 1842 on the newly-built line from Paris to Versailles. Fifty-two passengers died, most of them burnt to death in their (locked) compartments, the first reminder to the world of the possible danger of rail travel. (*Histoire de la Locomotion Terrestre*/Mary Evans Picture Library)

The collapse of the newly-built bridge over the estuary of the River Tay in eastern Scotland during a terrible storm on 28 December 1879 cost eighty lives and touched the country's imagination, as witnessed by this recreation of the tragedy in the film of A.J. Cronin's novel *Hatter's Castle*. (Hulton-Deutsch Collection/Corbis)

Rail bridges can still collapse today with tragic consequences. Four people died when the front carriage of a train was swept away by the swollen River Towy in west Wales on 19 October 1987. (PA News)

The funniest, the most creative, the most extraordinary of railway-connected films was obviously Buster Keaton's silent masterpiece *The General*. (BFI Films: Stills, Posters and Designs)

Most symbolic – and one of the most effective – of all cinematic railway crashes was that of the bridge over the River Kwai in David Lean's 1957 film of the same name. (The Ronald Grant Archive)

(Left) Over one hundred people were killed in Germany's deadliest post-war railway accident. On 3 June 1998 an ultra-modern ICE train derailed at Eschede on the line between Hamburg and Munch when a wheel came apart and caused the train to crash into a road bridge. (PA News)

(Left) The media's exploitation of crashes is as old as the railways themselves. Here the *Illustrated London News* creates its own dramatic reconstruction of the aftermath of the crash at Thorpe near Norwich on 10 September 1874. It killed twenty-two people in one of the worst crashes in history on a single-track railway in Britain. (Mary Evans Picture Library)

(Right) More old-time sensationalism. The *Petit Parisien* went to town in its almost certainly exaggerated depiction of an accident on the Ligne de Sceaux in the suburbs of Paris in 1905 when three people were killed. (Mary Evans Picture Library)

The dramatic fall of a locomotive from the Gare Montparnasse in Paris in 1895. There was only one casualty, and that an unlikely one: an old lady selling newspapers outside the station. (Mary Evans Picture Library)

together. A couple of the lead locomotives separated but the passenger cars remained intact and the train skidded to a stop.'

As was the normal procedure, the bridge had been inspected after the storm but no obvious damage was reported – the foundations were not visible because the water level was so high. The inspector was further reassured in that a freight train had passed over a neighbouring bridge at the same location, which carried the track of trains travelling westward, in the opposite direction to the Chief.

'The continual rain' says Rick Downs, a specialist in railway crash-worthiness, 'caused a heavy water flow under the bridge and had eroded away the side support structure on each side, causing the bridge to slowly collapse, that is to drop down a small amount. An approaching train crew would see a small dip in the track as they were approaching the site.' The crew of the locomotive 'did see the dip in the track as they approached the bridge and immediately made an emergency brake application in an effort to stop the train. Of course, because they were travelling at some speed they were not able to stop in time and passed over the bridge.'

The engine and half of the carriages jumped the gap and the entire train stayed upright. Amazingly there were no deaths or serious injuries, but 116 people had to go to hospital.

The accident was spectacular. The fire chief for the city of Kingman, had responded to the call even though it was not, strictly speaking, within his jurisdiction. He had already dealt with numerous calls from people affected by flooding caused by the storm: 'Everybody was winding down from calls in our community and I had gone home and was getting ready for bed when the call came in for the train derailment. We'd been up since about mid-night on calls in the community and that call came in at approximately five o'clock in the morning.

'When we approached the spot it was just turned daylight and the sun was just starting to highlight the crest of the mountains. You could see the light of the train and the passengers had been given glow sticks. They were a fluorescent green so you could see the outline of the train and these green lights bobbing around up and down the railroad. I wasn't aware that they used them in that quantity on those type of incidents, so for a few seconds I was wondering what those lights were and then after I approached I could see that the victims were holding the lights.'

The incident should have killed everyone on board the train but, to start with, the train didn't break up. 'It uncoupled between the locomotives', says Rick Downs, 'and that's not surprising given the anticipated dynamics of the train passing over a bridge that is slowly collapsing underneath it . . . The first three locomotives separated from each other and continued down the track, the fourth locomotive, however, did not uncouple from the car behind it, nor did the cars immediately behind that car uncouple, they all stayed connected and that fourth locomotive passed over the bridge and travelled down the railroad apparently in a derailed mode, causing the rest of the train to derail behind it. The train came to rest with a sleeper car that happened to be spanning the gap of the now collapsed bridge.'

When Downs inspected the crash site, he 'immediately observed a length of rail which had separated from the track and had become embedded in the fourth locomotive, which was still attached to the rest of the train. This rail had penetrated the under-structure of the locomotive, had travelled down its side sill, a box-type structure, to where the rail actually travelled down this channel, going in one end of the locomotive and coming out the other and penetrating into a baggage car, which was located to the rear of the locomotive.'

The design of the locomotive played a major role in saving lives. It was, says Downs, 'a monocoque design where the fuel tanks are integral to the car body itself. That means that the fuel tank is up inside the locomotive rather than suspended from the frame beneath the locomotive as we've seen in older models.' It is located 'in a position where there's quite a bit of ground clearance available between the bottom of the locomotive and the track. This allows for the debris which often results in a derailment to pass harmlessly beneath the locomotive until it comes to rest.'

More specifically, the positioning of the fuel tank saved it from damage from the individual rails that had become detached from the rail bed by the force of the crash. 'To have a rail penetrate a locomotive like that and not cause substantial damage was unusual', says Downs. In the event, he continues, 'The rail punctured the underside of the locomotive, had travelled down the length of the unit and punctured the baggage car but because of the ground clearance underneath, the fuel tank was not punctured, hence there was no fuel loss' – and no fire.

So what was supporting that sleeper car was not the track but was actually the bridge. As Downs explains, 'It was the ground and road bed beneath the car. The rails were damaged but still in place. However, the car was not sitting on them.' Overall, he says, 'in this particular case there were relatively minor injuries as compared with what might have been had the equipment been a little bit different . . . There was a lot of energy absorption by the coaches and the equipment rather than by the people.' So today man can counter, to some extent, the damage nature still inflicts on railways and those who travel on them.

8
Blood on the Tracks

As you get older you see your own children and grandchildren when
you are dealing with young bodies.

Peter Rayner, *On and Off the Rails*

Historically, after accidents rail operators have looked to their own short-
comings, their trains, their track, their signals, their staff for an explanation.
But safety on the rails depends also on people outside the system. For, as
the railways themselves get safer, it is increasingly the action of outsiders
that ends up spilling blood on the tracks. In most cases the blood is their
own. In 1999, in Britain alone, 120 people were killed and 149 injured after
trespassing on the tracks.

From the very beginning, however, potential suicides have found railway
lines incomparably convenient. In the 1870s there was an average of forty
railway suicides annually in Britain and today, on British rails alone, there
might be a suicide a day. Railwaymen have found their own way of coping
with the traumas. As the veteran railwayman Peter Rayner wrote, 'We
laughingly blamed it on North Sea gas, which no longer kills as coal gas used
to, or we joked about it in other ways but, underneath, railwaymen and
women who have to deal with death on the line experience a very real stress
and each learns to deal with it in their own way.' He wrote of the first body
he encountered, 'If I was sick once, I was sick ten times.' Although he, like all
other railwaymen, learnt to cope, increasing age does not help. Far from it.

Nineteenth-century novelists exploited the inherent drama of a railway
suicide to great effect – as Tolstoy did in *Anna Karenina* and Anthony
Trollope with the adventurer Lopez in *The Prime Minister*. Lopez wanders
around Stanway Junction, a station clearly modelled on Willesden Junction
north-west of London, and his last moments are chillingly described: 'With
quick, but still with gentle and apparently unhurried steps, he walked down

before the flying engine – and in a moment had been knocked into bloody atoms.'

Not just human bodies but almost anything can, and has, from stray animals to objects thrown on to the tracks by vandals, got in the way of trains over the past 170 years with tragic results. In the United States – especially in Philadelphia and Baltimore – it is not unusual for Amtrak's employees to find household objects like fridges, sofas and bicycles lying across the rails. And all too often these cause accidents. A runaway luggage trolley, carelessly left too near the track of the Midland main line at Wellingborough fell into the path of an express. The engine finished up on its side facing the way it had come, while the driver, fireman and five passengers died as the leading coaches were wrecked. Animals on the tracks are commonplace in India, but stragglers are not confined to the subcontinent. In 1844 a train ran into a cow on the line between Newcastle and Carlisle, the train was derailed, the driver killed; 140 years later a cow caused a derailment on the line between Edinburgh and Glasgow and thirteen passengers were killed; in 1967 a herd of buffaloes on a track in southern Italy collided with a night express and five people died – though fortunately the death toll was reduced by the strength of modern rolling stock.

Human stragglers are the worst. They cause serious problems in countries where the rail bed forms a convenient, and possibly the most practical, footpath in deep country. In 1924, of the 2818 people killed on Indian railways 2029 were trespassers; today the problem is exacerbated by overcrowding on the trains, which means that many passengers are riding outside the carriages, and not only on the roofs. In the eighteen months to the end of 1956 more than eight hundred people riding on the footboards of trains were killed.

Any attempt to separate the tracks from the public is confronted with two problems: it is clearly impossible along the thousands of miles of lines in open country and even when it is vital – as with the DC electrified systems that depend on live rails – the railway companies are confronted by what the insurance industry calls: 'an attractive nuisance', meaning that barriers like tall fences with spikes, which invite daredevils to prove their capacity to overcome such an obvious obstacle. In open country any form of protection would also mean establishing tunnels or other crossings for wild animals.

Then come the vandals. 'The perpetrators of such crimes,' says German railway investigator Erich Preuß, 'can be divided into three broad groups: first, the so-called "schoolboy pranks", that is, the minor and relatively harmless cases, and, second, those for whom money is their prime objective. The third group are politically motivated, such as opponents of the transport of nuclear waste to reprocessing plants.' But schoolboy pranks can be dangerous: in one case near Berlin a train was derailed after school-children had put concrete blocks on the line, though the prosecutor did not press charges. Very different, though, was the case of a crash in the summer of 1994 on the line from Glasgow to Greenock. This is typical of many lines in run-down urban areas. As Jim Murray, the Greenock Railtrack spokes-man, says, 'People use it sometimes as a playground and as a location where they're going to fly-tip.' He adds, 'It's not just a railway problem, it is a social problem.' On a routine Saturday-night journey from Wemyss Bay a train was derailed while running through Greenock at high speed. The driver and one of the eight passengers were killed. The guard was lucky because some instinct had prevented him from going into the front carriage to check the ticket of its solitary occupant – the only passenger who was killed. Fortunately, when the train hit an electrical support the bump signalled that someone had interfered with the electrical power and alerted the police.

According to Jim Murray, a lump of concrete forced the train to its left: 'As it moved along the line it derailed, it hit off a bridge abutment. That pushed the train up off the tracks and in underneath the bridge. In doing so the train knocked down a number of overhead structures, which pushed it across to the other side and knocked down two more structures.'

'In passing the buttress,' says John Malcolm, head of Greenock CID, 'the side of the train was torn open like a tin can and peeled back to about a third of the way down the carriage.'

Actually, says Jim Murray, it's very difficult to derail a train, 'because this very heavy mass is travelling at speed along rails and is connected to the rail at every point along the wheel . . . You've either got a problem with the track, you've got a problem with the wheel, or you introduce something that's gonna break the wheel away from the track.'

The investigators found distinctive debris from chunks of broken concrete at the side of the track too far from a nearby bridge to have been thrown from above. They were 'troughing lids', which covered a gully that ran along the tracks. Some of the lids, each weighing 35 kilos with their reinforcing rods, were missing. It was not the only debris under the bridge: 'There was graffiti and spray-painting on the paintwork, which showed signs of bottles and cans,' says John Malcolm. 'People had used that particular section of track as a private den', a picture characteristic of railway lines in deprived urban environments.

The police sealed the area and started house-to-house enquiries. Malcolm and his team soon established that during a period of about half an hour between when the train passed by on its way to Wemyss Bay and its return journey, the blocks had been placed on the line by vandals, almost certainly by one of the gangs of teenagers who roamed the area. They could, he says, 'build up a picture of a group of youngsters who lived in the general area and who would be expected to hang about the corners or indeed the bridge itself at that time'.

Although many of the locals were reluctant to come forward, some were prepared to be interviewed. In the end Murray 'was trying to track down two couples, two boys and two girls, who had been seen to walk up Peat Road and reached the bridge within the time frame of the train having gone to Wemyss Bay and before it came back.' In the event, 'The two girls strongly suspected the boys did it but didn't know how to manage the information so they managed it by ensuring that we had to find them.' The girls 'hadn't seen what had happened on the railway line. On their return to the street, one of the boys made the comment to them that the next thing that would happen would be that a train would crash', but it took a whole week to find them. Eventually the youngsters were convicted of culpable homicide (as there had been no murderous intent, under Scottish law the crime could not be classed as murder) and were each sentenced to fifteen years' imprisonment.

But still the vandalism continues. In early 2000 vandals launched three petrol bombs at a train travelling along the south coast of England between Brighton and Eastbourne, an area far less deprived than that in and around Greenock. Fortunately only one smashed through a window and exploded, injuring a passenger with flying glass, before an off-duty conductor travelling on the train put out the fire with an extinguisher.

Terrorism has always been a menace for the railways. Inevitably trains, especially those carrying important personages, have always been natural targets for those who consider themselves at war with society. In October 1888 nihilists laid a mine under a train carrying Tsar Alexander III through southern Russia – which led Stalin to station a soldier at every junction on any route on which he travelled. Most recently, in northern Sri Lanka the Tamil Tigers have caused numerous disasters in their rebellion. In the single worst such incident thirty-six were killed in an ambush when a train was wrecked after mines had been placed on the track and the guerrillas had fired on the passengers.

Over the years the Indian railways, ever a symbol of the power of central government, have been regular targets for saboteurs. A crash that killed twenty-five people in July 1928 eight miles from Calcutta was the eighth in ten months. Four days later another train was derailed, though the saboteurs missed their probable target, the famous Punjab Mail. In October there were two other attempts at derailment and soon afterwards a special train carrying the governor of Bombay also had a narrow escape. Sometimes, of course, terrorism is criminally rather than politically inspired: in 1942, dacoits belonging to a criminal Sind sect known as Hurs derailed the Punjab Express, attacked the survivors with axes and shotguns then stole their money and valuables. After that and similar attacks, trains were provided with armed escorts.

After Indian independence in 1947 the Communist Party tried to cause chaos by sabotaging the railways. In the first few months of 1950 there were no fewer than ninety-one cases of attempted sabotage culminating in the derailing of the Punjab Mail in Bihar, killing ninety-two people, while in August the Toofan Express crashed into a goods train that had been derailed on a bridge near Benares.

In 1947 the wave of strikes organized by the Communist Party in France led to a number of cases of sabotage, which culminated in a series of incidents on 3 December, one of which – a crash near Arras in northern France – killed twenty-one people. Saboteurs had unbolted thirty metres of the main line from Paris to Lille, while ensuring that the signals remained at clear.

The motives of saboteurs vary wildly, as can be seen from the experience of the German railway authorities over the years. In 1926 an express travelling from Berlin to Cologne was derailed with the loss of twenty-one lives after a rail had been loosened. The police traced the sabotage to two young men who had planned to stop the train and rob the mail van, but had run away unnerved by the severity of the crash they had caused.

Over seventy years later more than forty threats of sabotage were made against the German high-speed system alone in the first six months of 1998. Most came to nothing. In December – five months after the dreadful accident at Eschede (see pages 163 to 168) – the German railway company, Deutsche Bahn, received letters from a group calling themselves 'The Friends of the Railway'. They threatened to derail a high-speed train unless they were paid a ransom. Later in the year slabs of concrete were placed on the track of a high-speed ICE train running from Hanover to Berlin, the points were jammed and several bolts were loosened. The train hit the concrete but was not derailed. The saboteur, says Dr Jürgen Seigmann of the Technical University in Berlin, 'first raised the track by ten centimetres over fifteen metres, which gave a fairly marked ramp effect.' But this in itself would not have been dangerous – the passengers would only have felt a jolt. What was dangerous was that 'Whether intentionally or not, the saboteur had also widened the gauge by six centimetres. This meant that the axle no longer had a side guide – an axle wobbles as it moves along', and if the wheel needed to be guided 'a change in course of even a tenth of a millimetre could lead to a derailment'.

The sabotage required not only considerable technical expertise but even a special ratchet unobtainable in a normal DIY outlet – in the event it transpired that the saboteur had been trained as a track-layer. Fortunately, says Seigmann, he 'was interrupted while he was working on it. He had set up the jack and raised the rail. Then he must have seen the train coming and had to get away as quickly as possible so that the train ran into one of the stands that had just been used to lift the rail. It was smashed into little pieces and the ICE was damaged in the front when it hit the jack.'

The accident increased the pressure to pay the ransom because there had been a number of incidents within the space of a few weeks and no one knew where the saboteur would strike next. Ten days later a freight train was derailed at Anklam in Mecklenburg. This proved expensive, but only in material terms. A passenger train had been due to pass the other way – on a stretch where the tracks were very close together – shortly after the derailment, but happily that day it was late and the driver was warned in time.

Immediately after the police had held a press conference one Herr Sabota phoned, claimed he was the saboteur and demanded ten million Deutschmarks – around three million pounds. The police immediately agreed to pay. They also, says Erich Preuß, 'succeeded in gaining the confidence of Sabota by promising to supply a car with the money and that there would be no observation or escorting by the police.' They also succeeded in talking him out of his first plan to have the money transferred outside Germany.

When Sabota arrived at the agreed rendezvous, a motorway service station near Munich, members of the GSG – the German equivalent of the SAS – arrested him, three days before Christmas. At his trial, where Sabota admitted that he was the only 'Friend of the Railway' and that he alone had been responsible for the sabotage, his remarkable life story came out. He was truly an 'all-German' criminal. Born in the West, he had moved as a boy with his father to the East, where he completed his education, married, divorced, tried to escape to the West, failed, and was imprisoned for the attempt. After he was released he moved to the West and started a number of businesses, most of them unsuccessful. Nevertheless he managed to persuade the prettiest girl in the town in which he was living to become his second wife. When he began his sabotage efforts he clearly needed money to keep up not only his lifestyle – and pay off some of his debts – but also to help his wife, who was the secretary of a man later imprisoned for investment fraud.

In the event he was sentenced to life imprisonment. But even the severe – to some over-severe – sentence passed on Sabota did not deter potential blackmailers, two of whom subsequently and unsuccessfully tried the same trick on DB.

The variety of causes – and results – of derailments can be shown by contrasting some of the many such serious accidents in the United States. Twenty-four people were killed in August 1939 when the Union Pacific's City of San Francisco was derailed after a rail had been deliberately misplaced on the outside of a curve. Over half a century later, at 1.20am on 9 October 1995, Amtrak's Sunset Limited passenger service from Miami to Los Angeles was derailed in the Arizona desert. 'It's out in no man's land, it's desert,' said the area's senior law enforcement officer, Sheriff Joe Arpaio. 'There are a couple of small towns in the vicinity but it's very difficult terrain to get to . . . As the Sheriff I cover nine thousand square miles. That's why we have helicopters, Jeeps, horses and so on.'

'If someone were planning to do a derailment,' says FBI investigator John Waugh, 'this would be an excellent choice; it's one of the most remote areas of all Arizona and one of the most remote areas that the Amtrak train travels over in its journey.' The precise location was also ideal: because of the curve, in theory the train would continue straight – although the guilty parties were not necessarily aiming at one of the two passenger trains that passed each week along the tracks. It is also within an area that contains extremists 'not happy', as Sheriff Joe puts it diplomatically, 'with the United States government'. 'These are not the most co-operative of people,' noted FBI investigator Roger Ripley. 'They just wanna live their life and be left alone.'

Fortunately the train derailed in an unusual fashion. About a hundred feet before the trestle bridge, says John Waugh, 'the derailment was effected by moving one of the rails inward approximately a foot. That involved moving a lot of spikes – about twenty-nine – and then physically pushing the rail, which is quite heavy, inward. It was secured by pounding a couple of spikes into the wooden ties to make sure it didn't resume its original shape.'

A further clue to the saboteurs' sophistication was the way in which they had interfered with the signalling system. This consisted of trackside signal lights that provided a warning when another train was ahead or a rail was broken. When the saboteurs removed the steel rod connecting the rails on the bridge they would have broken an electric circuit that would have turned the signal to red and warned the driver of the Amtrak train of the danger ahead. But they connected the ends of the rails they had separated with an electric cable, thus completing the circuit that leaves the signal at green – a trick that showed some knowledge of railway signalling. They also knew the area, and this makes Sheriff Joe very angry. They did it, he says, 'knowing that it would be very difficult to bring in the ambulances, the helicopters, the search and rescue'. They knew 'that the trains would fall into a ravine'.

In the event, says John Waugh, 'The outside wheel on the left side of the train fell off the rail and the wheel assemblies on the locomotives fell off the rail and the train became effectively a monorail.' This was lucky because it 'caused the train to follow the curve over the trestle rather than taking a straight line. If it had gone off at a tangent the locomotives would have gone into the wash, falling down perhaps twenty-five or thirty feet.' The carriages would have followed and the damage would have been far worse. In the event the train began to buck as the locomotives travelled over the trestle, though in the end some of the carriages did fall into the wash.

It was a spectacular crash with carriages and bodies lying all over the cacti and the sand. One Amtrak employee lost his life and seventy-eight passengers were injured. It was the first time in thirty-eight years' service, that Sheriff Joe had seen anything like it: 'It was sort of a shock because you only see this kind of thing on television or the movies.' By dawn, says Neal Halford, a passenger on the train, 'It was like the opening scene of M.A.S.H. There was a helicopter sitting on virtually every hilltop, there were paramedics going up and down, and helicopters, they're taking off, other ones are coming in.'

Inevitably the derailment became big news: it happened only six months after the bombing of a federal office building in Oklahoma City. The feeling of conspiracy was reinforced when two letters were found under a rock in the desert sand. Halford was wandering around to escape from the heat of the train – even in October it is hot in Arizona – when he spotted a piece of paper. At first he walked past it but then 'The little wheels start clicking in my head. The windows don't open on trains . . . we're a long way from anywhere . . . it's really odd that this piece of paper should be lying out here.' When he started to read it, 'I only really got through the first two or three sentences before I just let go, "Oh, my God." What was just an accident a few moments earlier went from being that to someone has just tried to kill every last person on this train. It's a very strange moment in your life to realize that someone had you in his sights and they barely missed.' On the other side of the train he saw another note, placed under a rock. But even when he had handed them in he was worried. Halford's father had been a policeman and he knew the drill: 'I have my fingerprints all over this note now! And so I've ruined a piece of very important evidence.'

In the end four identical notes were found. 'Essentially,' says John, 'there were "two pairs of notes", one set just down the tracks and the other side of the trestle, very close to where the rail was split. And another set approximately three miles away, again in close proximity to each other and in a location where they were clearly meant to be found . . . One of the notes was on the ground under a rock. All the notes are somewhat ambiguous, in that they do not make reference to a train or to a derailment or to any action.' So they might have been a red herring, because 'We don't know precisely what the motive was for this derailment. They were all signed "Sons of the Gestapo"' and poured scorn on the FBI's attempts to storm the compound of the Branch Dravidians at Waco in Texas, and a cabin at Ruby Ridge in Idaho where an outlaw had holed up. But there was no sign in the files of a group of that name.

'There are many theories on who was responsible,' says Sheriff Joe. 'Was it a single person? Was there more than one? Was it an organization? Was it a disgruntled employee?' A similar case had been reported in a railway magazine in the early 1930s of a crash in which the same technique had been involved, which resulted in a large number of deaths.

The crime remains unsolved. The only hard evidence came from a truck driver, who had been sleeping in his vehicle near the incident. He told the FBI that during the night he had been woken up by loud metallic bangs. A heavy hinged metallic device was recovered nearby. It was a 'derailer'. But there was no evidence that anyone had actually used it to cause the derailment. So far as the timing was concerned, a gap had been cut in a fence during the forty-eight hours before the crash, showing the window of opportunity. At the same time the pilot of a light aircraft had noticed a truck complete with overhead lights directed at the tracks. Other evidence came from the owner of one of the closest homes to the site, a mere sixty-eight miles away. He had seen a vehicle stop at about 9.30pm and the driver check its lights before moving on. This gave the investigators some idea of the time at which the rails had been shifted and the sophisticated measures used. But that's about all, despite the efforts of the FBI. Sheriff Joe is probably not alone in feeling that only an informant, attracted by the $320,000 reward will solve the case.

Sabotage demands a deliberate effort but in contrast there is one point at which accidents are inevitable without any positive action on the part of man. Level crossings are unique: they are the only point at which two major forms of transport – road and rail – compete for the same space. Throughout railway history they have always been recognized as danger spots. In most cases the fault lies with the driver of the road vehicle, or the layout of the crossing, yet rail attracts the blame. In Britain attempts to make crossings safer started early. The 1842 Railway Act required that gates be placed across the road involved not the railway.

Historically, level crossings were discouraged in Britain, but in Charles Francis Adams' home state of Massachusetts, as elsewhere in the US, 'They were practically insisted on,' and, of course, as the rails spread west across the endless prairies there was no reason not to let the two tracks cross, given the rarity of any traffic. As a result accidents at level crossings have always been far more numerous in the United States than in Britain. Typically, in the US in five years during the mid-1870s, there were 104 collisions while in Britain in eight years of the same decade there were nine.

This contrast continues today: in 1997–98, says Stanley Hall, there were twenty-four accidents at level crossings in Britain, leading to two deaths, both of the drivers of the road vehicles. The accidents affected all types of crossing. In the United States, despite decades of safety improvements, a motor vehicle and a train collide on average every ninety minutes. This is partly because of sheer numbers. In the United States there are around two hundred thousand level crossings on public roads. These account for approximately four thousand accidents a year, involving five hundred deaths and up to two thousand injuries. On crossings that have proper warning systems, such as gates or flashing light signals, 'accidents are reduced but they still have half the accidents, simply because these crossings are the most used. In three-quarters of the cases the accident has been attributed to the inattention or impatience of the driver of the vehicle involved.'

As Dr Stephen Richards, an expert on level crossings, points out: 'You can go out to practically any crossing and observe [that] up to 30 per cent, sometimes 40 per cent, of the motorists will drive through the lights or around the lowered gates' arms.' Another problem, he says, is that 'A significant number of motorists believe that a train can stop as quickly as a large truck – but it takes a train up to a mile to come to a stop.' And, of course, in the United States, unlike Europe, there are very few trains: 'Motorists can go through a crossing several times a day,' observes Richards 'and never see a train. What this means to the average motorist is a negative expectancy that's built up over time.' In other words, they simply don't expect to see a train.

The problem is compounded by the rhythm involved in level crossings. If the lights flash and the gates are down but there's no sign of a train, motorists become impatient. Their frustration increases when the mechanism is faulty and the gates stay down. They are designed to be fail-safe – better safe than sorry – and because some of the installations and the tracks are up to thirty years old there are many false activations.

Under normal conditions, 'A minimum warning time of twenty seconds is recommended,' says Richards, but if motorists have to wait more than fifteen seconds, they 'lose faith in the devices and start to drive past the flashing lights and even around the gates. Once the warning time pushes beyond a minute you see a wholesale exodus of motorists from that stop line at the crossing. I've witnessed crossings where you literally have up to 80 or

90 per cent of the motorists who arrive at the crossing drive round the lowered gate arms. I've seen school buses, I've seen emergency vehicles, I've seen transit bus operators all take it upon themselves to drive round lowered gate arms.'

His perceptions were confirmed by researchers at the University of Tennessee, who studied the behaviour of 3500 motorists at 445 level crossings. They found that most motorists expect a train to arrive within twenty seconds after the warning light has begun to flash, and if they have to wait more than thirty or forty seconds they engage in what the study describes as 'risky crossing behaviour'. Even if they see a train approaching, this does not necessarily stop them. People find it difficult to calculate the speed of a train: 'The larger an object is, the slower it appears to be travelling,' says Richards. This is the case with jumbo jets as well as with trains. In the worst case, 'A full-sized freight train may actually be pulling 150 railcars. You add the speed [up to 30mph] to the length of the train and it can result in an eight- to ten-minute wait. That is an extremely long time for a motorist sitting in his or her car. Unfortunately, some drivers simply will not tolerate that kind of wait and if they think they've got a little window of opportunity to beat that train to the crossing they then try to do it. And the results can be catastrophic.'

Larry Mann, a lawyer specializing in US railroad legislation, spells out the figures. 'It takes a 150-car train going 59mph over a mile to stop, so when a car or a truck goes through that crossing, that train can't stop, it's just impossible. The engineer is not at fault in that situation in most cases, I would say 99 per cent of the cases. But the *rail carrier* may be, for various reasons. Perhaps the crossing itself is not maintained properly – there could be high reeds or bushes obscuring the sight of cars or traffic – the signals might be functioning improperly, there might be cars along a parallel track obscuring the view. There are a lot of areas where the responsibility is with the railroad company itself and not the train crew.'

The situation has grown more complex with automation, and a vast increase in the length of track covered by a single signal box or control centre. In the old days signalmen above many busy crossings could see the road and judge when to set off the warning signals and to lower the barrier. But with the elimination of signal boxes the decisions were made at an ever-increasing distance: to be safe the controllers allowed an ever-longer time lag. Hence the increasing frequency with which impatient road-users 'jumped the gun'.

To deal with the problem the Americans devised what they called the 'thumb-wheel' system, an automatic mechanism that measures the speed on an oncoming train as it approaches a crossing and calculates its exact time of arrival. It then sends the appropriate signal at the time. (It's called a 'thumb-wheel' because in its control box is a small wheel, its diameter the size of a thumb, that adjusts the timing of the warning.)

As small signal boxes were replaced by fewer, more sophisticated, more distant boxes, two types of automatic crossing were installed in Britain: the Automatic Half-barrier Crossing, first installed in 1961, and the Automatic Open Crossing, first installed in 1983. 'Half-barriers' have gates across the left-hand side of the road, so that crossing-dodgers have to zigzag across to avoid the descending gates, while in the open crossing there are no barriers. Both are controlled by a track circuit triggered by an approaching train, giving a warning time of twenty-seven seconds, allowing for a minimum of twenty-four seconds red. The timing looks dangerous, but experience shows that any longer interval leads to impatient drivers jumping the rails. Moreover, in a further effort to reduce accidents, the cheaper AOCs can legally be installed only where there is relatively light traffic on both the roads and the railway lines and where the speed limit is relatively low. In general both AHCs and AOCs have worked admirably, even though, as Stanley Hall points out, 'They transfer the responsibility for safety at the crossing from trained and reliable railway staff to road-users who may occasionally act recklessly, irresponsibly or carelessly.'

Whatever the system, the problems involved with level crossings are compounded because of the vast variation in the size and speed of trains and of the road vehicles – and the nature of their contents. Typically, seven passengers were killed and fifty-five injured when an express train from Le Havre to Paris crashed into a lorry in July 1985, on a crossing equipped with four half-barriers.

In Britain, one of the most famous recent accidents resulting from the meeting of road and rail involved one of the 'special' vehicles and loads that inevitably present problems. The accident occurred on a quiet weekend in January 1968 when a low-loading transporter began a short journey along the roads of Staffordshire carrying a heavy transformer a few miles from a factory to a depot at Hixon. The Ministry of Transport has always laid down that movements of such 'abnormal loads' follow prescribed routes and have a police escort.

Unfortunately, in this case, the route involved crossing the London–Manchester main line just outside Hixon. The fatal crossing was equipped with what was then a new system: automatic half-barriers, triggered by the approach of a train, which also set off a series of warning lights and bells. In theory there was a series of eight-second sequences: eight for the warning, eight for the barriers to come down and eight for the train to clear. But the inquiry after the accident found that neither the police escort nor the crew of the transporter had any idea as to the speed of the operation: they had not realized that the warning signals were aimed exclusively at road traffic and that there was no way of stopping a train if a vehicle got stuck on a crossing. As the load and its escort approached the crossing they were worried that the transporter might not clear the railway's overhead cables, so it slowed to a crawl as the crew checked the clearance. Unfortunately the 148-foot long monster was travelling at only 2mph, totally insufficient for the twenty-four seconds allowed for traffic to pass.

The inevitable happened. At 75mph, with about four hundred yards to go, the driver of the express saw the transporter ahead. It was too late. In the subsequent crash the transporter was split in two, the train was derailed, finally coming to a halt a hundred yards from the crossing, the leading coaches zigzagging across the track behind it. Three railwaymen and eight passengers died.

The accident was deemed so important that a judicial inquiry was set up, the first to investigate a railway accident since the Tay Bridge disaster of 1879. The inquiry heard that, after an earlier near miss at another crossing, British Rail had written to haulage firms telling them that they should telephone the signalman for permission to take big, slow-moving loads across level crossings. In this instance the hauliers had found the letter so arrogant that they tore it up, and similar letters to chief constables had not been passed to the police escorts. The Ministry of Transport had not even thought about the issue. By default the authorities had left it to the public to take responsibility for carrying heavy loads across level crossings, and they hadn't told the public what to do.

Historic and modern problems combined in an accident at Lockington in East Yorkshire in 1986. Lockington is on the line from Bridlington to Hull, which runs through flat countryside, so when it was built level crossings replaced bridges. Road traffic increased, and until 1985 the crossing at Lockington was supervised by a manned signal box and manually controlled barriers. But this was too expensive: in 1986 the signal box and barriers were removed and the crossing was opened up. There was no physical barrier, merely a sign and a warning light that flashed to warn road-users that they were approaching a railway line.

A morning train from Bridlington to Hull was approaching Lockington at around 70mph when, to his horror, the driver saw a Ford Escort van appear on the crossing. The buffers of the train ripped into the side of the van, just behind the passenger seat, tearing it into five sections. The passenger was killed and the driver badly injured. The train was in even greater trouble: the leading wheels derailed to the left and the leading coach ran diagonally down an embankment into a field. The force of the carriages behind it spun the coach round from end to end and tipped it on its side. Eight passengers were killed and sixty others, including the train driver, seriously injured.

The guard escaped injury and was helping the shocked passengers when he realized that another train was due from the opposite direction on the single track. He ran frantically up the track and, as he saw the train approaching waved it to a halt before it reached his wrecked train, narrowly avoiding a second collision.

The investigator, Major Tony King, soon discovered that a number of local people were dissatisfied with the crossing and had reported several failures in which trains had approached the crossing without the road lights flashing or that the lights had flashed when no train was in the offing. Even the driver of the van had been involved in these discussions, yet the lights were working correctly on the day of the accident. Perhaps he had been distracted, chatting to his passenger. Yet, disturbingly, King discovered that because the locals believed the lights weren't working properly some drivers would pass over the crossing even when they were flashing.

The crossing had only recently been modernized and Stanley Hall believes that the driver, who knew the crossing well, 'was driving as we all do on familiar roads, on automatic pilot, had turned out of a side road close to the barrier. The absence of gates meant to him that it was safe to pass, because he had not got used to the idea of the newly installed AOC.'

But the worst accidents at level crossings, as we have already seen with the 1868 crash at Abergele, occur when either the train or the vehicle involved is carrying a dangerous, especially combustible, load. So it was at St Foy-la-Gironde in September 1997 on the little local line between

Bordeaux and Bergerac. It was the worst accident in France – a country notable for the speed and safety of its trains – since the immediate post-war period. It was, moreover, a classic case of the lethal consequences of a crash involving a slow-moving truck carrying a dangerous load. A diesel passenger train collided with a petrol tanker that had crashed into the road barrier at a level crossing. The train scythed the tanker in two, it exploded into flames, engulfing both the train and nearby houses. Thirteen people were killed and thirty-one injured.

But the problems faced by Amtrak are unique. First, level crossings are far more frequent in the United States than anywhere else; train services, even on major lines, are far less frequent, thus inciting a casual attitude amongst already casual American drivers; and, perhaps worst of all, general speeds are lower, providing a stark contrast between the approach of a heavy but usually relatively slow freight train and a fast passenger train.

In recent years two of the most tragic results of this combination both occurred in Illinois, one at Bourbonnais, the other at Fox River Grove. At 9.30pm on 25 March 1999 the Amtrak express City of New Orleans was approaching Bourbonnais, fifty miles south of Chicago. The train driver saw a large truck at a crossing pulling out in front of him. A train like his, with fourteen coaches travelling at 80mph needs over a mile to stop. No chance. The twin engines swept the truck aside and smashed into two carriages on a nearby siding before coming to a halt fifty yards south of the crossing. When the locomotives halted, many of the carriages behind them ploughed into them, jack-knifed and piled up in a heap of twisted metal. Diesel leaked out of the fuel tanks and began to burn. The fire crept under the double-decked sleeping cars, which had been ripped open by the impact. There were eleven deaths and 116 people were injured.

The problem, says Dr Stephen Richards, of the University of Tennessee, is that 'At this particular crossing there's a number of sidings, industrial spurs, very close to the crossing itself.' As a result, drivers are used to slow-moving freight trains and the odd railcar, but not high-speed passenger trains. As Richards says, 'It's a very complex situation for a driver to assess exactly where the hazard or hazards are at this crossing,' a problem exacerbated by the fact that up to a thousand huge trucks a day pull on to the roadway near the crossing.

Richards guesses at the driver's frame of mind: 'As the lights first came on, our driver with this long load is just starting his trip is close enough to the crossing, so there's a moment of indecision. Do I stop or do I continue and go ahead – can I even have time to stop? One scenario is that the driver said, "Well, I'm too close to stop. I might as well go ahead and try to clear." The lights come on before the gates begin to move. Our driver might well have thought, "I can go ahead and clear the crossing before the gates actually start to move" – which would not have been unreasonable, given that he was only twenty feet or so from the crossing, and the warning time was between twenty and twenty-five seconds. Seeing the gate descend out of the corner of his eye he then starts to try to zigzag, hits the far-side gate, which was also coming down and the train reaches the crossing before he is clear.' To make matters worse, with a truck like his, says Richards, 'You don't get much acceleration out of the vehicle.' (The situation would have been different in Britain, where an amber light flashes for up to four seconds before the red.)

'The truck,' says Bob Lauby, an NTSB investigator, 'was carrying about eighty thousand pounds in weight of reinforcing rods for concrete. The load was overhanging the front and the back of the truck when the collision occurred . . . It's not usual for a train to derail but because of the dynamics of the heavy truck the train derailed in this case.' To make matters worse, as it derailed the train hit a string of freight cars sitting in a siding. Lauby had witnessed 'many train wrecks but so far as passenger trains are concerned this was the most severe I'd ever seen'.

The crossing, says Lauby, was 'a constant time crossing. This means that as a train approaches the circuitry can tell how fast it is coming and make sure that you have a constant twenty-five seconds of warning at the crossing itself. This is the most modern type of technology that we're using as standard in the United States.' Using 'predictors', computers that calculate the speed of a train and its distance from the crossing, ensures that 'you're not waiting excessive amounts of time for slow freight trains to come through'. But even this was not sufficient to avoid the accident. 'One of the most important questions about this investigation was to make sure that this type of accident doesn't happen again.'

Before such predictor-controlled crossings were installed, says Richards, 'Up to 80 per cent of motorists were passing through the flashing red lights . . . Even more alarming, up to six motorists per hundred were driving right in front of the train. A near miss situation.' After predictors were installed the level of potentially dangerous situations reduced by four-fifths.

The investigators interviewed a number of witnesses to try to establish the sequence of events. A crane driver said he had seen the lights flashing before the train reached the crossing. They devised a computer simulation, helped by the tyre tracks, from which, says Lauby, 'we can match the final position of the truck, the probable speed of the truck, the exact location of the truck when the collision took place'.

The truck driver, John Stokes, who had used the crossing regularly before the accident, claimed that he hadn't seen the train until he was on the crossing when the automatic barriers started to come down. He said that he was trying to get out of the way. The train driver claimed that he saw that the barriers were down and the lights flashing.

The NTSB investigators tested the equipment and the warning systems and found that they had been in proper working order. They then discovered that Stokes was operating on a probationary driving licence – his full licence had been suspended after he had picked up several tickets for speeding. In all probability he had gambled that the train was a slow-moving freight rather than a fast express.

In the event Stokes was not charged after the crash, though recent personality research shows that he corresponded almost exactly to the profile of the worst type of level-crossing risk-takers. He was a male who liked country music (yes, it counts), he was driving a truck – and thus was working. In his defence, other types of research show how difficult it is for the human eye to judge the speed of anything moving towards it, especially at night. Stokes might well have assumed that it was a freight train, looked to check, concluded that it was moving slowly enough and moved on to the crossing only to find the train upon him in a matter of seconds.

There were at least two accidents involving school buses in the last five years of the twentieth century. In the spring of 1998 a southbound Burlington Northern Santa Fe Railroad Co. freight train travelling through Montana struck a school bus at a crossing that lacked warning lights or even signs. There were six passengers on board the bus at the time of the accident, one of whom died. The railroad said the train blew its whistle and went into an emergency stop before striking the bus. In March 1999, less than a year after this collision occurred, attorneys reached an out-of-court settlement. Neither party would disclose the amounts awarded but one attorney said it was the 'largest settlement for the wrongful death of a minor in Montana ever, by a bunch'.

Three years earlier a more serious and far more heavily publicized crash had been responsible for the deaths of seven children. At 7am one autumn morning a school bus was making its usual run around the community of Fox River Grove. As the driver went over the railroad crossing on Algonquin Road, she found herself halted at a red light at the junction with US Route 14, which was just ahead on the other side of the tracks. Unknown to the driver, her bus had extended some three feet over one of the tracks. As the bus full of children stood waiting for the light to change, the crossing gate came down to allow the passage of a commuter train on its way to Chicago. 'At first,' says Jean Poole, an NTSB investigator, 'when the gate started to come down the children started joking and laughing about it because they just believed that they would be out of harm's way. When the train got closer and the gate actually hit the bus and broke off, they got scared . . . and they were yelling and yelling at the bus driver.' But she didn't hear them. Special sound-deadening material had been laid in the lining of the roof, the radio was playing, and one of the speakers was just by the driver's head. By the time the driver realized what was happening there was, says Poole, 'no time for her to react'.

In the event the barrier bounced off the roof of the bus. The train, its horn blaring, hit the bus at about 30mph even though its emergency brakes had been fully applied. The chassis and body of the bus separated. Of the thirty-four children aboard, five died instantly and two others were fatally injured.

Ironically the chief of police of Fox River and the area traffic signal engineer had both been in a parked car near the crossing at the time the commuter train smashed into the school bus. There had been a number of incidents at the crossing – twenty since 1994, nineteen involving cars or lorries struck by the gates as they closed, and there had been many complaints about the apparent malfunctioning of the signal.

The NTSB assembled an unusually large task force to investigate the accident, though many of its members, like Jean Poole herself, were from the highways investigation section. From the beginning, says Poole, the investigators believed that 'There was a problem with the signal system. Because the light didn't turn green for the school bus driver to get out of the way and the active grade [level] crossing equipment had already activated. In a way she was trapped between the traffic light and the grade crossing.'

The signal system was triggered when a train passed over what they called a 'shunt'. 'A signal,' says Poole, 'is then sent to the crossing equipment to warn motorists to get off the railroad tracks in time . . . At the same time another signal is sent to a traffic-control box . . . to put it into a pre-emption phase where all the traffic on the major highway Route 14 is going to get stopped so that these people can get off the side road, Algonquin Road, and get away from the railroad tracks. That's what's supposed to happen. We couldn't figure out why the light didn't turn green or why it wasn't perceived to have turned green.'

From the accident reports they read of complaints that the green phase on the signals was not long enough. They talked to the police chief, who had received the complaints and the accident reports and who had referred them to the engineers from the railroad and from the highways department. They in turn had examined their signal systems and found that they worked perfectly.

They then examined the thumb-wheel system whose setting had been changed two weeks before the accident, reducing the length of time allowed by five seconds to twenty-five seconds. This proved to be a blind alley, albeit a revealing one since it demonstrated a culture clash between the railroad engineers who, in Poole's words, 'did not believe that the thumb-wheel setting had caused the accident and the highway engineers who believed that this was the cause of the accident'. But the railroad engineers were proved right when repeated tests proved that there was ample time for the slowest vehicle to pass even with the reduced time setting. Moreover the accidents had started well before the thumb-wheel setting had been changed.

As the pile of information mounted, so the speed of the train came into question, but that factor was soon discounted. Meanwhile, Poole, who was charged with writing the report, was ploughing through a pile of papers and realized that the culture clash revealed over the thumb-wheel discussion was profound. Typical was the highway engineer who 'turned to the signal system and set the timing for it as he would have done at any other highway intersection without regard to the signal system of the railroad at all'. Neither highway nor railroad engineers 'knew how the other's signal systems worked, nor were they using terminology that meant the same thing to both groups'. As it was, both systems were working, but separately.

This lack of co-ordination was a vital clue, that and the relative neglect of the whole question of pedestrians. This was an unsurprising omission, given the low number of pedestrians who used the crossing. Until 1994 there was no set programme for pedestrians, who simply pushed a button when they wanted to cross, but that year, says Poole, 'Twelve seconds of pedestrian crossing time was programmed in to occur automatically all the time.' It was that year that the problems had started, for it was because of the time left for pedestrians that there was not enough time at the lights where Algonquin Road met Route 14 for the driver of the bus, or of any other slow-moving vehicle. As it was, the driver had only two or three seconds to get through the lights. It was only after the accident that they installed a big sign on Algonquin Road proclaiming 'DO NOT CROSS THE RAILROAD TRACKS UNTIL THE LIGHT IS GREEN'.

The final piece of the Fox River jigsaw emerged with the discovery that the driver 'was not the normal bus driver,' says Jean Poole. 'She was the assistant director of transportation and when there would not be a bus driver to take a route she would fill in and help. On this particular day the original bus driver for that route had called in sick, and her normal substitute bus driver had already been given another route.' Unfortunately the assistant director had never driven on the route before. Indeed, she was so unfamiliar with it that, according to Poole, 'She asked the first child she picked up to help her with the route.'

What the child could not tell her, says Poole, was that the regular drivers had all 'figured out on their own because they had driven this route so many times, that they don't fit into the space. So they had devised their own scheme to stay on the other side of the tracks until the lights turned green and they had to gauge whether they'd have enough to get out of the roadway on to Route 14 before the lights caught them again and turned red on them, leaving them trapped.'

Unfortunately, 'They did not bother to tell the transportation director, who had a system to take care of this had they told him, nor his assistant who was driving the bus that day. If they had let everybody know and communicated with each other – another communication failure – maybe this accident wouldn't have happened.'

But level-crossing accidents are by no means confined to the United States. Railned, which manages the infrastructure of Holland's railways, studied 6152 incidents at around a thousand locations between 1985 and 1997: about fifty deaths a year were caused by trains crashing into road vehicles. The most common offence was zigzagging around closed barriers, which accounted for one in six of all the incidents, followed by deliberately trying to cross after one train had passed when the offender knew that another was due which accounted for nearly as many. Of the remainder, half were due to misjudgement or inattention, mostly by car drivers, while in nearly a quarter of the cases the road vehicle was trapped by other traffic, or had stalled. Only one in fourteen were due to the railways, mostly when trains were flagged with the barriers up.

The young were over-represented among the guilty, most of them pedestrians, or riding bicycles or scooters – it is much easier to dodge round barriers on a two-wheeler or on foot than in a car. And since nine in ten of those involved in collisions used the particular crossing regularly, it was clearly not ignorance but familiarity that caused the problem.

Railned has now come up with a programme aimed at reducing casualties by a modest 25 per cent – clearly any more ambitious target would simply not be cost-effective. Priority is being given to blocking off the paths used by pedestrians and cyclists so that getting through them becomes more difficult. Red warning lights are being made more visible and carriageways are being divided so that drivers cannot zigzag between lanes, while kerbs will prevent cars from being driven off the side of the crossing where they might become stranded. And the average cost? A modest sixty thousand guilders – a little over twenty thousand pounds – for each of the first fifty high-risk crossings involved.

Nevertheless, and whatever the precaution taken by the authorities, the psychology of motorists, as well as their sheer number, ensures that collisions will continue, until the level crossing is a thing of the past – as, of course, it is already on specially built high-speed lines.

9
The Mechanics of Disaster

Was the train crashworthy? You're asking me to say how bright is the sun. I have nothing to compare it to.

Rick Downs

Trains, the locomotives, the carriages, the tracks they run on and the signals that control them make up an exceedingly complex system. The failure of a single element – a broken rail, a faulty wheel or brake, a severed signal cable, a bridge weakened by floods – can be a killer. The long history of the world's railways provides many examples of every possible mechanical fault.

Amongst the inevitable crashes involved are dozens of examples of 'tombstone technology'. To take a handful at random, it was a crash in New York in 1913 that led to the introduction of coaches made of steel rather than wood in the United States. Another crash, at Sevenoaks in Kent in 1927, which left thirteen people dead, led to a rethink on the design, and above all the stability, of locomotives. And after forty-eight commuters died when a train plunged into Newark Bay in 1958, the safety of drawbridges became a priority.

In so complex a system the failure of the smallest link can, literally, be fatal. The classic event, involving the railway equivalent of the 'for want of a nail' syndrome, occurred in 1915 with an accident that killed ten people. The subsequent inquiry soon found that a split pin, at a crucial point on the coupling mechanism, had been improperly replaced and had fallen off, losing the coupling rod. The cure was simplicity itself: to ensure that the washers on such pins were secured in the opposite direction to that of travel so that they tightened, rather than loosened as the engine rocked them back and forth.

Poor maintenance also causes acidents. Herbert Hamblen paints what we would now think of as a third-world picture of some nineteenth-century

American railroads. On one penny-pinching line he worked for, 'Brake shoes were never renewed while a vestige remained, several wrecks were caused by inability to stop trains . . . Cheap oil that would not lubricate cut out journals and crank pins . . . Cotton waste was no longer issued so that the engines became coated with grease and dirt, making it next to impossible to detect a fracture in any of the parts . . . The quality of the fuel became so depreciated that it was impossible to make [up] time.'

In the early days of railways major progress was already being made in the rails themselves. The original material used, cast iron, was brittle and treacherous, while wrought iron was too expensive, and it was not until the 1860s that steel made in modern Bessemer-type furnaces became available. Today, longer, welded rails, made of ever-stronger steel (much of it still produced at Workington in Cumbria in the mill that has been making rails since the 1850s) combined with ultrasonic testing ensures that all rails *should* be safe.

But rail breaks continue and, indeed, the number on Britain's railways has increased since privatization. But this is nothing new. Canon Roger Lloyd, one of a long line of English clergymen fascinated by railways, recounted how he was involved in an accident during the Second World War on a train from Liverpool to Euston in which, fortunately, there were only two minor casualties. Somehow the driver 'had hauled his fifteen coaches for nearly half a mile from a speed of seventy miles an hour to a dead stop on a track which was simply sleepers and ballast and jagged rail ends, and under a bridge, which the rear coaches had struck, and he had contrived to halt the train with every coach upright and every coupling intact. It was a marvellous feat, and to his skill alone several hundred people owe their limbs and their lives.'

Even if the rails themselves were strong, there was an obvious source of weakness in the 'fish plates' joining the rails together – one reason why the longer the rail is the less chance there is of an accident. The rails, bolts and nuts had to be flexible, but not too flexible. The problems involved – especially when a stretch of line is being modernized – were shown in dramatic fashion in a serious derailment at Hither Green in south east London in 1967 when a piece of rail a mere six inches long broke away just as a crowded twelve-coach diesel train was passing over it. The front wheels of the third coach derailed but continued to run for another third of a mile before they hit crossings from another track and caused the rest of the train to derail. Four carriages overturned, leaving forty-nine people dead and eighty injured. According to Peter Semmens,

> The stretch of line was a busy one and took a lot of pounding from the motors of the multiple units which had their engines suspended on the front. The crash occurred where two short so-called 'closure rails' had been laid between two lengths of Continuously Welded Track (CWR), which was being installed as part of the upgrading of the line. Because of inadequate support from the ballast the rail joint had become over-stressed by passing trains and fatigue cracks in the rail and one of the fish plates caused both to fail through brittle fracture just as the diesel was passing over them.

After an inspector had found that 'the general maintenance of that stretch of line was inadequate,' a speed limit of 60mph was imposed, the installation of CWR speeded up, and the use of 'closure rails' stopped. Most main-line systems are now laid with continuously welded rails without a joint sometimes for hundreds of miles, and most also boast a centralized traffic-control system operated from a despatching centre. With this system a rail break, however small, would immediately show up on a despatcher's screen.

The strength of the materials used has always been of crucial importance. Even before steel had become commonplace, scientists and engineers had already come to grips with the phenomenon we now know as metal fatigue. The tragedy at Versailles in 1842 had been caused by a broken locomotive axle. In the words of Wolfgang Schivelbusch, 'One of the experts assigned to the study of the causes of the accident, the engineer Laignel, saw the physiology of the travellers and the material part of the railroad as equally subject to the same concussions when he said that "the shocks and vibrations fatigue the travellers and destroy, in effect, all the material, and particularly the wheels and the axles".'

Twelve years later a lecture was given to the Institute of Civil Engineers in London entitled 'On the Fatigue and Consequent Fracture of Metals' which proposed the motion that 'There are reasons for believing that many of the appalling, and apparently unaccountable, accidents on railways, and elsewhere, are to be ascribed to that progressive action which may be termed "the fatigue of metals". This fatigue may arise from a variety of causes, such as repeated strain, blows, concussions, jerks, torsion or tension.' (Quoted in Wolfgang Schivelbusch.)

By the 1860s, August Wohler, a German scientist, had started to quantify the strains involved, thus initiating the scientific definition of metal fatigue. His first object of study was the axle of locomotives, and he went on to propose more stress-resistant materials. Railways were not, in fact, the first object of such study. The Americans, appalled by the regular explosions on board steam-powered boats which had been a feature of the 1830s, had already been working on improving the strength of the materials used. Both lines of enquiry – which culminated in the investigations that followed the crash of a number of Comet aircraft in the mid-1950s – were based on the relatively new idea of 'dynamic' strain resulting from regular use, as opposed to the sort of 'static' strain imposed on structures.

Obviously the track itself also has a role to play in the stability of the trains that travel along it. The broad gauge of the old Great Western Railway provided an extraordinary degree of stability. By contrast, the limitations imposed by the narrow loading gauge on the line running to Hastings provided a loss in lateral stability causing the carriages to sway. This was nothing new. Before 1939 the Southern Railway had been notorious for the lack of care it took over the maintenance of its tracks – one particular class of large tank locomotives swayed dangerously on its tracks but proved perfectly stable even at high speeds on the tracks of other companies. In many instances short pieces of track were used to patch and mend, proving an additional source of dangerous weakness.

If the rails mattered so, obviously, did the strength, design and reliability of the locomotives running over them. In the early years of railways, boiler explosions attracted considerable publicity although they accounted for only a tiny percentage of accidents, and the combination of stronger steel and welding largely removed the danger. Perhaps the most important hazard of steam locomotives was that it was difficult to see ahead through the small windows at each side of the boiler, and the driver's view was often obscured by the steam. In multiple units and in most diesel engines the driver sits right at the front of the train, and in a modern streamlined electric locomotive he has before him only a long low bonnet.

Unfortunately, in the days of steam, advances in locomotive design often hindered rather than helped the driver's view. In 1910 there was a rash of crashes in France, many of which were traced to the invisibility of signals to the drivers of the newly introduced Pacific locomotives. Indeed, Pacific-style locomotives might have been the very last word in locomotive design of the steam age but the driver's view was often restricted by the size of the boiler casings. The one involved in the Lewisham disaster of 1957 was of a class known as the 'Spam can': in these the cabs had been narrowed to pass through the Bo-Peep tunnel near Hastings, further restricting the view and forcing the driver to move to the other side of the cab to see some of the signals.

As far as the carriages were concerned, the steady replacement of wood with steel greatly reduced the death toll in accidents – although, in Britain anyway, wood was not entirely abandoned until the early 1950s. Moreover, old-fashioned compartment carriages tended to be weaker than corridor stock because the doors provided for each compartment weakened the structure of the carriage.

A terrible accident in eastern France – the worst in the history of French railways in peacetime – just before Christmas 1933 vividly showed the contrast between wood and steel. Two hundred and thirty people were killed when an express travelling from Paris to Strasbourg ploughed right through a train from Paris to Nancy. Virtually all the casualties – including families laden with Christmas presents – were in the wooden carriages of the Nancy train, five of which were reduced to smithereens. But there was virtually no damage to the steel carriages of the Strasbourg train, several of which remained on the track and sustained so little damage that they were used to carry survivors to Paris.

The following year saw a serious crash near Warrington, in Lancashire, when a signalman forgot that a local passenger train was standing by his signal box. Nevertheless the death toll that resulted when a Blackpool–London express crashed into it would have been far greater than twelve if the express had not consisted of all-steel carriages and been fitted with shock-absorbing buffers and electric lights.

Time and again modern coaches, with an integral construction and a self-supporting strong box structure, have proved their worth in crashes. In February 1980 an express passing Bushey, north of London at 100mph derailed because a welded rail joint had fractured, leaving enough of a gap to ensure that when wheels clattered over it the rail bent and the whole nine-coach train was derailed. The carriages were thrown in all directions and the middle ones separated, but all had integrated steel bodies so, apart from broken glass, they held together and no one was killed.

In 1986 Peter Rayner was involved in an accident when an express travelling from Liverpool to London at 100mph crashed into a train that was nearly stationary. Of the 658 people on the two trains only the driver of the express died. This, wrote Rayner, was 'something that will come over the years to be considered an exceptional tribute to the design and construction of modern railway stock. Had the crash occurred with non-crashworthy stock and without the buckeye-coupling gear, there is no doubt there would have been more deaths.'

By contrast the 'slam-door' stock still used on many commuter trains around London instead of more modern carriages with doors that shut automatically is old and rickety, and should have been replaced long since. Safety has been used as an excuse for speeding up the process, which should have been carried out anyway for quite other reasons such as speed and comfort. In the older stock, doors left open can injure passengers, who also tend to jump on and off while the train is moving. These trains also need fully staffed station platforms to ensure that doors are shut before the train moves off, which was normal in the 1950s when many of these trains were built but is not so today. In fact production continued until the mid-1980s, partly because BR was strapped for cash but also because of a tradition inherited from the Southern Railway – that the quickest way to discharge hordes of commuters quickly was through lots of individual doors. According to figures given by the distinguished veteran railway writer Richard Hope, in the *Railway Gazette International* of May 1992, in the years from 1988–90 'the number of passengers KSI [Killed or Seriously Injured] while entering or alighting from trains, opening or closing carriage doors, or falling out of carriages was 283, which is 46 per cent of BR passengers KSI from all causes. Such accidents are all but eliminated by adopting power doors.'

An even greater but less well-recognized danger is presented by flimsy carriage bodies. Among the worst are those of the bus-based Pacer DMUs introduced by British Rail in the early 1980s when it was even more short of funds than usual. Their vulnerability was clearly demonstrated in a crash at Winsford in Cheshire in 1999 when a Pacer simply crumpled while the electric locomotive involved was barely scratched.

The best modern carriages are 'energy absorbing' with a 'crush element', similar to the design of modern cars with a strong passenger compartment. 'You design the structure,' says Rick Downs, 'to absorb the energy involved in an accident in order for the vehicle to come to rest where you sacrifice portions of the vehicle and allow it to be crushed in order to absorb the energy of any collision and keep the areas that are occupied by people relatively intact.'

The carriages, says David Tyrell of the Volpe Institute, are 'designed to collapse in a particular way. Basically the area where the occupants are is significantly stronger than the area where the crush elements are. These are designed in such a way that the load is distributed going into the volume for the occupants. There's an end frame that helps distribute the load going into the crush area and the crush elements are specially designed, you use fairly thin sheet metal structure as box structures with little dents, little holes to make sure that they crush in a particular fashion.' In the event of a crash 'both ends of it remain essentially parallel, things don't skew out and also the material stays intact. There is no tearing or fracturing of the material as it collapses back. This basically lets the car remain in one piece and again helps to keep the cars in line, to stop one car from coming up over the next or one car moving out to the side relative to the other car.'

'At Kingman [see Chapter 7] when the locomotives were basically tearing up the track, there were large compressive forces acting throughout the train and what these compressive forces do is to force the ends of the cars to go out laterally so that now the corners of the cars are hitting each other. The sides of the cars will then start to impact each other. Once that starts to happen one car can basically wipe out the next by crushing all the space where the passengers are.' But at Kingman the modern carriages proved capable of absorbing the shock.

In a crash, it is not just the construction of the carriages that matters: it's also the ease with which passengers can get out. The crash at Silver Spring in Maryland led to considerable improvements in the ease with which people could alight from a train: signs became clearer, better emergency lighting and emergency exits were installed and upgraded door-release systems. There was clearly room for improvement in the design of the coaches used by the MARC, the commuter service involved at the Silver Spring accident: Earren Kearns, a survivor, says, 'I noted there were some kids still trapped in the train and that's when I proceeded to jump on the Amtrak train to kick out the MARC window, or tried to anyway, and it was impossible. This glass was so hard I couldn't kick it out, I even jumped down and picked up some stones and threw them at the window. The kids on the other side of the glass were banging, too, but there was really nothing I could do at that point to help them.'

The problem of getting out of the train was not unique to Silver Spring. Of Kingman, the head of the local fire brigade points out, 'The only entrapment that occurred on the train was from doors that, because of the derailment, had twisted the frame of the cars and wouldn't easily open. Firefighters and sheriff's deputies had to use sledgehammers and pry bars in some cases to open them.'

Larry Mann, who is acting for some of those involved in the disaster at Silver Spring, claims that the MARC car 'was not crashworthy. The occupants were unable to exit that car for several reasons, one being the almost impossibility of opening the doors. There were few signals or signs notifying persons on how to exit or what to do.'

'Some of the problems involved in getting out of the carriages,' says Bruce McGladry, an NTSB investigator, 'were because the smoke from the fire made it difficult to see. There's one of your first problems – you need signage or lighting that makes that somewhat easier to see. There were emergency exit windows on each MARC car but not every window. There are "strip-out" windows that have a rubber gasket. You pull out the rubber gasket then operate another handle and you can remove a window, but some of those windows hadn't been maintained so it was difficult to get them open. The windows are also made of a plastic that doesn't break so firefighters trying to get in from the outside had a great deal of difficulty with them.'

'Now of course you can go through a door but the doors were closed and there are no handles on the outside of the door, no sign that says, "Open here." There is an emergency release, which is underneath the side of the car in the general vicinity of the door but those were not identified for what they were. Train personnel know about them, of course, but the emergency-response people did not. There had been no drills or exchange of information prior to the accident that would have prepared them for this kind of event.'

The doors could be opened from the inside but the mechanism was 'behind a panel, the panel had a couple of screws and the screws could be opened with a coin but you had to have a coin and you had to know what you were looking for once you opened the inside panel. In the event, although the emergency services arrived within five minutes nothing could have been done to reduce the death toll.'

Within a year, thanks to recommendations from the NTSB, MARC had revolutionized the design of the inside of its carriages. Of course designers don't want to make it too easy for passengers to get out unless at official stops through either the door or the windows but now you can open the doors from inside without a coin. Today, says McGladry, 'There are instructions on the outside of the panel and there's a drawing, and when you open the inside of the panel the lever you need to move to make the doors open is now red, the only red item in there.'

'We have also incorporated emergency door-release systems in the vestibule, says John Kopke, a safety expert for MARC trains. 'Formerly these release systems were confined to the car exterior for emergency responders and on the interior close to what we call the body-end door. We found people walked right by these and looked for a release in the vestibule.'

They changed the glazing methods too so that it now takes less than a minute to break open the windows rather than the five to ten minutes in the old system. Also, says Kopke, 'The escape time is improved considerably because we have several times the number of emergency windows as were originally in the car.' By providing six times as many such exit points 'We've multiplied by a minimum of six the number of people who can get out of the car at the same time.'

Kopke and his colleagues went further. 'We actually sat in the car and redesigned the signage, interior and exterior, to be a little more passenger-friendly. We came up with the idea of luminescent [signs] in order that if we lost lighting in the car, if the batteries were torn off from underneath the car and we had no emergency lights, the signs would glow in the dark.'

Even the wording was changed after Kopke and his colleagues had realized that the signs were not 'sufficiently friendly to the commuter. There were terms like glazing. The average commuter doesn't identify with glazing, he identifies with glass. There were too many steps in the emergency procedure. We reduced the number and put it all in a great big red sign with white letters that glowed in the dark . . . I feel that the signs should be large enough and specific enough that they draw your interest while you're travelling and I hope that you will not have to try to read them in an emergency but already be familiar with them.'

The changes have meant that Bruce McGladry himself now happily rides a MARC train to work every day. 'There are posters at the end of each car giving you a number of instructions, there are messages from the train crew on every single run, talking about those instructions, explaining where they are, what they are. There's lots of retro-reflective signage, and they've done a nice job in designing the car to do a much better job of providing egress than existed at the time of the accident.'

As we have seen terrible accidents were caused by primitive couplings. David Tyrell explains that couplings perform a double function: 'In service conditions the couplings pull the individual cars along as the locomotive is accelerating the train – they transmit the load down the length of the train and help pull it along. Under braking conditions when the cars start to slow down the couplings take a compression load that pushes them together and helps the whole train slow down. In collision conditions the couplings act to keep the cars together. In addition to the loads that are acting along the length of the train there are also loads that are acting sideways, that are trying to push the cars apart laterally and there are also loads trying to push the cars apart vertically. If the cars do separate vertically, as most of the structure of the car is at floor level there is the potential for a very strong structure at floor level to hit a fairly weak structure above that level. One car can potentially wipe out another car by overriding – or telescoping, as it's termed.'

Inevitably the couplings have to cope with tremendous loads, both vertical and horizontal, obviously far greater in a collision when the modern freight-type coupler, which allows for some vertical movement, may uncouple. But they may also cause passenger carriages to telescope. Since the early 1920s tight-lock couplings have been normal, at least in the United States. Stanley Hall describes such an automatic coupling as 'a buck-eye coupling, which was like two hands grasping each other. In Britain several of the companies adopted this type of coupling, which was far stronger than the screw coupling and far less liable to break in two following a collision. In recent times it's enabled trains to remain intact and upright following derailments, resulting, of course, in no passengers being killed and injuries being generally of a minor nature. Many of the railway companies in Britain were slow to adopt the buck-eye coupling until British Railways in 1948 adopted it as their standard pattern.'

What the Americans call the tight-lock coupler provides a very firm connection. As Tyrell says, 'It forms a single link between each of the passenger cars.' At Kingman, specially strengthened couplings meant that the train stayed in one piece instead of breaking into sections. Tyrell goes on, 'The earlier couplers that were used in passenger equipment allowed substantial vertical motion – as a matter of fact they were pretty much unrestrained. If you took a car that was in the middle of a train and tried to lift it up you'd have had no difficulty doing that because the couplers allow almost free vertical motion. One might expect in a situation like Kingman that if you had those kinds of couplers the cars would indeed come undone and that at the far end of the bridge you'd end up with a large pile of what used to be passenger cars.

'When the locomotive is slowing down very rapidly, you've got high compressive forces throughout the train: the train is trying to squeeze together. One of the effects of the couplers under those conditions is to push the cars out and let the train adopt a zigzag pattern. In addition to the high compressive load the couplers are also subject to a high vertical load, which is trying to separate the cars.' At Kingman, 'The couplers were effective in keeping the cars connected when the train was decelerating, when the locomotives were tearing up the track and there were high compressive forces in the train squeezing things together. The coupler arrangement essentially forced the train into a buckled position where the cars each adopted a zigzag pattern. For a higher-energy collision this kind of condition is not desirable.' In other collisions, 'You've got the corners of the cars impacting each other rather than remaining in line. The structure of the car at the corners is not as strong as it is in the centre so two weak parts are hitting each other. As this progresses it can go out into an amplitude buckle and the whole thing can come together in an accordion fashion. We've seen this in several other accidents, accidents really that are at a higher speed and have more energy associated with the collision.'

At Kingman, however, says Tyrell, 'The couplers allowed the carriages to remain in line so the strong part of the cars came into contact with each other rather than the ends popping away from each other.'

Of all the links in the railway chain the wheel is probably the most significant, if only, as Markus Hecht, professor of Engineering at the Technical University, Berlin, points out, 'because there is no so-called redundancy. All other parts of a vehicle may fail and there is a back-up system to help avoid a critical situation.' With wheels there are no back-ups. So wheels should not only be made of the most durable material available, they also need regular testing. Enter the old-fashioned wheel-tapper. There used to be a popular, if rather satirical, series on British television called *The Wheel-tappers and Shunters Social Club*. But laughable as the idea of the wheel-tapper appeared in the 1960s and 1970s to the British public he performed a crucial function, akin to that played by a piano-tuner testing individual notes, for a wheel-tapper's hammer could detect any flaw in the combination of wheel and steel tyre.

The failure of the wheels or tyres on a train is not a recent phenomenon. There have been some major accidents in British railway history attributable to such a flaw, a famous one in 1873 at Shipton-on-Cherwell, north of Oxford; another occurred near Lytham St Annes in Lancashire in 1924 when fourteen people lost their lives. In the mid-1960s there were two crashes on the railways in Switzerland, supposedly among the most safety-conscious in the world, one in the Borgallo tunnel under the Apennines, the other in the St Gotthard tunnel, both due to the breakage of the tyre – though, happily, in the latter case, there were no casualties.

One particular type of train has been involved in two major crashes, the most recent of which involved a flawed wheel. It carries a whole circus round the United States. In 1903, twenty-two people, two camels and an elephant were killed when a train carrying the Benjamin Wallace circus was passing through Michigan. Ninety-one years later, on 13 January 1994, the Barnum & Bailey train, a monster of nearly a mile long, weighing 4000 tons and pushed by four locomotives, met a similar fate. Its fifty-three carriages held 400 people – clowns, midgets, trapeze artists – as well as sixty animals. But the train was not only big, it was special. 'The circus train, that's our home,' says Tom Dillon, master of one of the circus' trains, the so-called Blue Unit, 'It had been my home for eight years and for many people that much longer. We have a tight sense of community, we tour the United States together and we never worry about packing because our home is with us . . . this is a nomadic lifestyle.'

But as the train passed through the outskirts of the town of Dover, in Florida, on its way to Orlando, an off-duty detective noticed that one of its wheels was on fire and radioed police headquarters urgently. The train was halted and the driver walked back to the wagon involved but saw nothing amiss so the train proceeded.

An hour later a factory worker who had paused to watch the train go by saw two pieces of a wheel fly off into trees nearby. The incident was followed by sparks, a dustcloud and a grinding noise. On board, two clowns realized that something was wrong. They went in search of the train master, but couldn't find him.

After the accident Mike Martino, the lead NTSB investigator, was 'told by an employee of the circus that he and a young lady both were on a car and they had heard a very loud clang, which we found out later to be the point where the wheel came apart, and then they heard ballast or rocks being thrown up against the under-carriage of the car they were on. Both of them decided that they needed to inform someone, so they proceeded toward the train master, the senior person on the train. As they were doing so, the other wheel in the same axle derailed and was furrowing or ploughing through the area between the two tracks, the two rails.'

As Raf Vittone, an ambulance driver, 'looked towards the end of the train I could see what appeared to be smoke coming from one of the wheels and I didn't think much of it at first but as it got closer the smoke seemed to get worse. When it got close enough where I could see what it really was, the wheel had come off the track and the track was dragging next to the car. It was digging up the gravel on the side of the railroad track and that's what was causing the smoke. So I realized almost immediately that somehow the train needed to be stopped or it was possibly going to derail so I called our despatch and asked them if they could get hold of somebody with the railroad company who'd be able to get word to stop the train.'

Moments later the train crossed a set of points and derailed in a spectacular pile-up. One of the clowns – still fruitlessly searching for the train master – was killed, as was an elephant trainer. The carriages were left sprawled across the tracks in a curious zigzag pattern. 'Three or four cars came through the fence into our yard,' says Sena Naismith, who worked near the tracks. 'We began to see people, not animals, little children. There was a gentleman that was killed in the first box car that had come through the fence. He had two young sons and I believe he was a Russian man and they were screaming in their native tongue for their father. They knew he was in there. People were trying to comfort the boys but they just ran from person to person, begging for their father.'

When Mike Martino arrived the next day he found that 'The inside of the train was very disarrayed . . . The personal items that you would normally have in your apartment were on the train and appliances such as TV sets, stereos, had not been secured firmly and had been thrown about in the interior.'

Not surprisingly, says Jeffrey Steele, then the circus' performance director, 'The company was devastated at first . . . but when Mr Feld [of the family who owned the circus] arrived, he identified something that all of us knew but none of us had said. He said the most important thing we could do was get a show on there and he was absolutely right, not because we needed to make a profit but because that's what we do and that's the only normalcy we know.' Miraculously, the circus missed only three performances. After the crash, 'The audience was on its feet at the end of the first show just because we'd managed to do it,' says Steele. It was especially emotional when they came to a stilt-clown routine, which had involved Cecily, the clown who had been killed. Equally difficult was the arrival of the elephants, whose trainer, Ted, had also been killed. 'Those,' says Steele, 'were tough things for us to do but it was what pulled us through as a unit. It was from that point that we started to come out of the shock.'

For Martino, 'This case was special because I'd spent two years with Ringling, in fact with this particular train . . . When I went to the investigation I knew a lot of the people there.' The train of events that had led to the derailment was soon obvious, he says. 'I was walking southward away from the train and saw that there was a distinct marking where a rail wheel had been on the inside of the gauge and it had broken several of the railroad ties. Also when I got to a road crossing I could see where it had been torn apart by this dragging wheel – the dirt was fresh and the marks were freshly cut. We followed the line that this derailed wheel created to a point where the wheel had come off the rail and it was in the same vicinity as where we found the pieces of the broken wheel. Hence we were able to conclude that the point of derailment was about four to five miles south of the accident and it was right at the time when the wheel came apart that this caused its sister wheel in the same axle to derail.'

From day three of the investigation they 'knew that the wheel was a factor in the accident but it was a couple of months afterwards, when we had been able to disseminate all the information from the other disciplines, that we determined that the causal area to be focused on would be the mechanical portion, or the wheel.'

Investigators from the NTSB puzzled over what had caused the wheel to break and derail the train. Already, says Martino, they had 'a theory that the stamping was affecting the wheel. In this particular case the wheel had a number four on the inside of the flange. In previous accidents the Safety Board had investigated cases where a straight plate wheel had developed a crack where a stamp was on the inside. Based on that previous knowledge we felt that this was a scenario like the previous accidents we'd investigated and that we were on to something. When you put the pieces together one of the cracks was right at the long part of the four so this was definitely an area that we wanted to look further into' – especially as the number had been stamped on the rim, the weakest part of the wheel.

Then they realized that 'Heat would enhance this type of crack and really what we had was a heat fracture or heat crack, and the heat would be introduced again by the braking motion to the wheel.' For over two decades freight trains had been fitted with curved plate wheels, which allowed plenty of air to flow over the curve of the surface of the wheel. But the circus train was of a custom-made design that still used straight plate wheels, whose flat surface did not allow air to circulate: when the brakes heated the wheel, it didn't cool again.

Without mentioning their theory, they sent the wheel to the independent transport testing station in Colorado, where Dan Stone quickly found the same phenomenon as Martino and his colleagues: 'a crack which grew into a shape like a clam shell' until it failed when 'the brake proceeded into the centre of the wheel and around the plate of the wheel, separating the outside of the wheel from the inside'.

Finally spectrum analysis revealed that the raised number four was indeed at the heart of the problem, although it had been exacerbated by the braking system. Stamping the metal had weakened it, the frequent braking at relatively high speeds had overheated and distorted the wheel until a fatigue crack had appeared. During the course of the journey the tiny crack had lengthened dramatically until the wheel had split and disintegrated.

As a result of the investigation, says Bill Misura, director of domestic transportation for the circus company, 'We changed all of the wheels that had rim stamps.' On the train's tread brakes – similar to the drum brakes formerly used on motor vehicles – 'The brake shoe rubs against the wheel and can heat the wheel. Now the wheel is made to withstand a certain amount of heat but on long steep mountains you have gradients that cause the train to need to brake extensively and there can be some overheating at that point, so it behooved us to change our braking system to a disc braking system similar to what's on an automobile. It has a disc and callipers and pads that squeeze the disc and all of the braking then or all of the heat dissipation comes out of the disc and the wheels are not heated at all.' They also installed a better communication system after a trauma that prevented the train from going back into service for two years.

Axles and axle bearings have always been a crucial stress-point. The ends of axles are carried in boxes with oil-impregnated pads. Formerly the wheel-tapper would put his hand on the axle box to see if they were too warm, for 'hot boxes' have started many a fire or cracked the box casing.

Wheels run on bearings, and there again the story is of irregular advances. Technical improvements are sometimes greeted with cynicism and so it was with the installation of roller bearings. Their absence from the axles of a dining-car of a train involved in a major accident in 1943 near Philadelphia was blamed, probably wrongly, for the fatalities after an axle running on plain bearings overheated. In the subsequent derailment a coach tilted and hit a signal gantry, leaving seventy-nine dead and 103 injured. But even then some cynics attributed the blame for the accident to the manufacturers of the new roller bearings anxious to increase their sales.

Sometimes bearings, which are designed to help axles run smoothly, are *too* smooth, as appears to have been the case in a crash in Canada on 12 August 1996. In the previous five years, 190 cases of runaway wagons had been reported to the Canadian Transportation Safety Board, seventeen of which resulted in main-line track collisions. In this instance a seventy-three wagon train was crossing the McLeod River near Edson, 120 miles west of Edmonton in Alberta. Just after crossing the bridge, the three-man crew saw a line of twenty grain cars that had rolled smoothly off a side line at the Edson yard fifteen minutes earlier and had joined the main line directly in front of them travelling at 40mph. They pulled the brake lever too late, leading to a crash at 50mph.

(The crash was also due to absence of 'derails', portable metal devices that direct cars off side tracks before they reach the main line. The derails used to be dropped off by the conductor in the caboose, or guard's van, and were eliminated when Canadian Railways eliminated cabooses previously needed on all sidings. In this case the derail would have deflected or stopped the runaway wagons before they reached the main line.)

The impact drove up the nose of the lead locomotive to crush the cab and the crew, the engine flew off the rails and landed south of the tracks, where its diesel tanks exploded. The result was a major fire, while cans of fruit juice and boxes of Kellogg's Raisin Bran spilled from the derailed boxcars with a load of dried peas that lay five feet deep on the ground around the wreckage.

The runaway cars all used hand-brake systems, an old-fashioned big steering-type wheel and a handle or lever mounted at the back of the car.

Their bearings, however, were far more modern, and their sophistication contributed to the accident. According to Randy Gram, chief of rail accident investigations for the Canadian Transport Safety Board, 'Cars have a well-designed bearing system, it takes little energy to get them going downhill.' In fact, the bearings are so sensitive that strong winds can often push an empty car along a level track.

In any crash, investigators need to know what really happened, and since an accident in 1996 many American trains are now equipped with automatic data recorders, the black boxes famous from air crashes. According to Larry Mann, 'The rail workers were instrumental in getting that adopted. In fact they wanted even more indications placed on the event recorder. Right now there are eight indications, such as speed, location, braking etcetera, but the rail workers wanted something more encompassing, One would be a hot-box detector . . . and a signal indication. We, the rail workers, attempted to have that included in the event recorder regulation. It was opposed by the rail industry. Another that comes to mind was whether or not there should be a detection of what is known as emergency brake applications. Currently there is no indication of that and the Federal Railroad Administration chose not to include that . . . The other issue which has now arisen, is why the initial regulations did not encompass crashworthiness. We've had a number of accidents where the trains had event recorders but they were crushed or water was involved and you could not read the data. Through this rail safety advisory committee the FRA is now considering crashworthy-type event recorders, and I think that this will be adopted in the near future. . .The rail industry has opposed it up to now because of the cost involved' – not unreasonable, given the tough price competition with the road haulage industry.

The next step, of course, would be voice recorders. In the Silver Spring accident the investigators were lucky that the driver of the crashed train, who was killed, had talked to his controller in the minutes leading up to the crash, but, says Bruce McGladry, 'It would have been somewhat easier, somewhat more positive in determining the events in the cab, if we had had a recording device that had captured those conversations', notably in finding exactly why the driver made the mistakes he did. 'There are, however, issues that need to be discussed with respect to voice recordings. There are voice recordings in aviation that are used by the NTSB in determining accident causation but they're fairly restricted in how they can be used, who can use that information and what the information is used for . . . For recording devices similar to those in aviation to be on vehicles in other modes of transportation, like locomotives, some of those issues need to be discussed. Are there going to be disciplinary actions, for example, based on what occurs in conversation in a locomotive cab, who has access to that information, what are they going to do with that information? Those issues have been discussed but have not been settled, and currently there is not widespread use of voice recorders.'

The unions object because as Mann points out, 'The workers, of course, are in a train for up to twelve hours a day, day in day out with the conductor . . . You're going to be talking about any number of things, like football games. Now, you're not supposed to do anything on the train but operate it . . . do nothing but focus on the rail movement. You're obviously going to talk about other things, even though your primary focus is to operate the train safely. Nobody questions that, but being subjected to penalties for that causes great concern to the rail worker.' The American rail industry is afraid of the legal consequences. Suppose, says Mann, that 'I am injured in an accident and I have access to this recorder, which shows hours of chatting between the crew about the baseball game or what their wife is wearing to church. You can see how that would play in front of a jury and there would be great concern that it could be used in a punitive fashion possibly by plaintiffs. If I were a rail manager I would certainly have concern about it.' Nevertheless he believes that voice recorders will be introduced but with restrictions governing their use in court.

In theory, the widespread use of another modern tool, the mobile phone, ought to be a useful back-up feature in improving communications between trains and their controllers. But not inevitably, as was seen in the first days of 2000 in an accident that resulted in the deaths of twenty Norwegians when an express collided with a local train on a stretch of single line near Hamar. It might have been averted had the controllers, who were aware of the impending crash, been able to contact the drivers – but they had the wrong numbers for their mobile phones.

10
Let's Blame the Driver

A locomotive driver stands with one foot in the grave, the other in prison. The total inflexibility with which extreme consciousness of duty, absolute punctuality and reliability is demanded of a driver, indeed from every railway worker, appears dramatically. If he once fails, then years of the most careful work in his profession, and an irreproachable mode of life, are not much use to him . . . It is surprising that individuals can still be found who, in spite of the tremendous demands, dare to come forward for service on the foot plate.

Ascanio Schneider, 1968

The driver is the central figure in most rail crashes. He is also the easiest person to blame, partly because he is likely to have been a victim and is no longer there to defend himself or provide explanations for actions that may sometimes seem bizarre or just plain dangerous. However, as Stanley Hall wrote, 'Drivers carry a heavy responsibility, and 'they are not given the status they deserve, nor the pay' – just look at the comparison with airline pilots.

But once upon a time – indeed, I suspect, until steam disappeared from the world's railways – many schoolboys wanted to be engine drivers. As Bill Withuhn observes: 'Just as today little kids dream about piloting the space shuttle or perhaps being a famous race driver, kids at the turn of the century looked up to the locomotive engineer. Being able to run a train at sixty, seventy miles per hour was just so exciting that every kid thought it was great.'

'The train engineer, or driver, became a heroic, kind of mythic figure,' says Lynne Kirby, 'especially in America, where trains drove the economy and also for the first time made transportation available to masses of Americans. That the train was also a very dangerous thing to conduct, to drive, to engineer made the heroic status of the engineer that much more grand, that much more mythic.'

Throughout railway history there are stories of heroes among engine drivers. In February 1871 an express from New York crashed into a disabled freight train. The driver of the express died at his post. According to Charles Francis Adams, the fireman, who had jumped to safety in time, told a court, 'the next I see of Doc Simmons [the driver], he was dragged up days afterwards from under his locomotive at the bottom of the river. But it was a good way to die. He went out of the world and of the sight of men with his hand on the lever, making no reply to the suggestion that he should leave his post, but "looking ahead and watching his business".'

In 1937, Joe Ball, a driver, and his fireman, Cormack Higgins, were in charge of a Euston–Liverpool express. When they entered Primrose Hill tunnel, little more than a mile after they had set off from Euston station, they were unaware that a deflector plate on the smoke box had been insecurely fastened, allowing the plate to fall across the blast pipe of the engine. When this happened the cab was engulfed in flames. Ball and Higgins stayed by their posts for over three miles, stopping only at Willesden Junction, where they knew help would be available. Both men died from their burns.

But heroes are in the minority, and in most cases of alleged driver responsibility, speed has been the cause of many, perhaps most accidents. Such was the case even before competition from the motor vehicle and the aeroplane pressured railways to increase speeds not only of passenger trains but also of the traditionally leisurely freight trains. Throughout railway history runs the thread summed up in the simple phrase 'The driver was late and making up time.'

This book provides innumerable examples of trains coming off the tracks simply because they were travelling too fast, especially where there were temporary changes in a line, caused by repairs or a diversion. One of the worst came as late as 1951 when eighty-four people were killed in New Jersey after some of the track had been slewed to allow work to be carried out on a nearby road. In 1985 a train was derailed in the middle of France causing forty-three deaths while travelling too fast over a stretch of line that was being upgraded, while in early 2000 eight people were killed and 149 injured, many of them seriously, when an express travelling from Amsterdam to Cologne came off the tracks at Bruehl, ten miles south of Cologne.

The crash occurred as the train travelled at 75mph over points intended to divert it past construction work. The engine's black box indicated that the train had initially slowed down to 20mph but had then accelerated to the speed that would have been normal in the absence of the diversion. The locomotive and five carriages left the track. Two of the carriages plunged down an embankment, landing in the living room and front garden of an elderly couple, who, miraculously, escaped unharmed.

In the past the problem of excess speeds at sharp curves or diversions from a main line was exacerbated, at least in Britain, by the fact that, until well into the post-war period, few cabs were fitted with speedometers. Moreover, until the 1970s, drivers received little or no warning that they were approaching sharp curves. It took an accident – the death of five passengers and a ticket inspector when a night sleeper tried to go round a curve at Morpeth north of Newcastle at double the recommended 40mph limit – for such warnings to be provided. And that was as late as 1969.

Many of the most famous crashes were often due simply to the excess speed at which engineers were driving, showing how much lost time they could make up and often resulting in the deaths hymned by balladeers. So it was with Steve Broady, hero (or anti-hero) of that famous ballad 'The Wreck of Old 97'.

> Steve knew what he had to do:
> They gave him his orders at Monroe, Virginia,
> Saying, 'Steve, you're way behind time'.
> This is not Thirty-eight, but it's old Ninety-seven.
> You must put her in Spencer on time.

Unfortunately Steve went off the tracks, due to excess speed, at a known danger spot – a curve on a descent between Lynchburg and Danville – where the brakes failed.

> He was going down grade, making ninety miles an hour
> When his whistle broke into a scream [Woo Woo]
> He was found in the wreck with his hand on the throttle,
> And a-scalded to death with the steam.

The ballad on the death of George Alley told a similar story, of how his mother warned:

She said 'My darling boy, be careful how you run,
For many a man has lost his life in trying to make up lost time,
But if you run your engine right, you'll get there just on time.'

George Alley replied,

'Dear Mother, you know I'll take your heed.
I know my engine, it's all right, I know that she will speed
So over this road I mean to run with a speed unknown to all,
And when I blow for Clifton Forge, they'll surely hear my call.'

Despite sensing that there was a rock on the line, Alley sped to his death. He shared the fate of the single most famous driver in railway history, Casey Jones, a dashing figure, black-haired, grey-eyed, six foot four inches tall. He was the eldest of four brothers, all crack 'engineers' on the Illinois Central, and died in a wreck at Vaughan, Mississippi, in April 1900 when he drove the locomotive heading the Chicago Fast Mail, popularly known as the Cannonball, from New Orleans to Chicago, into a standing train. His fireman saw what was about to happen and jumped off in time. The conclusion was that 'Engineer Jones was wholly to blame for the collision'. In fact, says Bill Withuhn, 'Casey was speeding in the fog and slammed into a train ahead that hadn't quite cleared a siding. It might have been a tragic wreck but only Casey was killed so the crash was not that horrific in terms of loss of life and limb but a couple of composers got a hold of the idea and created a song. "The Ballad of Casey Jones" was a popular hit and suddenly Casey was a folk hero.'

Come all you rounders for I want you to hear
The story of a brave engineer.
Casey Jones was the fellow's name,
A big eight-wheeler of a mighty fame.

Then followed the chorus:

Casey Jones, he mounted to his cabin,
Casey Jones, with his orders in his hand!
Casey Jones, he mounted to the cabin,
Took his farewell trip into the promised land.

Put in your water and shovel in the coal,
Put your head out the window, watch the drivers roll,
I'll run her till she leaves the rail,
'Cause we're eight hours late with the Western Mail!
He looked at his watch and his watch was slow,
Looked at the water and the water was low,
Turned to his fire boy and said,
'We'll get to 'Frisco but we'll all be dead.'

Casey pulled up Reno Hill.
Tooted for the crossing with an awful shrill,
Snakes all knew by the engine's moans
That the hogger at the throttle was Casey Jones.
He pulled up short two miles from the place,
Number Four stared him right in the face,
Turned to his fireboy, said 'You'd better jump,
'Cause there's two locomotives going to bump!'

Mrs Jones had a 'pink' that her husband would die but told her children,

'Go to bed, children; hush your crying,
'Cause you'll get another papa on the Salt Lake Line.'

The majority of serious accidents in which the driver was largely or entirely to blame remain unexplained, typically that at Salisbury in June 1906. One of the classic tragedies of the early years of the twentieth century, this was supposed to have been the result of the race between the Great Western Railway and the London and South Western for carrying passengers and mail to London from liners docking at Plymouth. The GWR route, via Taunton and Reading, was longer, but the L & SWR, via Salisbury, was steeper and controlled by GWR signalmen, who habitually tried to delay their rival's trains.

As Norman Pattenden describes the accident – which had such an impact that a plaque inscribed with the names of the victims was erected in Salisbury Cathedral – 'Boat trains started running in 1904 from Plymouth to London in connection with ocean liners coming across from New York. They . . . catered for passengers and also mail. Both had the option of disembarking at Plymouth by tender rather than carrying on with the vessel to Southampton. By using the speed of the railway between Plymouth and London it was possible to save a day and, in 1904, the American Line liners started to call at Plymouth . . . The London and South Western conveyed passengers and the Great Western Railway conveyed mail traffic. The liners operated at uncertain times but trains were laid on to meet the arrival of the liners . . . On the train that night there were forty-three passengers on board, all off the American Line ship, New York, all first-class passengers . . . At the eastern end of Salisbury station there was a very sharp curve to the left, which started at the London end of the platform . . . there had been a speed restriction of 30mph applied there some years before the accident took place, and in fact quite strict instructions had been issued to adhere to the limit because of the sharpness of the curve. The boat trains were rather unusual in that they were more or less the only trains that ran through Salisbury without stopping.

'The driver of the boat train had been a driver for eight years and had driven regularly between London and Exeter, but he'd not worked a boat train before so it's quite possible that he'd never driven through Salisbury without stopping. Just before two o'clock in the morning of Sunday 1 July 1906 the boat train approached Salisbury station. About a mile west of the station the driver sounded the whistle to give notice of his approach, which was normal, and then continued to run at full speed towards the station instead of reducing speed. To the consternation of staff in the signal box and on the station he hurtled through the station at probably 60–70mph until the train reached the sharp left-hand curve at the east end of the station. Centrifugal force started to turn the locomotive over towards the right and as it turned right over, it hit a milk train which was passing. In a matter of seconds the boat train was just a tangled heap across the eastern end of Salisbury station.

'The scene was one of utter devastation, a five-coach train had been reduced to a heap of wreckage. Twenty-four passengers were killed, as were the driver and fireman of the boat train, the guard of the milk train and also the fireman of another engine nearby . . . The first four vehicles of the passenger train [had] wooden bodies and they were just reduced to matchwood and the only vehicle that survived virtually unscathed was the rear guard's van.'

Within a month (what a contrast with the slow progress of today's inquiries!) the inspector, Major Pringle, had concluded that, as Pattenden says, the crash was caused by 'excess speed on a curve. It was unusual in that the train actually tipped over . . . I've done similar types of accident inquiry and usually the train has burst off the track and become derailed . . . There's only one other accident I know of where there was a clear tipping over of the train on a curve.'

The accident came at a time when speed was much in the news, only two years after the first time that a train, headed by the locomotive City of Truro, had exceeded 100mph on British tracks (GWR ones at that) and the shock was considerable. A rather bad poem was written to commemorate the tragedy and postcards of the wreckage were much in demand. There were also some long-term effects. Pattenden says, 'the fifteen-mile-an-hour speed restriction, which was put on at the east end of Salisbury station after the accident, is still there today. The curve is exactly the same.' Even today 'All regular passenger trains always stop at Salisbury station. There has been no running through non-stop since that terrible night in 1906.' The only exception to this, apparently, is the Royal Train.

Nevertheless Pattenden destroys one myth: 'There was a strong suggestion at the time that the train may have been racing to beat the Great Western, who were opening a shorter route to London that day. There doesn't appear to be any evidence of that at all. The overall timings of the boat trains had not been altered for several years and drivers who worked the boat trains knew full well that if they arrived in London early they would actually be taken off their locomotives as a disciplinary matter. Certainly in the conversation that the driver had with the station inspector at Temple-combe earlier that night, he said quite clearly that he'd got no intention of arriving in Waterloo early, so I suspect it was one of those stories that goes around after a major accident, not founded on fact at all.'

But there were many other theories: that the driver was not used to the route or to the relatively new locomotive; that the two companies had induced their drivers to break the speed limits; and even that the well-heeled American passengers had bribed the driver to go faster.

The Salisbury crash demonstrates that many possible factors might lead drivers to travel too fast. Several explanations were also put forward for a mysterious crash at Grantham less than three months after the Salisbury disaster. The driver, the fireman, eleven passengers and a postal sorter were killed when a fast mail train was derailed after hurtling through the station and ignoring two danger signals. According to L.T.C. Rolt, a signalman saw both driver and fireman 'standing motionless, one on either side of the footplate, each staring ahead through his cab spectacle glass . . . A moment later [he and his colleagues on the platform] heard a great noise like an explosion and then the night sky over the north yard was lit with flames.' In a book on *Britain's Greatest Railway Mystery*, Philip Green surmises that the accident was caused by the severe sciatica from which the driver, Fleetwood, was suffering. Green invites us to join Fleetwood and his fireman, a 'gentleman apprentice' called Talbot,

> in the hot, swaying, increasingly noisy cab of No. 206. Fleetwood is tired and in pain and increasingly anxious as precious minutes are lost . . . Maybe a few sharp words are exchanged – these are not two old ladies at a tea party, after all. Both men are certainly tired, disgruntled, fed up. By the time they have slogged their way to the top of Stoke Bank they are not speaking. . .Is this simple fact of human nature the reason why they are staring straight ahead but apparently seeing nothing? . . . Call it the indirect result of sciatica plus a culture clash, or simply momentary inattention. But whatever it was it was responsible for the death of fourteen people including Talbot and Fleetwood.

The sense of unease remains when one or more of the key factors behind a crash are missing and the driver seems to have been determined to commit suicide. This was clearly the case when an underground train smashed into a dead end tunnel at Moorgate station in the City of London at 8.46am on 28 February 1975 after the driver had been seen accelerating as he passed through the station – which was at the end of the line. Witnesses said that the driver, like the crew at Grantham, was standing bolt upright at the controls looking straight ahead as if paralysed. He had clearly not tried to stop, indeed his hand was on the accelerator at the moment of impact. Forty-five people died in the worst accident ever seen in the near 150-year history of London's underground system. The train was so badly crushed inside the tunnel that it took five days to remove all the bodies. Naturally there was speculation about suicide on the part of the driver, though there was no evidence of depression or personal problems. Tests for alcohol were inconclusive because there had been natural fermentation in his body in the five days between his death and the time his body was recovered. At the inquest the jury returned a verdict of accidental death, though at the time a respected journalist put forward the theory that just before the crash the driver had been told that he had contracted a disease which rendered him impotent.

Descriptions of accidents tend to underestimate, or even ignore, the psychological factors behind crashes. Apparently the only really serious accident on Great Western Railway in the twentieth century, at Norton Fitzwarren in Somerset in 1940, was due to the driver having confused the signals, despite the automatic warning system installed by the GWR. Luckily 'only' twenty-six passengers were killed, even though the train was crowded with 900 people. It was said that the driver had erred because the signals were in the 'wrong' – that is, unexpected – place since there had been no room to put them where he would have looked for them. But perhaps the real explanation was that the driver's home had just been destroyed in a German bombing raid.

Or the explanation might be mechanical. In the autumn of 1947 twenty-eight were killed and ninety-four injured at Goswick, near Berwick in Northumberland, when an express was derailed because the driver failed to slow down sufficiently to allow for a diversion from the fast line. It was a typical muddle: the driver had an unauthorized passenger on the footplate and failed to see the distant signal that showed caution. He should then have crossed to the other side of the cab as the locomotive (a Pacific) had right-hand drive. This was one of the accidents that led to a system known as 'Approach Control' on diversions that require trains to slow down. The stop signals only change when the train is relatively close, thus ensuring that it is travelling at an appropriately reduced speed.

If the driver survives, his ordeal is only just beginning. As they say of pilots in similar circumstances, 'If the accident doesn't kill the pilot then the inquiry will'. One of the drivers involved in the famous crash in the snow at Abbot's Repton, on the main line from Peterborough to King's Cross, in January 1876 was destroyed by the accident and the subsequent inquiry. As David L. Smith wrote in *Tales of the Glasgow & South Western Railway*, 'He took on himself blame where there was none, his health suffered, and some years later he committed suicide.'

Just as bad is when the driver has done everything he could to prevent an inevitable accident. Peter Rayner was in the cab in just such a case when a train hit a ganger who had taken no notice of the driver's warning whistle. 'The terrible thing, I know from being present that time,' he wrote, in *On and Off the Rails*, 'is the inevitability of the accident, the long period of brake application, the noise of the brakes, the whistling that brings no reaction and the noise of you and your companion shouting at the person on the track. The mere fact you are four hundred yards away and inside the cab does not stop you shouting.'

There is no end to such stories. To take an extreme case, after the terrible crash in 1933 at Pomponne in eastern France the driver and fireman of the express train involved were arrested and the driver was forced to stand between two policemen for several hours while the bodies of the dead were carried past him to be laid out in rows in a field. Even today, few railway companies follow the excellent example set by East Japan Railway, which Masaki Ogata explains: 'Sometimes mass communication in the newspapers, television, blames the driver but at the same time they blame the company and we never put the responsibility on the driver only . . . We have to share, I think. That's our company's attitude, and most important thing is to find out the real cause of that accident, then we try to ensure that such an accident will never occur again.'

Worse than the inevitable inquiry is the possibility of a prosecution, even if the driver is eventually found innocent. One of the most bizarre such cases came in 1988 after fifty-nine people died when a local electric train ploughed at 60mph into a commuter train standing at the Gare de Lyon in Paris. The investigation revealed an extraordinary chain of events. Five miles from the Gare de Lyon a woman passenger had decided that she was on the wrong train. She pulled the emergency handle, the brakes locked, and she got off. The passengers grew restless as the driver spent half an hour releasing then resetting the brakes. Eventually they set off again – at 60mph to make up for lost time. Then the driver realized that he had disconnected the entire braking system, and it was downhill all the way to the Gare de Lyon. He radioed the station master, warning him to clear the tracks and the platform, but a minute later came the impact. The driver was tried for manslaughter, as was the woman who left the train. In the event the driver was sentenced to four years' imprisonment, of which he served six months. Not surprisingly, his sentence provoked a strike by France's railwaymen.

There were two such prosecutions in Britain in the 1980s, neither satisfactory. The first came in 1984 after the crash at Morpeth in Northumberland when a sleeping-car express crashed through a permanent 50mph speed limit at between 85 and 90mph. No one was seriously injured but the driver was prosecuted because, it was alleged, he had been drinking beer and whisky before he started the trip. The inspector's report, which came out only after he had been cleared of the charge of endangering life, concluded that 'Approaching Morpeth [the driver] may have fallen asleep, or become so drowsy that he completely forgot the approaching curve.' The inspector, Lieutenant-Colonel A.G. Townsend-Rose thought this by far the most likely explanation for the disaster.

A more sensational one came in 1989 after a crash when an express passed a double and then a single yellow light at Purley, near London, without the driver applying the brakes. By the time he reacted to the red signal it was too late. He hit the rear of a train from Horsham a glancing blow and the train plunged down an embankment. Five passengers were killed and thirty-two detained in hospital. The driver was charged with manslaughter, which, as Peter Semmens points out, was 'hardly the way to encourage open co-operation'. He was sentenced to eighteen months' imprisonment, but there was a public outcry and the sentence was reduced on appeal.

The crash and the prosecution produced a sensible comment from Stanley Hall in a letter to *The Times* of 21 February 1989:

> Time and again it is clear that responsibility for most accidents cannot be attributed to an individual failure, be it of man or machine. The present trend for seeking a scapegoat and revenge for serious transport accidents is unwholesome. Rather than cause any improvement in real safety standards, it is likely to result only in people and institutions seeking to cover their tracks. What purpose, other than revenge, is served by sending to prison a train driver who inadvertently failed to stop at a red signal? Does it make the railway any safer?

Another of the rare cases where a driver, or signalman, was sent to gaol – cases rendered fewer because English juries tend to sympathize with drivers who have already suffered greatly from the crash and its aftermath – came when the driver held responsible for the crash at Aisgill in 1913 was imprisoned for two months, a sentence reduced because the Midland Railway was criticized by the court for the strictness with which it punished delays. As a result, says Ascanio Schneider, the driver had been 'more afraid of such a failure than of breaking the safety regulations'. Sometimes the whole system is guilty not just of imposing a reign of terror but, even worse, of lacking control over its drivers and allowing them to continue in charge when severe doubt has been cast on their capacity to function adequately at work. This has been shown clearly by two recent crashes on the underground systems in Toronto and New York.

In 1995 a certain Robert Jeffrey joined the Toronto Red Rocket subway system, supposed to be the safest in North America, as a driver. On his first day on the job he ran through a double red light. On his second day he shot through a caution signal, then a red danger signal, even though an automatic brake device, activated by a trip arm, should have kicked in. He was now heading downhill at 35mph. He passed two more red lights, then a further red signal, which should have stopped him automatically. Amazingly he didn't brake and none of the safety devices stopped him. He drove straight into the back of a parked train. Three people died and dozens were badly hurt. Investigators found that a small protruding piece of metal on the train wheel had deflected the trip-arm safety devices. It has since been altered to prevent a recurrence. But why Jeffrey sailed though four red lights without touching the brakes remains a mystery.

An even more extraordinary case had occurred four years earlier when Robert Ray was in charge of a ten-carriage train with 125 people aboard on the New York subway. At the point where he came off the tracks, says Bruce McGladry, 'There was a general work order that required him to go from an express line to a local line so he was going from one track to another through a crossover, due to maintenance work on the express line further down the track. He was supposed to make that crossover at no more than 20mph but was expected to go at about 10mph.'

He had been driving so fast that other crew members had sensed danger, and even a passenger had asked him to slow down. He refused. As they approached Union Square station at 50mph, the automatic brakes cut in but the train derailed. 'When he tried to negotiate the crossover at that high speed,' says McGladry, 'of course he was unsuccessful. The train went off the tracks, hit support pillars, split open the car. Five people were killed and nearly a hundred injured, eleven of them seriously. Some of the injured were trapped for hours in the pitch black. The accident raised basic questions not only about the driver – and the fact that the management allowed so unsuitable a person to drive – but also about the strains of driving, especially on metros and commuter services where the routine can be deadly.

'When they tested him for alcohol' says McGladry, 'he was three times over the limit, even though he was tested thirteen hours later because of problems with getting the requisite court order and with the testing equipment.' The biggest puzzle for the NTSB was that ' the amount of alcohol in his system should have made normal activities, walking and talking, difficult. In fact he reported to work, signed in, had a brief discussion with the despatcher and operated a train for approximately half an hour. Now, even though he made some operational errors in that half-hour, like over-shooting a station, at least he didn't wreck the train. How is that possible with someone with such a high alcohol content? It's only possible in someone who has a relatively high alcohol intake on a regular basis. You become conditioned to the alcohol and you can perform some functions, albeit not up to your full potential. This created issues for us at the Safety Board in trying to figure out how it was possible that someone with such a high blood-alcohol content was allowed on to a train in the first place.'

According to McGladry, the alcohol level was exacerbated by 'the level of fatigue that the operator had. In piecing together his activities over the last day before the accident he had had about four hours, maybe four hours and fifteen minutes maximum, of sleep.' To make matters worse 'It wasn't continuous four hours either. It was in two segments. That would produce someone who was fatigued, which reduced his capabilities, like alcohol reduces capabilities. Combine the two and we have someone who didn't work out very well' – surely one of the understatements of all time.

Ray came from a New York ghetto, started working as a cleaner for five years, and was looking to better himself – 'maybe, even rise to be a supervisor,' he says. Nevertheless, he found he had problems even after three years as a railwayman. 'You've got to have the trains out on a certain time. Sometimes a person may not come in or calls in sick, and you have to work double shift. You may get stuck in the tunnel for hours waiting for a cross to come across or you maybe have to go in a yard. You have to work a lot of hours. It's like a domino effect, you know – the supervisor gets hit, then he comes down on the motorman and the motorman goes to the conductor. I was often separated from my family because of the overtime. I would come home early in the morning, my children wanted to come around me and I was so tired, I just wanted to go to sleep, and then when I get a few hours' sleep, you know, the phone was ringing. When I finally got up and I had just enough time to brush my teeth, get a bite to eat and then run back off to work again. This went on for a long time and I was planning on going from the night shift to the day shift and figured that would work out a little better.'

The day of the crash, he says, 'was just a day like any other day . . . By the time I got up to go to work I was rushing, I was kind of tired. I checked all the signals, made sure everything was in order . . . As I was operating I realized I was having problems with the brake but it was nothing to me that seemed unusual because that happens all the time if you're rushing . . . I was running a little late and trying to pick up speed, and I remember I overshot a couple of stations. The procedure when you overshoot a station is, you can't back up a train but you can block the doors if your train is over to the point where people can fall out. They can get out of another car.'

By then Ray was running a little ahead of schedule but was getting increasingly concerned. 'I said to myself, I said, "Oh man, I've got to pay more attention." I was at maximum speed which is, like, fifty-five or sixty miles an hour, depending because from 28th Street going into 42nd Street is like a down grade,' despite a speed limit of 10mph on one particular curve.

'The last thing I remember when leaving 42nd Street, was . . . thinking it was kind of hot. Now mind you have to have both your hands on the control, so I thought I'll wait till I get into the station and then I'll remove my sweater . . . but I got a dizzy spell. I remember passing the station at 28th Street and the heat. When I was a kid I used to have seizures and somehow I just blacked out. I saw 28th Street and I looked and 42nd Street was ahead of me. The last thing I remember I was out and I had my head down.

'I looked around, it was massively dark, it was cloudy, smoke all over the place. The first thing in my mind was to operate the controls. There was no movement, nothing. I got on the radio, I tried to call my conductor, I tried to call the command centre. That's when I noticed the whole side of the train was gone so I said, "Man, we must have had an accident or something", and I heard people moaning and I figured I had to get out of here because the smoke was like burnt rubber. As I was going to exit the front door it was locked, and I remember there was a police officer. She says, "Are you the motorman or the operator of the train?" and I said, "Yes, I am," and she says, "OK." I went to reach my hand to one of the cables because there was nothing else to hold on to because I was dizzy and she said, "No, don't grab it because it's a live wire," so I put my hand down. I got up to the platform and I said, "I've got to get out of here, it's too hot." I was feeling like I was going to pass out again so I went out to the street and the air was making me feel a little better and that's when I knew they were going to fire me because all accidents are inexcusable. Being the breadwinner and a role model for my family, I felt that I was a failure for a moment – all the study I put myself into and it's just gone overnight.

'The only alcohol I had in my system that day was maybe a couple of shots of vodka but now I realized I had to get something to drink because I wanted to just block everything out. I went and got a beer and I don't know how many beers I had. I just wanted to just drink myself to a stupor. When I finally got to the Bronx where I was staying with my fiancée, the unmarked car came and pulled over in front of me and they said, "Are you Ray?" and that's when my brother and my fiancée came out and grabbed me and told me what had happened.'

After that, 'The system tried to plant crack bottles under my cab and the crack bottles were so neatly put together that it was obvious somebody planted them there. My lawyer offered me a plea bargain where I could get five to fifteen years and at first I took it because my fiancée didn't think she would stay with me for twenty-five years if I was in prison for that long.' His new-found religious faith prevented him from taking what he came to regard as the coward's way out. His reward was a life sentence.

But the crash was not exclusively the driver's fault. For a start, his fitness to drive was not properly checked. As McGladry points out, 'The amount of time that's available for the despatcher to make his decision on someone's fitness for duty is relatively short, especially in this particular case where the operator showed up a little late and had to rush to grab his radio, sign his name. In that short time-span the despatcher had to make a decision: was this someone capable of doing their job or not? One of the responsibilities of the despatcher is to observe operating employees, conductors and opera-tors, motormen, for their fitness for duty. But that's a rather ill-defined term and in fact the despatcher said he was observing to make sure the operator was properly attired for the evening . . . Now he's also a busy man, he has other things to do as well. What is the likelihood that he would expect someone to come to work intoxicated, where he would have to make that kind of decision? Not very likely.'

The system did not help. 'It's very boring just driving down a track with tunnels,' says George McDonald, a union official. 'They're taught that if there's a red light or some reason you have to stop, there's an automatic stop system. If a signal's red you have a trip-up, which stops the train. They're told if they see anything in front of them to just let go of the handle, they call it the dead man's feature and that will apply the emergency brake to the train.' But there's also a service brake, 'which will stop the train hundreds of feet quicker than the emergency brake. But the lawyers in the New York City Transit Authority feel it's better to say that you've put the train into an emergency and the train was now not in your control and the emergency braking system took control and did what it was supposed to . . . But crucially the emergency braking system would not stop the train as quickly as the service brake.' As a result, he concludes 'This accident was foreseeable.'

But, above all, the blame lay with management which, says McDonald, has the 'responsibility of giving a fitness-for-duty test to every worker. A lot of things have been said about the driver in that accident, that he might have been on the drugs or medication or alcohol, so how did he get on that train? It's management's responsibility to see if the driver looks like he's fit for duty. I can see accidents happening where people are using either pre-scription medication or illegal drugs, if they're not monitored and watched. It's up to management to stop that person from boarding a train by giving them a fitness-for-duty test and we have been yelling for this for a long time. They do the hiring, they do the assignments, they do the scheduling.'

'We asked the National Transportation Safety Board to come down,' says McDonald. The NTSB 'has no authority but can make recom-mendations and stop federal funding. They recommended to Congress that there should be drug and alcohol testing for all drivers of school buses, trains, public transit vehicles. The Federal Transit Administration and Congress passed a regulation for drug and alcohol testing which is now randomly administered. If anyone is caught with alcohol or drugs in their system they would possibly lose their job.'

'The fitness-for-duty test that resulted from the Union Square accident requires management personnel actually to talk to an individual beginning a shift and identify anyone who looks unfit because they are overtired, or maybe using drugs, alcohol. If they feel that the person is using alcohol or drugs then they do not assign them to duty. They send them for drug testing or they question them and see if the person has a problem.' Although this weeding out process has ensured that far fewer unfit drivers are allowed on to the system, it came too late to help poor Robert Ray.

11
When Tiredness Kills

I believe if the rail industry were to tackle fatigue in a competent way that you would see a significant drop in rail accidents and injuries.

Larry Mann

As Bruce McGladry pointed out, Robert Ray's problems were partly due to tiredness, a theme that emerges in a high proportion of accident reports. Time and again tiredness, strain or personal worries are at least partly responsible for the misjudgement of a driver or a signalman – indeed, Casey Jones himself was almost certainly overtired since he had agreed to take the Cannonball on a double shift back from Memphis to Canton. Today drivers' hours – and, above all, the anti-social shifts so many still endure – continue to take their toll.

Examples are scattered through railway history. In 1942 after the driver of a goods train overran a signal near Neuchâtel in central Switzerland and crashed into an oncoming passenger train, it was found that he had been so tired on the outward journey that he had fallen asleep more than once. He had been asleep when he ran through a station at full speed, and was awakened only by the crash.

Six years later the first serious accident after Britain's railways had been nationalized in January 1948 happened when a foolish soldier pulled the communication cord to stop a train near his home at Winsford in Cheshire. A signalman then allowed another train into the section occupied by the train. As the normally unsentimental Ascanio Schneider wrote:

He must take the principal blame, yet here, as so often in this book, we also stand before a little professional tragedy. He was sixty-two years old and had serious symptoms of the then typical occupational diseases of a signalman: he had a hernia, the result of heavy work of the mechanical lever system, and suffered from stomach trouble, the consequence of meals hastily swallowed between passing trains. Besides that, he had a cold and was concerned about his seriously ill wife . . . When the express arrived he was cooking himself some supper on a small stove in the corner of the box. Tired and fraught, he failed to look outside the box to see the express and allowed a goods train through.

One word recurs constantly in the reports of accidents in which drivers were the obvious guilty party: fatigue. It is a world-wide phenomenon. As Martin More-Ede of Circadian Technologies says: 'Because of the increasing time pressures, we're seeing a society where everything's speeded up, where efficiencies are being squeezed out. The number of crew members is being reduced to the lowest possible numbers to save costs. We're seeing that schedules and timetables need to be met and much less of any changes of the timetable . . . Because of all these pressures fatigue is often one of the consequences. People have too little time to sleep, there are too many other things going on, too many other pressures, and when you have too much fatigue, you have too little attention in critical safety-sensitive situations on the rails and accidents come from that.'

Such crashes occur all over the world and a few examples show the geographical spread. Indian trains are almost invariably crowded and the system is under-equipped with safety devices. In January 1988 a passenger train travelling at 40mph sped past a red danger signal and rammed into a train that had stopped after running into a deer in dense fog at Hardoi, 200 miles south-west of Delhi. There were 1500 people on board the two trains, ten carriages were wrecked, forty-nine people were killed and sixty-two injured. The driver was held principally to blame for the crash, which was so serious that a special railway review panel was appointed to examine it. It was headed by a Supreme Court judge, and highlighted precisely the problems of fatigue, shift patterns and unsuitable rest facilities that find their echoes elsewhere.

The dry words of an NTSB report shows how the problem continues in the USA:

About 3.25am, mountain daylight time, on June 8, 1994, the second of three eastbound Burlington Northern (BN) freight trains near Thedford, Nebraska, had stopped behind the first eastbound train when it was struck in the rear by the third eastbound train. The lead unit of the striking train derailed, coming to rest on an adjacent track where it was struck by a westbound train. The engineer and conductor of the striking eastbound train were killed and the engineer and conductor of the westbound train were injured. Damages to track, equipment, and lading were estimated at $2.5 million . . . The engineer had failed to obey a restrictive train signal because, based on his inappropriate reliance on peripheral cues, he anticipated the signal would change; and the inattentiveness of the conductor to train operations, as a result of fatigue.

In a smash at Beresfield near Sydney in 1997 three people were badly injured when a coal train drove straight into the back of a standing passenger train. The driver had passed through a signal at caution then another at danger. The investigators found that he had fallen into 'automatic behaviour syndrome' – when someone is so tired that they can go through the motions of a work routine but fail to respond to new and vital information.

The overwhelming importance of sheer tiredness as an explanation for many crashes is emphasized by Larry Mann who, as he says, has 'handled a tremendous amount of court litigation over the years . . . In my investigations in most cases it's because they are fatigued. The rail industry works the crew an inordinate amount of time. I'm aware of situations where certain carriers are working crew members thirty days straight without a break and you're talking about working a maximum of twelve hours a day, day in, day out. You can see that a person is tired.

'Under the Hours of Service Act, a federal statute, the employees are allowed to work up to twelve hours a day. The railroad industry works a crew eleven hours fifty-nine minutes so that the crew member is required to receive eight hours of rest. If they were to work the employee twelve hours the crew member would get ten hours' rest.' But by working the driver only a few minutes less than twelve hours, the railway company is allowed to give him only eight hours off. 'Now, during that rest period the employee has to get home, he has to eat, wash, he has to be with his family.' Because a driver is virtually always on call, 'as a practical matter a typical employee gets only about five hours' rest, day in, day out. This has been recognized by the National Transportation Safety Board as the top safety issue in the rail industry and it's been a long history of fatigue in the rail industry.'

Fortunately, as Martin More-Ede explains, 'The US Department of Transportation and also the Federal Railway Administration is really recognizing fatigue as the number one safety risk in the rail industry and in transportation in general, and because of this, and because of the data showing that we probably have ten to fifteen major rail accidents a year where fatigue is a major contributory cause, and those accidents are costing lives – and on average a million dollars per accident in terms of the damages – it's becoming a huge issue all around the world.'

Perhaps the most important incident in changing attitudes to fatigue – and in revolutionizing the approach to a major railway system – came in Canada after a crash at Hinton, Alberta, in February 1986. There had been two other cases of accidents involving driver fatigue in Canada, 1985 before the Hinton disaster. In February that year the driver of a train at London, Ontario, 'probably experienced a sleep episode' – in the words of the official report – and 'not only missed a critical restrictive signal indication but was unable to intervene as the train approached and struck stationary cars'. In October, at Greeley in British Columbia, there was a collision 'when the crew of one train did not take appropriate action in response to railway signals . . . The crew had become impaired by fatigue due to excessive waking hours without a restorative rest period' – a situation not helped by dense fog.

The Hinton crash occurred at 6am when an enormous freight train was crawling along the tracks. It was time for a crew change. Stopping the train would be a hassle so the new three man crew climbed aboard while the train kept moving. Half an hour later with the train rolling downhill towards Hinton, it had picked up speed to 50mph, twice the limit, approaching a point where the double track was singled. The guard was aware of the danger and tried to radio the driver. There was no reply. The guard could have pulled the emergency brake but that would certainly have caused extensive damage and might even have derailed the train.

It was probably too late anyway. The freight train, which was enormous even by Canadian standards – a mile long and weighing 13,000 tons – ploughed into a passenger train bound for Edmonton. Sulphur in the freight wagons ignited. The crash and the fire together killed twenty-nine people including the driver, whose actions remain a mystery.

The crew of train 413, the giant that crashed at Hinton, had had only a short night's rest and, according to Joe Kolodrubsky, an investigator with the Transportation Safety Board of Canada, the engineer's health 'was highly suspect. He was found to have diabetes, he was plagued with pancreatitis, he'd had a colostomy, he was an alcoholic and he had high blood pressure, quite a conglomeration of illnesses . . . I don't think it's a regular practice that someone with that many illnesses would be working.' According to the official report he had been drinking so heavily just after Christmas that his wife had thrown him out.

Kolodrubsky believes, 'Probably the engineman was dozing, from where they located his remains. I think he was on his way down to the toilet, which is in the nose of the cab. The conductor said he was trying to call him at the time but nobody heard him.' All this despite the presence of a safety device known as 'the dead man's pedal'. This, says Kolodrubsky, should 'ensure that if the engineman becomes incapacitated the train brakes are applied. It is a little lever, a pedal on the floor, and the engineman is required to sit there with his foot depressing this pedal. If he takes his foot off there's ten seconds, then a warning, and if the pedal is not depressed again the train brakes go on.' Unfortunately the inquiry soon revealed that enginemen often nullify the pedal: 'They would use their lunch pail or overnight bag, or whatever, and just put it on the pedal and then they have no worries.' And the reason? Human nature and human physiology. 'Can you imagine sitting there with your foot holding down this pedal for six or eight hours?' asks Kolodrubsky. 'And if you wanted to go to the washroom you'd have to get somebody to come over and step on it while you left or take over your position. It is an onerous thing.'

Ironically, the second locomotive on the train 'had the latest up-to-date device installed. It's called a reset safety control and it works differently. The engineman must touch the brake valve or the throttle, or blow the whistle or ring the bell – any little movement and the safety control resets itself. If there's no movement it starts to clock off ready to initiate a flashing light to inform whoever is there that you haven't touched the brake valve or haven't blown the whistle and you'd better do something. They'll just touch something and that resets the control . . . If there is no motion by the engineman on any of these devices in the cab, the flashing light becomes more intense as time goes by, and then they get an audio alarm, which starts low and goes up to a high intensity, and if there's nothing done after that, the train brakes are set on emergency and the train stops. It's a far more sophisticated deal than the dead man's pedal.'

Unfortunately the union had prevented the installation of the new device in the driver's cab. 'The lead unit was classified as a comfort cab,' says Kolodrubsky, 'because of facilities that were provided within that locomotive, like a washroom and a hotplate. That cab had the old dead man's pedal as a safety device but because of an agreement they had with the locomotive engineers the comfort cab took priority and that was to be in the lead position at all times whenever possible. It is a mystery to me why they would allow a comfort cab to take priority over a highly controversial safety device like the dead man's pedal, which was very easily nullified and they knew that.'

The Hinton crash prompted research on behalf of a number of companies by Circadian Technologies of Cambridge, Massachusetts, experts in the nature and rhythms of sleep. Martin More-Ede explains: 'Hinton was a classic case of a freight train accident relating to fatigue. The accident happened at 8.15 in the morning because the crew of the freight train had been working through the night, had been operating on three hours of sleep or less. It occurred at the most likely point in the clock for these freight train accidents to occur due to fatigue, which is about eight o'clock in the morning, typically peak time. In other words people work all the way through the night and just lose it at that point.'

For this was not an isolated case. 'The most challenging work patterns,' says More-Ede, 'are found in the North American locomotive engineers. These people work extremely irregular schedules, they are always on call, they never know when they're going to go out. The work is therefore totally unpredictable. As a result they can't predict their sleep/wake pattern.'

Working conditions don't help to keep them alert. 'There's a lot of monotony in that type of environment,' says More-Ede. 'You are pulling a very heavy train, sometimes a mile long or more, going up a steep gradient where you may be chugging along at only ten miles an hour. It can be monotonous – it's not like being on a street with street-lights, then there's the smell of the diesel fumes. All sorts of factors are leading to a pretty soporific environment . . . There's very little else going on and you have moments of panic interspersed between hours of boredom. In the age of steam there was much more going on – there was a much more tangible sense that you were operating a train, more vibration, more noise.'

The track leading to Hinton was monotonous in the extreme. When the investigators sent a similar test train along the same route with a group of observers on board, they found, says Kolodrubsky, that 'when they got on this long incline one of them did fall asleep', even though, and notably unlike the drivers, 'these people were not tired. The test run was during the same time of the day so they were all rested up when they got aboard the train.'

In theory, says More-Ede, 'You are protected by an alerter device: it turns on a light and if you touch it, it will switch off again – just to prove you're awake. But in reality most people, after a few years of experience, will almost do it in their sleep.' For, as he says, 'The in-cab devices are not really designed to protect against micro-sleeps.* They will protect against the person who's fallen fully asleep. You can't do that with one of these devices because the lights flash and if you don't respond the klaxon will go off and wake you up and if you don't respond to that the train will stop. But a micro-sleep is so short that it will occur within a time frame that won't be captured by that alerter device.'

Hinton was a major wake-up call for the Canadian rail industry. It was the first accident in which fatigue was clearly identified as the major cause. The inquiry's findings were reinforced by another incident, 'in which,' says More-Ede, 'a number of crew members were found to be running trains in excess of twelve hours, very extended periods of time. That led to an emergency regulation being put in place which required expensive changes to the way crews were staffed at an estimated cost of a hundred million Canadian dollars a year.' Naturally they tried to find alternative solutions, which is where More-Ede and his colleagues came in.

The 'Canada Project', as it was called, involved testing 'the baseline fatigue level. To do that we wired up engineers with electrodes, measured the brain waves, put portable recorders on them so that we could record every moment that they micro-slept or had a brief lapse while they were running a train . . . The risk turned out to be around five to ten seconds of micro-sleep, total inattention, per hour of running the train. We then moved from there to put in a number of fatigue countermeasures, then retested and were able to show substantial improvements in terms of the alertness level of the crew members.'

* More-Ede describes 'micro-sleep' as 'a brief intrusion of sleep waves into the brain when you're in the middle of wakeful activity. In other words, you're struggling to stay awake. It lasts five to twenty seconds when you don't see the outside world. You may be unaware that you've had that gap in your vigilance. When you're driving a car your eyes might close for five seconds, but when you're running a train they're more often closed for something like ten to thirty seconds.'

When More-Ede and his colleagues were riding with the drivers in the cab, 'There were a number of occasions when we were out on a stretch of track with a series of signal lights ahead of us and the train moving along quickly through the night and we turned to ask the driver a question and found that his head was bobbing and weaving, his eyelids were closing. That was certainly a scary moment for me personally and yet it happens. If you talk to drivers they will say, "Yes, there are some times when on a trip I am really struggling with sleep," and on our confidential surveys we found somewhere between 10 and 25 per cent of drivers would report that this happened to them on a semi-regular basis. Many a driver would talk of an incident where they'd slipped through a signal at danger or had missed a station even, or had just missed the edge of the platform and got the train misaligned because they'd had this momentary lapse of drowsiness.' On one particularly frightening occasion, 'We were able to record one micro-sleep of twenty seconds in length in a passenger train moving at a hundred miles an hour, which meant that the train went half a mile down the track with the train driver at the controls totally unaware of his environment.'

Nevertheless he believes, 'You can cut the risk of fatigue by really addressing the fundamental sleep-deprivation problem that exists on the rails.' This derives from the way the brain works to a clock, set by the 'Circadian rhythms,' which are upset by shift working. 'We evolved,' says More-Ede, 'on a rotating planet with daytime light and night-time darkness. Because of that we developed cycles of adaptation to night-time darkness and daytime light. So we find that body temperature surges upward during the daytime and falls to low levels at night. We find that certain hormones kick in at dawn to wake you up in the morning and others, like growth hormone, kick in at dusk to help you fall asleep. These cycles are called Circadian rhythms.'

Unfortunately, as every shift-worker knows, 'We've moved from a pattern of regular night-time sleep and being alert during the daytime to a twenty-four-hour economy.' To tackle the problem of ensuring that rail-waymen can cope with the 'regular irregularity' of their Circadian rhythms, More-Ede and his colleagues 'started out with the premise that you have to run this business twenty-four hours a day, seven days a week. It's a given, so the issue is not to try to ban shift work or ban running trains at night. The issue is how you help people better adapt to it. The answer is to provide them with more predictability. In other words, we constructed schedules for them whereby they'd have protected hours of sleep but they'd also know when they're going to work, with an approximate window of time. We also built those schedules of work hours to enable them to adapt. In other words, we didn't ask them to flip-flop between daytime and night-time work in an erratic pattern – that would be like a perpetual state of jet-lag. At the same time we gave them tools to manage fatigue, one of the issues we dealt with was napping.

'Napping is, of course, one of the age-old solutions to being a little sleep-deprived, but there's enormous resistance in the railway industry to napping. In fact, when we first suggested it in Canada we were almost laughed out of the room by management, but it's turned out to be one of the most effective strategies for managing fatigue. If you understand how to nap, brief naps of ten or fifteen minutes are effective pick-me-ups. They give a person a chance to pick up their alertness and to keep on going through the night.'

Unfortunately, he continues, 'Train driving is an industry with a tremendous culture to it. Many people who drive trains, their fathers drove trains, their grandfathers drove trains, it's very much in the family. You grow up as a railroader and you stay a railroader, and because of that new ideas are quite a challenge to introduce. But we had to address the situation in which people were fired because they were caught asleep. That took some considerable time, and it was only when we were able to point out that people were napping anyway in an uncontrolled fashion but we were proposing to control it that it started to become acceptable. Today it's very much a standard operating procedure.'

One of the most obvious challenges 'was to find out when they could safely nap. They obviously couldn't nap while the train was moving but there was an opportunity because much of Canada is operated on single tracks. So trains often have to move into a siding and wait for an oncoming train, then go forward. They might wait in that siding off the main track for fifteen or twenty minutes, which is just the right amount of time to take a power nap and get refreshed for the next stint on the rail.'

Not surprisingly, More-Ede believes, 'You can't leave it totally to technology. What you need to do is address the patterns of work and rest. Is there a napping policy? Are people educated in how to manage their sleep rate patterns? Those things can do a lot to address the problem and cost a lot less than putting in expensive technology.'

In the United States a major accident in 1986 resulted in mandatory rests. Moreover, drivers stayed on the same shift for at least three months instead of chopping and changing from day to day. Today, says John Reynolds, of the Canadian National Railroad, 'They're better off adjusting their lifestyles to fit their job – they can attend more family outings, do different things, accomplish a job and feel alert at the same time. For instance, one guy told me he was offered a chance to take his retirement. He says he's going to stay another ten years because it's made such a difference in his life.'

But Britain has not yet caught up. When More-Ede and his fellow-researchers arrived in Britain, 'The first thing we did was to ride the trains, interview the train drivers, we studied over twelve of the train operating companies all around the country, we looked at commuter rail, we looked at Intercity, we looked at the London Underground. We investigated the patterns of sleep and wake, we investigated the risks, did interviews and surveys and collected data on how fatigued people were . . . and the findings were really quite clear-cut. We saw almost as much fatigue in the British train operators as we'd seen in the Canadian counterpart.

'We talked with over three hundred train drivers. We interviewed them in their depots, in the stations, we rode with them in the trains. We had a chance actually to have a lot of candid conversations, and because we stress confidentiality people were willing to talk and told us a lot of stories about problems of running through signal lights or missing stations or falling asleep at the controls.'

This was not just theoretical work. It might be highly relevant to the Paddington train crash of 1999. The behaviour of the driver on the com-muter train, More-Ede says, 'was certainly compatible with what we saw when we rode with train drivers who were in a fatigued state. They could travel for quite a distance without being aware of their environment while they're in the middle of the micro-sleep . . . We know from studying hundreds of train drivers that when you've got an early start you might be operating on only three or four hours' sleep. We know this Paddington train driver started early in the morning. He'd made several commuter runs before the accident. We know he lived some distance out of town. All that adds up to a person who might have been quite sleep-deprived at the time, and quite vulnerable to having that critical micro-sleep that ended his life and those of many others.'

'When we've looked at a number of the ways that the rosters are built,' he continued, 'we found far too often that people had coupling between late rosters, and early rosters and quick turnarounds between them. One of the things about this Paddington train driver was that he was a relative newcomer to that job. When you're a newcomer you get some of the worst rostering patterns. In other words, the people who've been there a long time get the first pick of the rostering patterns and it's the junior man who can end up sometimes with the most irregular work patterns. I don't know that that's all true, I don't know what the patterns were, but that's the sort of thing you have to look for when you're analysing an accident like this.'

12
A Culture of Safety

The absence of accidents does not necessarily indicate the presence of safety.

Dr John Lauder, NTSB

Throughout railway history the corporate culture of too many railway systems has been marred by institutionalized sloppiness, where drivers and signalmen in particular have been used to disobeying or ignoring rules. Railway workers' cynicism about the railways' attitude down the years is summed up in an ancient piece of American railroad folklore about a switchman called as a witness in a case involving a head-on collision. On the stand he described how he had seen two trains bearing down on each other on the same track at a terrific clip. When one of the lawyers asked him what went through his mind at the sight he replied laconically, 'This is one helluva way to run a railroad.' Even today, the most difficult problem in dissecting disasters is when a host of factors is involved, adding up to a condemnation of the whole structure of a railway company.

A healthy corporate culture, which, in railway terms, involves not just loyalty to the company but an overriding concern for safety, can be of enormous benefit. Over the hundred and fifty years of its existence, first as the Great Western Railway and then as the Western Region of British Rail, the corporate culture of the GWR was real and highly effective. In an analysis of accidents, safety expert H. Rayner Wilson concluded that 'Its remarkable safety record was not due only to the technical factors but also to the efficiency and *esprit de corps* of its employees.' Tragically that culture was smashed with privatization. The Southall disaster, to which we return in Chapter 13, was the result.

It takes a long time to instil a proper culture of safety. It also requires the overwhelming devotion of rail management and workers to safety, as seen in Japan. Westerners tend to laugh at the fact that Japanese engine drivers wear white gloves and carry a watch given to them on their first day of service, but today the Shinkansen high-speed rail network transports 134 million passengers a year in total safety on 285 trains a day with an average delay of 0.3 minutes, and there has not been a single accident on the system since it started in service in 1964. The French, whose rail workers are also proud of their industry, have enjoyed a similar record since their high-speed network, the TGV, started in service nearly twenty years ago.

Jim Hall, chairman of the NTSB, defined corporate culture, in a speech to a railway industry workshop in June 1997, as the 'stable characteristics of one company or organization. Or, put more plainly, "the way things are done around here".' He said that government was 'responsible for setting guidelines and standards'; that management was 'responsible for enhancing the compliance with those standards, while accommodating variations in individual experience, knowledge and skills'; and that the operator was 'responsible for using the knowledge, skill and experience to do the job in the safest way'. These definitions, deliberately, placed the onus for improved railway safety on management and unions.

His conclusions, based on hundreds of investigations conducted by the NTSB, on ships and aeroplanes as well as trains, were stark. The accidents he was describing all shared one or more of the following characteristics: the futility of a belief in an infallible technology; the lack of appreciation for the role of the human in a highly technical system; the lack of an avenue for divergent opinions; the arrogance of management that believed in its inherent superiority to government regulations and sound operating practices; the trade-off between revenue and safety, to the detriment of safety; and, above all, 'the establishment of an organization's culture that discouraged communication, divergent opinion and an appreciation for the importance of safety'.

Hall went on to give an example from real life:

A transit operator stops the train between stations and in doing so successfully avoids endangering the train and its passengers.
However, stopping the train without permission violates an operating procedure. The operator calls the despatcher to obtain permission but is told not to stop. He stops anyway . . . But now, by stopping and avoiding the danger, the operator has no way to prove that an

unsafe condition actually existed. The question is, what action does his superior take? Is the train operator disciplined reflexively for his disregard of the rules, or is he recognized for his alertness?

Hall's remarks appear to be general but in fact he was referring to the 1996 crash at Silver Spring between the Amtrak express and the MARC suburban railway system serving Washington DC (see Chapter 9). The driver of the MARC train passed a caution signal shortly before stopping at Kensington station. The caution should have warned him to expect a red danger signal soon afterwards. But the driver forgot. The train accelerated out of the station to a speed of 60mph. It careered headlong on to an Amtrak passenger train on an adjacent track. The three-man Amtrak crew were killed instantly. But, to make matters worse, the leading carriage of the MARC train had pierced the fuel tank of the Amtrak locomotive, spraying fuel in all directions. Within a few seconds one MARC car was on fire from end to end. It was full of students, and onlookers watched helplessly as they hammered at the windows of the blazing train, unable to get out. In all, eleven people died. Investigators concluded that the driver of the MARC train must have been distracted while it passed the signals.

'The whole aspect of train movements comes into issue as well,' noted Larry Mann. 'The Amtrak train was being controlled by a despatcher in Jacksonville, Florida, several hundred miles away, and trains were approaching each other. If the person in control of the train movements had been paying attention, that would have been observed, the trains would have been notified immediately to stop, there would not have been a collision. Even in the face of the impact I believe there were actions that could have been taken to avoid this accident. The Amtrak train accelerated in speed: had the engineer applied the brakes instead, it seems to me that we would have not had the catastrophe that we had because the speed of the impact would have been much lower . . . Also there were two different sizes of equipment on the same trackage. Obviously a huge Amtrak locomotive is going to crush a small commuter car. Whether they should have been on the same tracks at the same time is another question.'

Jim Hall continued his speech to the railway industry with a lengthy analysis of the accident:

At first it appeared that a train operator simply did not comply with his training. The different pictures emerged suggesting that a superintendent at the train-despatching facility ignored warnings and did not stop the train. Later still it appeared that an executive manager had acted capriciously when he changed a long-standing operating policy without consideration of the consequences.

This accident resulted not from singular actions but from an organization-wide set of beliefs about the infallibility of the automatic train control equipment, somewhat reminiscent of the perceived infallibility of an ocean liner's watertight compartments so many years ago. [To Hall, the loss of the *Titanic* was the best single example of a tragedy that resulted from an organization's culture.] The MARC accident occurred shortly after a major snowstorm had begun and trains had started to overrun station platforms at several of the above-ground stations.

Larry Mann also emphasizes that one element in the crash equation was that ever-present problem, the weather. 'It was snowing and maybe the crew could not see the signal properly.'

Hall added:

The accumulating snow and ice reduced the effectiveness of the train's braking system. All trains were operating in the fully automatic mode; that is, they were being controlled by the system computer, not by the operator on board the train or by controllers in the system's central control facility.

Shortly after emerging above ground on its way to Washington, train 111 [the MARC train] arrived at Twinbrook station twelve minutes before the accident. Although the automatic train control directed the train to stop at the platform, the train overran the platform. At Rockville, too, the train partially overran the station. Because the operator had to secure the controls to assist passengers at that station, the train had lost its automated command to operate at the reduced speed of 44mph. So after leaving Rockville, the train began accelerating automatically beyond that speed, heading for 75mph, still within the design limitations of the rails and signals, at least when weather conditions were favourable. The operator called the controller to report the overspeed situation and was told this was due to his overrunning the previous station and that he was to continue in automatic operation.

As the train approached the Shady Grove station, the controller, who could see the location of the train on his monitor, called the operator and asked if the speed had dropped. Because it had, the controller later told Safety Board investigators that he had a feeling the system was doing what it was supposed to do and didn't believe that he had to put his job on the line by telling the operator to go into manual mode.

At Shady Grove station, a gap [spare] train was parked 470 feet beyond the platform – despite an unwritten Metrorail order that these trains were to be kept on the adjacent inactive track . . . When train 111 arrived at the Shady Grove Station, it slid past the platform and struck the standing gap train. The operator was found crushed in wreckage near the cab door. There were no other injuries. The Safety Board investigation team was launched that night. Once the follow-up investigation work began, a fairly clear picture emerged for what had happened and why.

Hall provided a list of the underlying causes of the accident:

First: Metrorail had recognized that leaving the gap train on the incoming active track presented an unnecessary hazard. But we learned that the gap trains were frequently stored on the active track, apparently because of confidence in the automatic train control system.

Second: there was no formal training program for controllers at the center, other than an annual operating-rules examination. Consider that the controller knew of the accident train's overruns at two previous stations, he knew about the deteriorating weather, he knew about the unusually high speed of the train, and he knew the gap train was parked beyond the Shady Grove station. And yet he did not see a need to stop the train.

Third: equally disturbing was our finding that no one, including the superintendent of the central control center, had the authority to intervene and stop the accident train unless a collision was certain. The controller felt that he would be putting his job on the line if he were to allow the operator to take manual control of the train.

Fourth: because manually operated braking was being blamed for a perceived flat-wheel problem, which would indicate poor braking technique, a decision was apparently made by the Deputy General Manager to eliminate all manual operation, even in inclement weather. No train operator knew of or was consulted about the change, and most of the management including the General Manager did not learn of the decision until after the accident.

It would be tempting to blame the conditions and circumstances of this accident on one person, the Deputy General Manager. But this would not have recognized corporate culture as a safety problem. The logic for substantive causation of this accident only holds together when we consider the extent to which management and operating personnel believed the automated train control system would protect them, and that the system would provide adequate margins of safety regardless of the quality of the decisions and policies.

It was a mindset that, again, reminded Hall vividly of that pertaining at the White Star Line, owners of the *Titanic*.

The investigators needed a voice record to be sure of what had gone on in the cab and which alerts had sounded, and the accident prompted the most radical single safety recommendation in the recent history of US railroads, the installation of black box voice recorders in all US train cabs (see Chapter 9). But, even more importantly, it led to an agonizing rethink by MARC of all its operating procedures in what amounted to a revolution in its corporate culture.

Sometimes the only way to overcome the perceived deficiencies in one culture is to call in a superior one. This is what happened on the New York subway system. 'In the seventies especially,' says George McDonald, 'there was no money for the transit system, and the first thing they stop is the maintenance. Most of the money was spent on new equipment, subway cars which were faster, longer, more modern. The system was built in the early 1900s and the rest of the system wasn't built to keep up with the technology of the subway cars. The signal systems were antiquated, the switching systems were antiquated, the safety systems were antiquated. We expected a disaster to happen, and no matter what we said about keeping up with the maintenance and the technology, the maintenance just fell to an all-time low. They laid off maintenance workers and they just stopped keeping up with the technology of one part of the subway. Then when an accident happens, like that at Union Square, the National Transportation Safety Board comes in, which does not have any power or authority. The New York City Transit Authority is like a country of its own – they're not under rules and federal regulations, they make their own rules and regulations as an authority. The only way we were able to get them to do the right thing and make it safe, keep up with technology on the track and the signal system was because we get a lot of federal money for transit and that money could be stopped by the National Transportation Safety Board or government. So they were forced to use that money to ensure that the technology on the signal system and the tracks matched the technology and the speeds of the subway trains themselves.'

Inadequate corporate culture is not confined to Britain and the United States. A report on a derailment in Finland that killed eleven passengers identified not only that the driver was tired – and probably making a cup of coffee at the time – but also pinpointed management inadequacies, including a careless attitude towards safety requirements that jeopardized train safety. But the most spectacular recent case of a failure in corporate culture was that of the German rail company, Deutsche Bahn. It was compounded of arrogance, the Not Invented Here syndrome which prevents many large organizations accepting ideas from outside, and panic leading to a refusal to listen to evidence even from its own employees. It led to the worst railway disaster in Germany since the late 1940s. On 3 June 1998 at Eschede, on the line between Munich and Hamburg, 101 passengers were killed and eighty injured in an ICE express, the DB's pride and joy.

The ICE had been travelling at 175mph when passengers began to feel a strange vibration. The train continued on the track and the vibration stopped. Then, as the lead power-car emerged from beneath a road bridge over the track, two kilometres from Eschede station, the driver felt a tug on his locomotive. He looked back and, to his horror, saw that the locomotive had separated from the train. The traction motor stopped and the brakes were automatically applied. Several hundred metres behind him a drama had erupted: the train had derailed.

Two kilometres further on the derailed carriages hit an over-bridge* and

* A similar unhappy combination of circumstances transformed the derailment of a suburban train near Sydney in 1977, caused by poorly maintained track, into a disaster that killed eighty-three and injured two hundred. It happened at a road overbridge and the derailed coaches struck the piers of the bridge, which collapsed on to them.

the other carriages piled up. At first the investigators thought that a road accident had caused a car to fall off the bridge, hit and derail the train. But the real cause soon emerged: six kilometres behind the scene of the crash, part of a train wheel was found, at the point where the passengers had felt the vibration. The broken wheel had come from the leading axle of the first car. The train had continued until it was about 300 metres from the bridge, which is where the coach derailed to the right of the track. A hundred metres further on, the next carriage derailed, forcing the third carriage off the rails. They then hit the bridge support and the train split up. After the fourth car passed the bridge, it collapsed on to the rest of the train.

Petra Sebastian, a passenger on the doomed train, first felt uneasy 'when I had this sensation that the train had just run over something . . . Then there was this strange movement as the train swayed right then left. I probably held tight because of the sudden pull, and I remember thinking, We can't be derailing, that's impossible!' Then there was this huge bang further ahead, followed by this sudden pulling, as if a gigantic Hoover was trying to suck me in . . . I opened my eyes and looked around me. There was grit in my mouth and everything was reduced to rubble.'

For Joacsim Gries, a local who went to the help of the survivors, it was 'like a spot where a plane had crashed down because the whole train was totally broken. There was all kinds of material in a large field, on the bridge, under the bridge, behind the bridge, so it was very hard to see the whole situation . . . We tried to help people inside the broken train but it was very hard. There's very thick glass in the windows so it was very hard to get into the carriages to free the injured people.'

The tragedy can be traced back to the situation within Deutsche Bahn. As Markus Hecht explains, until 1994 'DB was a state-owned enterprise and it had the image of not being as innovative as it should have been.' In 1994 DB was not privatized but it was converted into a company and was thus in a period of considerable cultural upheaval. For the new management the ICE 'was a new product that should improve the image of DB'. The train was not only fast but luxurious, soundproofed, with picture windows and information displays to ram home to the passengers the train's performance. For three years after 1991 when it was first introduced, it was enormously successful: it halved the journey time between Munich and Hamburg to three hours, and as a result rail usage rose by over a third while air traffic dropped by a tenth.

But the ICE became a victim of pressure to provide a perfect train quickly due to the increasing success of the French TGV, which had been operating since the early 1980s at speeds of up to around 300kph (186mph). To the Germans the idea of French technological dominance was intolerable – as was the fear that the French might capture the world market for ultra-fast trains, particularly in the Far East. The result was that the speed of the German entry into the race was greatly increased while the train was still being designed and built. 'The ICE,' says Hecht, 'was originally intended to run at a maximum speed of 200kph and at a late stage of the project this speed was increased to 250kph. This high-speed new track was used where there was little experience and therefore they made it rather stiff with the intention to get a long-lasting track.' Crucially the track had also to carry heavy freight trains, which required additional strength and rigidity.

Logically this meant that a relatively flexible wheel was required to ensure a smooth ride. As Hecht points out, 'On the road you have the pneumatic wheel as a cushioning device and the road can be regarded as rigid. On a railway system, especially a high-speed railway system, you have to have a soft track.' But the ICE started running on a rigid track with an orthodox monobloc wheel, made from a single piece of steel that provided the necessary strength at the expense of flexibility.

The result is described by Arne Kühnel, whose company, ADBM, built the coaches. 'Whenever a vehicle comes into circulation,' he says, 'there are always teething troubles, such as toilets that don't work. A somewhat worse thing that came to light after a relatively short time was that the ICE coach started to vibrate or hum . . . most of all in the dining car. This led to the cups rattling and the glasses wandering from the table. This wasn't very nice. But the question that weighed on people's minds at the time was about comfort and luxury, not safety.'

The diagnosis was simple: the wheels had warped after a short time in service, which caused the rattle and rumble. This problem was due to the way the track had been constructed. 'It was packed much harder than usual.' says Kühnel. 'This led to more strain on the monobloc wheels, and that's why they became misshapen while moving. This in turn produced the vibrations.' It would have cost too much to alter the hundreds of miles of new track so they had to change the type of wheels. 'Because the track was stiffer than it should have been,' says Markus Hecht, they needed a softer wheel 'to provide a cushioning device very close to the contact point of wheel and rail.' The type of wheel they chose was 'a rubber-cushioned wheel. You have a wheel rim, then rubber blocks and the hub of the wheel and there is a very small movement between the rim and the hub. They are in a dimension of a tenth of a millimetre but thanks to this movement alone, there is a reduction of vibration amplitude and also energy absorption by the rubber element,' which, as Kühnel says, 'was previously absorbed by the line'.

'The wheels that were chosen had been a proven design for tram-cars for decades,' says Hecht. They 'were modified for high-speed operation.' Unfortunately 'they were developed under a very great time pressure.' As a result, Hecht admits, 'Not enough time was spent on durability calculation and also on how to operate and maintain these wheels.' The pressure was greater because DB was having to maintain the alternative monobloc wheels frequently, while 'the passengers were complaining because of the low-frequency vibrations inside the ICE'.

Unfortunately, says Kühnel, the new type of wheels had only been used on slower, orthodox trains and were not adequately tested on the ICE trains. This worried the DB engineers and those from the train builders. But the company was in a hurry. As Kühnel says, 'DB was very late in introducing the ICE . . . so it was, above all, a matter of prestige. At all costs they wanted to prevent the train from continuing to suffer this poor image.' And, for a time, the new wheels seemed to have provided a solution.

The first clue that something was wrong came from an unlikely source: the company running the tramways in Hanover, which had used these so-called 'duobloc' wheels since the early 1970s for the same reason as the DB: they gave a better ride. The tram company checked the wheels every six weeks. 'In former times,' says Dirk Sarnes, 'we checked only the wheel and we saw how many millimetres we had in the profile, but nowadays we check this by ultrasonic. This way we can to look into the metal of the wheel and see little crevices before they develop into cracks.'

'In the summer of 1997 we had two cracks, which means that this metal wheel was broken. We had a big problem because the tram was out of action so we looked for solutions.' In the summer of 1997 they asked the German equivalent of the Health and Safety Executive to help. The first symptom 'was a rhythmic noise sounding like tock, tock, tock, after a short period the tram was immobile.'

'After we had the three first cracks,' Sarnes continues, 'we contacted the Deutsche Bahn. The company should have been alarmed, if only because the tramway ran at a maximum speed of 50kph, less than a quarter of that attained by the ICE.' Nevertheless, 'They told us they don't use wheel blocks, they only use these kind of wheels in the special restaurant car to reduce and soften the vibrations . . . They had no information about any problems with cracks and crevices, and therefore we developed a solution for ourselves and we were alone in the whole world.'

The tramway engineers 'examined the old wheels and by ultrasonic metering they found very small crevices'. The crucial change to strengthen the wheel was small: 'At the beginning the wheels had a dimension of sixty millimetres and the engineers advised us not to run down the wheels thinner than twenty-three millimetres' – as opposed to twenty millimetres, the thickness of a matchstick – 'and now we don't have any problems . . . When we had our solution we informed the other companies. Before Eschede, nobody was interested but afterwards everybody was interested' – and duly went away to check their own wheels.

DB should have reacted to the warning, for it had other sources of information. 'Because the wheels are crucial to safety,' says Hecht, they 'were inspected visually every day by maintenance personnel and also with measuring equipment. The wheel profile, the roundness or shape of the wheel, and sometimes also the surface cracks were inspected . . . But the method that was used was not very effective. Each wheel has some non-critical cracks and the ultrasonic device could not distinguish between the critical and non-critical defects. A crack inside the rim could not be detected with this ultrasonic device.' Although 'There was no ultrasonic inspection method available that could have detected the failure that occurred, there was other information mainly that the wheel was out of shape. That was a strong hint that something was wrong.'

Even the train crews realized that something was not as it should have been. 'The ICE trains are equipped with on board monitoring systems. Part of the equipment makes diagnoses directly to this system but also the train crew can feed into it observations they have made. Stable running is an observation which is not automatically recorded but must be fed in manually. The train crew fed in this information several times but it was regarded as a comfort problem and was delayed for action until there was more time to replace the wheel set.'

Nevertheless, on eight separate occasions the train crew warned that something was wrong with the train's suspension. In addition, says Hecht, 'Deutsche Bahn had a regulation which said that if the wheel is misshapen more than 0.6mm it should be replaced, and six times that distinctive wheel was recorded to be more misshapen than this limit. This information was neglected because the maintenance people thought it was a comfort-element limit and not a safety-element limit.'

After the crash the DB had to go for the expensive solution they had refused to adopt in the beginning, As well as replacing the wheels on the hundred or so ICE sets, they renewed the track and softened the pads between the sleepers and the rails to improve the ride.

13
The Politics of Safety

The law could require that we all drive new Volvos and have them serviced every fortnight. It would save hundreds of lives every year. But at what financial cost?

Head of Safety at Railtrack

The origins of the often hysterical arguments over rail safety – or, rather, its supposed lack of safety – that have swept Britain in the last dozen years of the twentieth century date back to the 1960s. Stanley Hall says that the more businesslike approach to BR introduced by Dr Beeching in the 1960s 'had only one victim – safety. Business managers failed to listen to experienced operators, whom they regarded as hidebound traditionalists unwilling to change, which resulted in several unsatisfactory and potentially unsafe track remodelling and resignalling schemes. There was a lack of firm purpose and direction in the planning of safety improvements' – a gap that widened a hundredfold after privatization.

Peter Rayner* came across one particular case in which safety was of secondary importance to profitability: a derailment was caused when the alternator from an electric locomotive weighing over a ton dropped on to the track. The reason: it had come loose, which had not been noticed because the interval between inspections had been greatly extended. 'In pursuit of business goals to drive InterCity into profit in response to government spending targets,' he wrote, 'costs had to be reduced. Engineering standards were to play second fiddle to bottom line accountability.' When he raised the point, a young engineer muttered about 'cost-effective maintenance'.

*In the 1980s his insistence on the maintenance of proper safety standards made him so unpopular with senior management that he was sidelined and, effectively, sacked.

But in the late 1980s safety came to the forefront. As a result of a number of highly publicized accidents like the sinking of the *Herald of Free Enterprise* in 1987 and a fire the same year at King's Cross underground station, which killed thirty-two people, combined with the increasing effects of the Health and Safety Act 1974, BR belatedly created a safety directorate. At much the same time the Railway Inspectorate was absorbed into the Health and Safety Executive and lost its political – though not its technical – independence. The move was made on the excuse that there weren't enough retired officers from the Royal Engineers to man the Inspectorate but was in fact made for the sake of administrative tidiness and the desire to modernize a 150-year-old body. One unfortunate result, as Hall notes, is 'of a publicly funded body (the HSE) prosecuting another such publicly funded body (BR) in the publicly funded courts, and being fined large sums of public money, which could better be spent on safety projects'.

All the time the pressure on the system, and above all on the drivers and the other railwaymen operating it, was building up as traffic and speeds increased. This was shown most clearly in the 1986 report on SPAD, Signals Passed at Danger – always a reliable measure of the pressure on drivers – in which Major Freddy Rose, the last of a long and distinguished line of totally independent chief inspectors, noted that the number of signals passed at danger was continuing to rise. This was not because the drivers were driving dangerously. In a study conducted with Peter Semmens, Professor Trevor Kletz worked out that the statistical chance of a driver passing a signal at danger was roughly a tenth of the level expected in a non-railway activity. 'On the other hand,' wrote Semmens, 'if traffic builds up as it did on Network South East in the late 1980s, drivers encounter far more signals at caution or danger, particularly in the rush hour. This increases the overall risk of SPAD and one can see how the need to cancel the Automatic Warning System each time might subconsciously become an automatic reaction to the hooter, rather than to check the aspect of the signal ahead.'

But help for hard-pressed drivers appeared to be at hand. In 1988 a study group of BR executives saw the Swedish ATP system in action. Given the atmosphere after the fire at King's Cross, the BR board decided to adopt the system, proposing to introduce it from 1992. Then on 12 December that year came the Clapham train crash on one of the busiest stretches of line into London. A crowded commuter train heading for Waterloo and travelling at around 50mph smashed into another train, veered to the right and hit another oncoming train in a rare three-train collision, leaving thirty-five dead and up to four hundred injured. A single wire in a relay room had made a false contact, causing a signal to show clear when there was a train on the block.

There have since been at least three other instances where miswired signals, like those at Clapham, gave a green or yellow light instead of a red one, though luckily without fatal consequences. In 1938 there was a serious accident on the District Line on London's Underground after a circuit-breaker had been wrongly wired.

The impact of the Clapham disaster was enormous because so few passengers had been killed in previous years. From 1970 to 1988 only ninety-two passengers had been killed on Britain's railways, an average of just five a year, which was considerably less than the weekly toll on Britain's roads. The Transport Minister at the time was Paul Channon, who panicked and ordered not a normal inquiry but a judicial one under a distinguished barrister, Anthony Hidden QC, who was innocent of any knowledge of the rail industry. While the inquiry was under way Hidden was also asked to examine the crash at Purley (in which five people died when a driver had ignored two yellow lights). His report confirmed that a single strand of live wire had been loose and able to touch nearby equipment thus short-circuiting a vital signal. The mistake had been made by an electrician who was overtired after working too-long hours and was unsupervised because his superior was in a similar condition – a constant problem in an industry which, since 1945, has never managed to recruit and keep enough skilled technicians.

Over the past twenty years the British, both the public and politicians, have overreacted to transport disasters with a number of lengthy and elaborate public inquiries into specific accidents. The system of judicial inquiries had been set up in 1871 but in recent years has been used with increasing frequency. The inquiry into the Hixon level crossing accident in January 1968 was only the second that had ever taken place, but both the fire at King's Cross and the accident at Clapham a year later were accorded a judicial inquiry, instead of being dealt with perfectly adequately by the Railway Inspectorate as had happened in the past with even more serious accidents.

'Following the Clapham inquiry,' says Stanley Hall, 'which lasted for sixty-five days, Hidden made a large number of recommendations, almost a hundred. Many of them were recommendations of procedures but there was one major recommendation that concerned the introduction of Automatic Train Protection . . . Now it was a big political issue and the secretary of state at the time said that the money would be found to apply Automatic Train Protection throughout the railway system. What he didn't know then was how difficult it might be. He merely made his broad statement that the money would be found but he didn't say how it would be found, who would pay it. He merely said it would be found.'

The ATP system, writes Hall, works like AWS:

The train picks up messages by induction from equipment laid between the lines by means of an antenna which is mounted under the train. These messages tell the driver that he needs to slow down or stop. However, the ATP system then goes on to check that the driver is actually reducing speed to the required extent, and that is the essential function which is absent from AWS. If the ATP system finds that the driver is failing to reduce speed it will jog his elbow by giving a short visual and audible warning. If that is unheeded by the driver, ATP will apply the brakes in time to stop safely.

'The British Railways Board set to with a will,' he says, 'and they gave contracts to two signalling companies for two trial sites, Paddington to Bristol and the Chiltern line from Marylebone. As these trials developed it began to be appreciated that there were significant technical problems in applying this computer-generated system to all the driving cabs in use on Britain's railways, of which there are many hundreds of different types, many of them with very rudimentary mechanical operation systems dating back forty years, and they were quite unsuitable for applying a modern computer system. You would have had to redesign and re-equip the whole cab and the whole system.

'They began to realize that the costs of doing this would be enormous and, at the same time, because the railways were covering safety in other directions, the justification in the terms of saving lives was beginning to be questioned. When it was looked into, it was appreciated that the potential life-saving based on the previous twenty years of applying ATP throughout the British railways was at the rate of about one a year. The costs were approaching a billion pounds, and the cost-effectiveness of ATP was questioned in those terms of a billion pounds versus one life a year saved.

The only thing that worried people was what if there was a big accident one day with multiple fatalities, as happened in 1999 at Ladbroke Grove, for example, when thirty-one people were killed. That distorts the statistics. But over a thirty-year period it only alters them from one fatality a year to three a year, so still the figures don't add up. By 1993 the British Railways board and the Railway Inspectorate were beginning to question the economics and the sheer technical feasibility of applying an ATP system nationwide and they suggested to the Health and Safety Executive and through them to the Department of Transport that the automatic train protection system as it stood at the present time wasn't cost-effective and really wasn't technically possible in its present form.'

What was even more unreasonably ambitious was Recommendation 46, which stated that ATP 'should be implemented within five years'. As Hall points out, 'Bearing in mind that the development of AWS, a much simpler system, took eight years and its installation on BR another thirty, it was absurdly unrealistic to suggest that ATP could be fully implemented within five, even if the money had been found which was unlikely.' Inevitably the idea of installing ATP was shelved by Channon's successors.

But Clapham left an uncomfortable legacy. This included not only the habit of overreacting to accidents, and a steep increase in the cost, complication and time taken to carry out signalling maintenance work because of increased precautions but also what Hall calls 'a rather unpleasant cult of looking for a scapegoat after an accident, as though that were more important than finding the cause'. This aspect of the Clapham aftermath was evident in the prosecution – persecution? – of the driver involved in the accident at Purley, which set an unfortunate precedent in which retribution came before analysis.

Overall the results show the inadequacy of politically inspired inquiries. To take another example, the report of the inquiry into the King's Cross fire made 157 recommendations. As Peter Semmens points out, they were 'rated into five different categories of importance, but, although there had been a dialogue on the subject with London Underground, it is not clear whether the classification was based on any sort of cost-effectiveness analysis, or an assessment of the speed at which they could be introduced.

'In the wake of these two accidents a widespread "over the top" attitude developed on safety matters. The concern about fire on the London Underground almost reached the point at which every item of machinery was expected to operate without lubrication, as any oil or grease was inflammable and so could start a fire.' As a result stations were closed more frequently than was sensible. This nearly led to disaster after seven trains were trapped on the Central Line in February 1991 when thousands of passengers had to be led to safety and seventy people had to be taken to hospital with heat exhaustion.

Then in the mid-1990s the atmosphere – and the reality – surrounding rail safety grew even more confused and unsatisfactory as a result of rail privatization, when British Rail was broken up into over a hundred operating companies in the biggest culture shock ever experienced by a major rail system.

In itself, privatization, or continuing private ownership of rail systems, need not necessarily lead to safety problems. Even the rigorous Rayner is prepared to accept that merely transforming railways into privately owned commercial enterprises is not itself bad for safety. 'There's always going to be a balance between the need to make profit and the need to be safe. I think that airlines meet that very well, and some private railways in various parts of the world. In Switzerland, for example, there's a very safety-conscious railway so I don't think privatization itself prohibits safety.'

The same was true in Japan where the privatization carried out in 1987 also came as a considerable culture shock. 'At that time,' says Masaki Ogata, 'all employees had to change their mindset. According to the privatization they began working for the company. Before the company was divided from the former National Japanese Railways they were working for the nation but I think in some senses their objective is a little bit ambiguous.'

Nevertheless, privatization has actually had a positive effect on railway culture. As Masaki Ogata says, the company's philosophy has moved 'from pursuit of responsibility to finding out the real cause of the accident, and our employees generally believe in that. We aim to find out the real cause of the accident and then the same type of accident never happens again. Every employee is most co-operative because they understand why we search for the real cause. I think this is a dramatic change from the Japanese National Railways era to the new East Japan Railways era'.

It has greatly improved the atmosphere of the industry, as has a change in corporate culture. 'In the Japanese National Railway era, before the establishment of our company, orders always came down from the top, from headquarters, and they just reached out to the branches. Then each branch sent orders concerning the accident to each depot or station. Today each employee tries to overcome the accident. They think about it, debate among themselves and try to find out the solution against accident for themselves.'

Since early 2000 there has been a parallel development in Britain: drivers will soon be able to use a confidential and independent reporting system developed in Scotland – similar to that used for some time by airline pilots – when they are disturbed by an incident.

In the United States, progress is described by Larry Mann, who, as a lawyer, has been involved in all major American legislation for thirty years: 'In the first areas of Congressional involvement in the early 1900s, Congress adopted laws covering specific items of a train, the locomotive and safety appliances – a very small area of coverage – and until 1970 the railroads were basically self-regulated. A series of accidents occurred in the late fifties and early sixties, train explosions, trains derailing, collisions, which made Congress realize self-regulation was not working. So Congress adopted the Federal Railroad Safety Act of 1970, which gave jurisdiction to the federal government over all areas of railroad safety. Since then the federal government has progressively adopted regulations and it's currently undergoing revisions. Safety has certainly been improved in the rail industry since the late sixties as a result of the Federal Railroad Safety Act.

'The rail industry has opposed virtually every proposal in Congress for adoption of a statute governing rail safety, including the Federal Railroad Safety Act of 1970. However, the Act passed Congress unanimously. It was a truly bipartisan piece of legislation, and in subsequent years where rail workers sought legislative improvements, the rail industry opposed it. At present there's a different philosophy involved. There is a new programme which has been adopted by the Federal Railroad Administration, known as the rail safety advisory committee, comprised of all of the interest groups in rail safety and they negotiate rail safety regulations. If that group can agree on a certain framework for a regulation then the Federal Railroad Administration adopts it as part of their enforcement procedures.'

Unfortunately, the sort of industrial co-operation under the benevolent eye of the government now seen in the United States is far removed from the bickering that seems inevitable after every serious accident in Britain, if only because of the fragmented nature of the privatized railway system. Of course, there is no theoretical reason why some such bipartisan approach as exists in the US should not have been hammered out. In theory, notes Stanley Hall, 'One of the prime concerns in the privatization process was the maintenance of a high standard of operational safety in a fragmented railway system.' The Railway Inspectorate duly produced a report called *Ensuring Safety on Britain's Railway* which, in Hall's words, proposed 'a complex, bureaucratic but effective system of safety cases, in which each train operator and every other organization concerned had to produce a safety case setting out how all risks were to be managed safely. Railtrack was charged with approving these safety cases. Railtrack's own safety case was approved by the Inspectorate.'

Nevertheless privatization has had a disastrous effect on British perceptions of the safety of their railway system, even though rail travel is, if anything, safer than ever before. But it is useless repeating this fact in the face of the way that there appears to be – indeed is – no single authority or organization to blame for a disaster, no single figure facing the television cameras and taking responsibility, as there was in the days of British Rail. This is why Railtrack, which owns the whole rail infrastructure and is by far the biggest railway company, takes all the flak for any disaster, even if – as at Southall – it is not to blame.

Under a unified system, of course, it is easy to pinpoint blame. Stalin had incompetent railway managers shot but, then, that was his habit with every type of person, innocent or guilty. Indian Railways sack senior managers – in 1997 the general managers of two major regions, the South Eastern Railway and the Central Railway, were both summarily dismissed after serious accidents. But in post-privatization Britain, responsibility is too diffuse for blame to be apportioned satisfactorily.

Peter Rayner is not alone in believing that 'Privatization was dogma-driven. It was something that the Conservative government under John Major wanted to do before leaving government and they did it, unfortunately on a hurried time scale. I have to say I wouldn't have objected to privatization had it been geographically logical, in which everybody is responsible for everything within a specific area, but it was done in a way that makes safety unworkable.

'I think where the railway has failed is that, unlike the motor car industry, which boasts of its safety features, since privatization they have not spent money on safety. Safety isn't the thing to spend money on. The thing to spend money on is saying have a nice day and you come back now, and that is where the emphasis has been wrong. I don't think privatization prohibits safety. I think the way *this* railway was privatized makes it almost impossible to manage it because it is geographically illogical, it's fragmented, and there are no vertical chains of command.

'If you go back to the previous system, there was one vertical hierarchical chain of command. Everybody had a precise place within that, and once it was established that, for example, it wasn't vandalism or terrorism that had caused an accident then the railway system would accept responsibility. Today you have eight or nine different organizations involved in an accident: one company owning the stock, another one running the trains, another one running the other train, vehicles owned by different people, maintenance and track owned by different people. It means that after an accident everybody consults a lawyer to ensure that they aren't disclosing too many of their own skeletons.

'The present system means that the track is owned by Railtrack. They hire contractors to maintain it. Those contractors frequently have sub-contractors and each of those organizations has to have its own safety case. Upon that infrastructure different trains are run by different people and these systems don't all respond to the same chain of command. It means that when something goes wrong you have trouble in getting a consensus. You also have trouble recovering from accidents or from even minor delays because there isn't the will to help one another.' Rayner notes that in 1991 Major Freddy Rose, then the Chief Inspecting Officer for Railways said, quite rightly, that 'The railway gets safer and each incident enables us to improve still further. These principles are now gone and each small piece of the railway endeavours not to share its problems for that is seen today as washing your dirty linen in front of your competitors, or worse still your shareholders!

'There are parallels,' he continued. 'When railways first started, different companies were set up and they competed with each other. The railways also started to have accidents, which meant regulations were needed. The then government brought in Her Majesty's inspecting officers of railways, who exist today in a different form under the HSE. They were needed to ensure that standards were met. The railways then became the national system and, of course, the inspecting officers and the nationalized railways worked together. The inspecting officers never had to be proactive because the railway was its own safety regulator. They were merely the referee. What has happened since privatization is that the railway has been unable to regulate itself properly. It's been at odds with itself, as a consequence of which the inspecting officers have had to issue instructions. Now I would argue that once you kick the ball you are not the referee, so the system has come into disrepute and it has to be put right. You have to put back a strict regulatory discipline.'

Under a state system, he argues, 'The government, whether it be Labour or Conservative, insisted that we identified how we spent the money we'd got and showed that we were either using it for real investment, that is new equipment, or we were using it to maintain existing equipment, and on signalling installations or on track, and we were obliged to be specific. The problem today is that Railtrack as a private company will say correctly that they have spent millions and millions of pounds in investment, but it isn't easy to identify whether they're spending it on track and signalling or on building new marble halls to sell pizzas and newspapers.'

Every aspect of the new system showed its worst side after the crash at Southall a few miles west of Paddington, at 1.19pm on 17 September 1997 when a packed InterCity train from Swansea to Paddington, operated by Great Western Trains, went straight past a signal at danger and slammed into a freight train. There were seven dead and 160 injured, even though the emergency services were on hand within half an hour of the impact. The first two coaches of the train had 'crumpled like tin foil'. The inquiry by the HSE learned that the track had recently been upgraded during the construction of the Heathrow Express line. This included remodelling junctions, improving the colour-light signalling and new high-voltage electrical installations.

'Responsibility for what happened at Southall stemmed directly from the way in which the railway was privatized,' says Peter Rayner flatly. 'The accident occurred because different people put different interpretations on what were previously clear-cut understandings and rules. It drifted into that situation as a result of privatization. I blame the previous government. The present government inherited the legislation privatizing the railways. Until they can put another Bill through Parliament they're stuck with it. All they can do is regulate it more stringently than it was before.'

The fragmentation impinged even on the priorities accorded to different types of trains running on the same tracks. Peter Rayner explains: 'The previous system of train regulation was based upon speeds of trains and numbers. Class one trains were express trains, class two trains were slow trains, class three trains were the express parcels trains, and so down through the line. These trains were regulated one with another so that you didn't delay the fastest trains. That system was changed under privatization, probably for financial reasons, to try to devise a system of penalties and a system of how people could all feel that they were getting a fair crack of the whip. I believe that increased the chances of collision opportunities. It was changed without much thought, I suspect because it was seen that everybody was commercially equal, and it was done for the wrong reasons.'

The whole penalty regime introduced an undesirable free-for-all. 'Penalties are paid to Railtrack if operators don't run trains or if their trains are presented late, and likewise Railtrack pays money to train operators if they delay trains. That system doesn't make for co-operation, doesn't make for common-sense decisions, doesn't make for saying, "Well, we'll cancel this train here and put all these people on that train, and that'll be one less train to go through the section". So the new system doesn't allow the best balance overall . . . We're back to the fact that flawed regulation and a badly operating railway means more red lights. The more red lights there are the more opportunity you have of passing one of them at danger, and therefore one should be looking not at signals passed at danger but at collision opportunities.'

In Rayner's opinion, privatization also led to the repeated violation of recommendation 50 of the Hidden inquiry, 'which said that commercial considerations should not be allowed to compromise safety, the desire to improve service should not be at the expense of safety'. Clearly, within the train-operating company the balance had been upset. 'I think,' he says, that 'there was a desire within Great Western Trains to run as many trains as they could and to get as much money as they could and that's quite a laudable thing to be doing, but to be doing it with the automatic warning systems – that is, a very critical piece of safety equipment – not working was, in my view, dangerous and incorrect. The fact that they had done it on more than one occasion was because they chose to interpret the rules in a way that permitted them to go backwards and forwards all day until the train went upon a maintenance shed.'

The InterCity 125 was equipped with a standard AWS system and also carried an experimental ATP system. Unfortunately it emerged that the ATP had been turned off and the AWS wasn't working. It had failed the previous day at Oxford, but its failure had not been adequately reported, so the train remained in service. But there were two other elements in that particular service: first, the AWS was working on the locomotive at the back of the HST train, though not on the one at the front, which was controlling the train. Turning it round at Swansea to ensure that the AWS system was working would have lost at least ten minutes at a time when the punctuality of trains was under the spotlight. The second element reinforced the power of the spotlight, for although the train itself was not special its passengers were: it was filled with VIPs and journalists returning from a major political occasion in Cardiff.

The pressure naturally told on the train's driver. Rayner says, 'He was presented with the train at Cardiff station with quite important people getting on it, and some of his own managers. It was an important day in Wales and I don't think it occurred to him that he could refuse. I believe that under BR there wouldn't have been any argument about it, he would not have taken that train and I don't think the previous driver would have brought it from Swansea, I find it amazing that he did because it was an extremely dangerous and foolish thing to do. If there is any criticism of Harrison [the driver] it is that he was persuaded because he believed it was now the norm to do something that was fundamentally unsafe.

'The reason the train wasn't turned at Swansea,' says Rayner, 'again comes back to the fragmented nature of the railway, that you would need to get permission from Railtrack to go over a piece of track that you wouldn't normally use to turn the train. It would require interfaces between different organizations whereas previously it would have just been under the authority of one person in Swansea who would have simply said, "Turn it the other way round before it goes back to London. If it's twenty minutes late going back so be it".'

Under BR, he says flatly, 'The train would not have been running at 125mph with its AWS not operative. I think it happened because at that point the signalling system changed. Driver Harrison, who had been concentrating without the benefit of signals at eye level, was suddenly faced with two that are high overhead. Those two signals were the first two that were less than perfectly sited. It was also an unusual signalling move that was made because it was with a freight train. Again you always have to have an innocent train for the accident to happen. Things came together. The only thing that really can be laid at the door of privatization is the fact that the automatic warning system wasn't working.'

Rayner also points out that 'Although the basic training for drivers has not changed since privatization, I think it was surprising to all of us about Southall that there was no desire by Great Western Trains to train their drivers in use of ATP. ATP was not considered one of the driver's competences: the evidence given to the inquiry made it clear that until the accident they weren't enthusiastic about learning automatic train protection.'

This attitude provides a marked contrast with the situation post-privatization in Japan. First, says Masaki Ogata, 'The typical employee spends one year at the station and he studies fundamental operations. After one year he moves to guard at the depot and studies what to do as a guard for one or two years. Then he moves to a driver's depot. He has experience of a station and he has experience as a guard so he's already a professional employee of our company. Before he becomes a professional driver he needs a licence, and after he gets his licence he goes to many depots and begins a real driver's life. But these new drivers need more knowledge and technique to drive each train and he has to learn everything needed for driving in each section, in each train. After he begins the life of a driver at each depot, on the train, he comes back to the regional instruction centre to refresh his knowledge and technique. We have on-the-job training and special training at the regional training centre, and sometimes at the central training institute.' And the final result? 'His attitude is towards punctuality, this is the first priority, I think, and also he has a pride in his profession. He is our company's man and he's a driver, and he carries, for example, three thousand passengers in his train. Such things make him proud of his work. So, first, punctuality and, second, pride.'

The perversity of the new British rail system was also demonstrated in the aftermath of the Southall crash. A full inquiry was ordered but could not start work until a decision had been made as to whether any person or company should be prosecuted for the accident. It was only in late 1999, two years after the accident, that the inquiry could begin, after the operators had been tried. In July that year Great Western Trains had been fined the record, but in fact meaninglessly small, sum of £1.5 million with the warning that 'Those who travel on high-speed trains are entitled to expect the highest standards of care.' GWT was charged with negligence because it had knowingly permitted the train to continue in service with the ATP system inoperative and the AWS isolated. 'It was aware of the risks but did nothing.'

When the report of the inquiry was published, in March 2000, it confirmed everything that had previously been said about the accident. But, as summarized by the magazine *Modern Railways* (April 2000), it also rubbed in the sheer number of faults and inadequacies in the present system. Yes, said the chairman, Professor John Uff QC, the primary cause of the accident had indeed been the failure of Harrison, the driver of the HST, to react to two yellow lights. But there had been other causes, including 'the failure of GWT's maintenance system to identify and repair an AWS fault, the failure of GWT to react to the isolation of the AWS, the failure of Railtrack to put in place rules to prevent normal running with AWS isolated, and the failure of GWT to manage the ATP pilot scheme to ensure equipment was switched on.'

The driver 'had not previously driven an HST without AWS operational – little attention had been given to the consequences of doing so and no GWT driver had received any instruction or training in doing so'. And why was the ATP system not switched on? Simply because Harrison was not 'currently qualified to drive with ATP'. Sermons might have been preached on the contrast with GWT's predecessor, the eternally safety-conscious Great Western Railway, God's Wonderful Railway.

If journalists had been responsible for throwing a powerful spotlight on to the Southall disaster, they and the police undoubtedly colluded to make the accident on the same line at Ladbroke Grove, only a mile from Paddington, on 5 October 1999 seem even worse than it was. The crash occurred just after 8am at the height of the morning rush hour when a local train to Bedwyn in Berkshire on a service run by Thames Trains collided with an express from Cheltenham Spa operated by Great Western, the same train-operating company involved in the Southall disaster two years earlier. The Thames DMU had been routed on to a bi-directional central relief line, installed as part of the 1992–93 modernization scheme for the approaches to Paddington, and was due to cross on to the fast down line after the express had passed. However the DMU passed signal 109 while it was at danger and accelerated to 45mph before running through the points on to the fast line at the spot where the dozen or so lines leading out of Paddington narrow down to the four-track layout normal on a major main line between stations. The effects of the crash were intensified because the combined speed of the two trains was over 100mph and because the diesel from both trains' fuel tanks exploded.

Vic Coleman, head of the Railway Inspectorate, described the crash as 'Wholly unprecedented . . . everyone's worst nightmare . . . nobody had ever experienced anything worse.' The shock was intensified by the number of casualties and because so few people had been killed in railway accidents over the previous few years, despite the complications introduced by privatization (in the years 1991–97 there were only six fatal crashes, including Southall, involving only fifteen deaths during a period when the railway system carried seven billion passengers).

Immediately after the accident the British Transport Police let slip to journalists that they were afraid the death toll was in three figures rather than the thirty-one that proved to be the case. Their worries concentrated on carriage H of the express in which, they feared, dozens of people had been burned alive. When they finally got through to it they found that, in fact, only one person had been killed since the others had escaped, albeit with severe burns and trauma. Such exaggeration was not new: immediately after the collapse of the Tay Bridge it was rumoured that three hundred tickets had been sold to travellers on the doomed train – exactly four times the real figure. At Paddington, though, the overestimate was reinforced by some dubious journalistic tactics, including counting cars left for several days after the crash at stations along the route.

The crash led to a hysterical witch-hunt, led by the press against Railtrack, whose employees were treated as murderers because it was supposed that the inadequacy of the signalling system was the cause of the disaster. This ignores not only the other factors in the tragedy but also that the system involved had been installed in 1992–93, one of BR's last and proudest signalling achievements, and had been designed in part to ensure that trains could retain their cruising speed as close as possible to Paddington.

The structuring of the approach combined with the resignalling were described as 'an engineer's dream but a driver's nightmare', partly because of the complexity of the layout even after it had been reorganized. Typically the Thames train was travelling on a bi-directional relief line installed as part of the 1992 remodelling. It was further proof of the dangers inherent in not separating the tracks used by fast trains.

After the preliminary examination of the scene of the crash, attention concentrated on signal 109, which the driver had ignored. There had been allegedly eight cases of SPAD involving the signal in the six years before the crash, and railway experts recalled a 1986 disaster at Colwich in Cheshire, also involving an express train and a missed signal which had occurred because the driver had been confused by a new layout. At Paddington, tests showed that the overhead electric wiring installed after the resignalling to accommodate the electrified Heathrow Express service had also complicated the driver's view. Moreover, the driver of the Thames train might have been dangerously tired.

But there is another explanation for the accident: that the morning light shining in the driver's face caused him to misread the signal's colour. This is not as absurd as it sounds. In September 1997 a freight train operated by Conrail rushed past a red signal at Hummelstown, Pennsylvania, resulting in a crash when the guard of the train in front was killed. The driver and the guard of the train that passed the signal both believed that it was in 'approach medium' mode, that is, showing yellow over green.

The accident was severe. According to Russell Gober, of the NTSB, the train, headed by five locomotives, 'had stopped at Hummelstown. They were sitting there waiting for a signal when a train came in from behind them and struck them in the rear. The impact was somewhere in the neighbourhood of fifteen to twenty miles per hour and as a result we had derailed locomotives and equipment. During the derailment the cars right behind the locomotive turned over and the conductor [guard] on the train was lost in the wreckage, he had been on the leading locomotive and when he saw the train stopped ahead of him, he and the engineer both ran out the rear of the locomotive and tried to vacate the train. The engineer cleared and the conductor disappeared. However, next morning they found that the equipment had rolled over on him and he was deceased in the wreckage.'

The poor driver had lost his friend and workmate, the guard, and was afraid of being blamed. Fortunately for him, the investigators from the NTSB found, as Gober says, 'That he attempted to slow down for a signal which was a double red. When he got to the signal it was not displaying a red over red, it was displaying a signal that he perceived as a yellow over green, which would allow him to continue. But the signal was not wired up to display that and it was not displaying that whenever we tested it. Due to contamination of the lenses the signal indication was displaying a false signal, a phantom signal, that made the locomotive engineer think, after discussion with his conductor who was later killed, that it was a signal OK to abide by, and they did. After they observed what they perceived to be a signal which allowed them to proceed at thirty miles per hour, they had released the brakes on the train and the train was operating, the engineer under the assumption that the track was clear ahead of him and that he could go to the next signal.'

The investigators found that 'The signals were wired up correctly, but after the accident we did sight-and-signal observation testing. We tried to see how far we could see the signals and what colour the signals were that we were observing.' Then they repeated the route of the fatal run with groups of observers 'stationed on the front of the locomotive where we could see as a train crew would see. We took turns back and forth, sitting in the locomotive engineer's seat to see what he could see. As we approached the signal, before it had been touched, two days after the accident, about the same time of day with the sun shining into it as it had been when the collision occurred, the signal was not displaying the signal indication that it should have.'

When the sun was setting and shining 'directly into the light lenses,' says Gober, 'the lenses were fogged up with rust from a water leakage. It filtered out the display. As the sun reflected on it when we approached it closer and closer, it changed and you could see green and yellow in the signals.

'We found that on our second test in bright sunlight conditions, which were the same as the accident train experience, the signals were not displaying a signal that would be identified in the way it should have been. It should have been red over red but it was displaying mostly a dark signal or no signal at all. The parties of the investigation were on the locomotive and included Federal Railroad Administration, the Conrail representatives, the United Transportation union, the Brotherhood of Locomotive Engineers and myself with the Safety Board and we observed flashes of yellow and green in the signals, which might have been misinterpreted by someone. According to the engineer on the train that had the accident, he observed it as yellow over green. We could not identify a signal displayed as yellow over green but we saw yellow and green in the signals and it would be called a phantom signal.' The engineer had said 'that he and the conductor perceived the signal as a good signal and they complied with it and as a result of that they had a collision.'

Gober had 'never heard of it being exactly like this before. However, I have seen signals that were out of focus and I've seen signals that were improperly wired, which would display an improper or phantom signal.'

Gober defines the phantom signal phenomenon as 'a signal which has a light source other than the light source intended for the signal, which causes it to display an indication or colour light that's different from what it is supposed to display.' After the investigation Conrail found that fifty-five signals, out of 9500, had water leaking into the system, which caused the lights to go out of focus. The insulation was improved on the lights.

After the Paddington crash the political reaction was much the same as it had been eleven years earlier after the Clapham crash. Once again a transport minister, in this case John Prescott, immediately said that the money would be found to introduce a full ATP system, although the railway industry had by then embarked upon a different system known as Train Protection and Warning System, or TPWS. This, as Stanley Hall describes it, 'will initiate a mandatory brake application if a red signal is approached at excessive speed or is actually passed. This is achieved by means of a speed trap and train-stop feature . . . Power is shut off and the brakes are applied automatically if the train is exceeding the safe limit. In other words, it provides an essential element in a safety system: the ability to override the driver's judgement without interfering with the normal operation of the train and thus risking the irritation and over-familiarity with the system which is a feature of some other systems.' It is always important that the driver should not feel that he has been reduced to a cypher, dependent on the system and unable to make any decisions of his own. TPWS is, of course, a cheaper system than ATP, with three-quarters of the benefits of automatic train protection, although that does not work at the sorts of speeds that are normal with modern high-speed trains. It is available now and could certainly be installed within five years, while ATP would probably take ten years to develop and another ten years to install.

Nevertheless, as Peter Rayner says, 'On the high-speed lines, when a high-speed line is resignalled and a new set of trains is introduced, as on the West Coast main line, for example, then it is reasonable to put in automatic train protection at the same time because you can equip your trains in the manufacturer's workshops. By all means let's have automatic train protection on those lines provided we can devise a workable, affordable system.'

Fortunately there was one major contrast in the aftermath of the disasters between Paddington and Clapham, as Michael Jones-Lee points out. Post-Paddington, 'There are journalists who are taking a more circumspect position with regard to these issues, asking questions about whether or not one should install safety-improvement schemes regardless of cost, asking whether there are ultimately trade-offs between rail safety and road safety so I think that there are signs that those concerned are now somewhat better educated, perhaps reacting in a somewhat more balanced way.'

In Japan it took only a relatively small accident to hasten the speedy introduction of an expensive safety system. The accident happened in 1988 – not, significantly, on the high-speed network – at Higashi Nikano station in Tokyo when a driver – the only fatal casualty of the crash – missed a red light, possibly because he was listening to a radio in his cab, and hit the train in front, which was standing at the station. The accident happened a year after privatization. 'At the time,' says Masaki Ogata, 'we thought it a very serious accident and it occurred in the central business district of Tokyo. After that accident we just decided to take many counter-measures against such accident.' The reason was simplicity itself: 'In Japan everybody believe that railways is a very safe transportation mode and we think so too. We employees of East Japan Railway Company must respond to those high expectations. Against such high expectations people became worried about the safety of the railway and that accident changed our policy.'

'Our company was established on 1 April 1987.' The Japanese National Railways system had already installed an 'automatic train-stop system for train control but soon after our company was established we wanted to increase safety on our lines. Just before the Higashi Nikano accident we had already decided that we were going to introduce a new automatic train-stop system, the ATSP.' After the Higashi Nikano accident, 'We decided to introduce ATSP much faster. We rushed to develop the ATSP, and also we established the safety research centre, a safety office at each branch and a regional training centre.'

The train involved in the Higashi Nikano accident had the Automatic Stop System. This sounded an alarm in the cab as a red signal but if the driver pushed a response button within five seconds the train could continue. This was what the crash driver did. 'Today,' says Ogata, 'we have introduced the ATSP system, which cost us $800 million (£500 million). P stands for pattern; according to the ATSP system, we have a pattern on the cab and the train operation follows that pattern. If the driver for example hits a pattern then the service brake automatically applies and the train reduces speed. The driver cannot exceed the speed of the pattern so the train automatically stops in front of the red signal with no possibility of repeal by the driver.' To operate the system, 'We have a transponder on the ground and the train catches a signal from that transponder located and after the train receives that signal the train has to just follow the pattern set, even though driver would like to exceed that pattern speed the driver can't do that, the driver just, you know, always operates the train under the pattern speed.'

Obviously, as Ogata emphasizes, prevention is better than cure. 'To prevent the anticipated accident, we have to analyse our weak points, then we find out the way to make it much safer.' Equally obviously, there is no such thing as the perfectly safe mode of transport. One estimate done by Stanley Hall shows that only nineteen deaths would have been prevented over nearly thirty years if trains then equipped with AWS had had ATP.

The problem is simple. There are so few railway accidents that providing a single, hideously expensive solution to just one problem, SPAD, is not going to improve the figures significantly. As Andrew Evans, professor of transport safety at University College London, pointed out, in the *New Statesman* of 14 February 2000, the causes of rail crashes 'are very varied: as well as the much-discussed SPADs which led to the Southall and Ladbroke Grove disasters, serious accidents in recent years have resulted from over-speeding, rolling stock defects (broken axles, shedding parts), infrastructure failure (landslips, a collapsed bridge), broken or buckled rails, faulty signal installation, mistaken procedures after signal failures and even trains hitting cows on the line.'

His words could be illustrated by an accident at Cowden on a foggy day in February 1994 on the single line Uckfield branch in East Sussex, which was fitted with AWS. The driver failed to stop at a danger signal even though he had acknowledged the warning provided by AWS. There were no radio communications so nothing could have stopped the train colliding into another. Both trains were derailed and both drivers killed, as was the guilty train's guard, who, it was suggested, had been driving the train. Now, such an accident might have been prevented by the installation of the hideously expensive ATP, but also, much more cheaply, if the drivers had been equipped with mobile phones whose numbers were known to the controllers and signalmen on the line.

Underlying any discussion is the basic, brutal question of the worth of a human life; safety, like everything else, is a matter of priorities. In the United States, as Larry Mann explains, 'There is a Presidential executive order which mandates that any federal regulation that is adopted must meet a cost–benefit analysis and if the costs outweigh the benefits, it will not be adopted.' Through its joint rail safety advisory committee the rail industry 'has already undertaken that analysis and if they feel that it is too costly for the benefit they would not approve that proposal'. The strength of the system is that all parties of the industry, workers as well as operators, have jointly agreed the figures. In 1986, says Mann, 'The federal government issued a report analysing that very point and they set a figure of two million dollars for an individual life.' There are exceptions: 'If you cause the death of an engineer and there's tremendous pain and suffering prior to his death, that case may be worth more than a few million dollars, so you have to take it case by case on an individual basis on what the actual damages were. An instantaneous death, though, has been valued at two million dollars.'

Much the same bleak but essential arithmetic could be done here. Michael Jones-Lee spells out the figures. He is an expert in cost–benefit analysis, which 'aims to take account of the preferences and wishes of those members of the population who will be affected by a particular investment or regulatory decision and, in the case of safety, what one aims for is to get a measure of people's strength of preference'. Crudely, this is measured by 'the amount that he or she would be willing to pay for it.' The aim: 'to get at a measure of the overall total sum that a group of individuals would be prepared to pay for typically small improvements in their own individual safety, improvements which, taken over a large group, can be expected to prevent a given number of fatalities. For example, if 100,000 people were each be willing to pay £10 for a 1:100,000 reduction in their individual risk of death during the coming year, the overall value of that safety improvement would be 100,000 times ten, or a million, and because it's 100,000 people each enjoying a 1:100,000 reduction in risk, the safety improvement could be expected on average to prevent one fatal accident. Under that approach the value of preventing that fatality would be a million pounds, and that would be a reflection of people's preferences for safety.'

For road crashes the preference apparently adds up to £1 million per death. By contrast Jones-Lee and his colleagues 'found that the value of preventing an Underground fatality was some 20 to 50 per cent higher than the corresponding value for the prevention of a road fatality . . . yet to our surprise we found that the value for the prevention of a rail fatality was some 15 to 20 per cent lower than the corresponding roads figure' – though this research was tackled outside the hysterical periods generated by major rail crashes. 'There may be other reasons for having higher values, political considerations, wider social considerations, but if one focuses exclusively on the preferences of members of the public, justification for much higher rail values just isn't there.' It is a decisive argument against rushing to spend upwards of £1 billion to equip the whole of Britain's railway system with ATP.

Moreover, 'and greatly to our surprise, the majority of members of the public take the view that the loss of thirty lives in a single accident is no worse than, and indeed no better than, the loss of thirty lives in separate accidents'. This is true although 'The large-scale accident gets tremendous media attention whereas the single fatality accidents producing the same number of fatalities over a relatively short period, say on the roads, get virtually no media attention at all.' Indeed they found that media attention was not a reason for increased spending on safety.

So rare are crashes that the figures for a single one can affect policy. Had the fatality figure for the Paddington crash been as high as was at first feared, says Jones-Lee, that figure 'would have fed into future decisions about the installation of safety systems on trains. Those systems would have been predicted on that basis to have prevented many more fatalities than they are currently predicted to do, therefore the cost per fatality prevented would have been lower and for given values of fatality prevention it would be more likely that the safety systems would in fact be installed. In hard-nosed terms, the more corpses there are, the more effective is safety improvement, therefore the more likely it is to be undertaken.

'There's a rather powerful case for saying that at least in the first instance the road safety improvement would be far more deserving.' But it would be even better, perhaps to spend the money on improving the railway system and thus reduce road accidents by attracting more passengers to the infinitely safer railways. Of course, it would be popular to force Railtrack to use even more of its allegedly inflated profits on safety. But, says Jones-Lee, 'If Railtrack is forced to spend some of its profits on the installation of very expensive safety improvement systems they might react by putting up fares. I don't think the public would be happy with the kind of fare increases that would be necessary to cover the installation of, say, ATP, but again one might argue that Railtrack ought not to be allowed to raise fares to make up for the profits that are being taken from them for safety expenditure. My suspicion is that in a commercial world they would understandably cut back on other things that passengers want, like time-keeping, convenience and so on. The reality at the end of the day is that while it's tempting to suggest that they should be made to give up profits to spend on very costly safety systems, other disadvantages would flow from that, which, if our estimates of values of safety are correct, would on balance be detrimental.

'If motorists, for example, or other road transport operators were required to take the same sort of safety measures as it's being suggested Railtrack should, then you could, in principle, cut road deaths dramatically. If you required all drivers to have their cars checked every couple of months, to change tyres as soon as there was a little bit of wear, to impose speed limits of, say, fifty miles an hour on all roads and twenty miles an hour in urban areas, I don't doubt that road deaths would fall. But motorists wouldn't wear it, any more than I believe rail users would wear the fare increases that would almost certainly follow the installation of a system such as ATP.'

But however high the expenditure on ever more sophisticated safety systems there will still be accidents. As Stuart Matthews, chairman of the Flight Safety Foundation, put it: 'The aviation accident rate is like the bar in a limbo dance. It can go lower and lower, but it cannot touch the floor.' Precisely the same argument applies to the world's railways.

Bibliography

My detailed descriptions of individual accidents are taken from the following select handful of books:

Adams, Charles Francis, *Railroad Accidents* (Puttnam, New York, 1879)

Hall, Stanley, *Danger Signals – An Investigation into Modern Railway Accidents* (Ian Allan, Shepperton, 1987)

Hall, Stanley, *Hidden Dangers – Railway Safety in the Era of Privatization* (Ian Allan, Shepperton, 1999)

Kitchenside, Geoffrey, *Great Train Disasters* (Parragon, Bristol, 1997)

Rolt, L.T.C., *Red for Danger* (Sutton Publishing, Stroud, 1998)

Schneider, Ascanio, and Armin Mase, *Railway Accidents of Great Britain & Europe* (David & Charles, Newton Abbot, 1968)

Semmens, Peter, *Railway Disasters of the World* (Patrick Stephens, Yeovil, 1994)

The following works also proved useful:

Coleman, Terry, *The Railway Navvies* (Hutchinson, London, 1965)

Dickens, Charles, *The Letters of Charles Dickens*, Vol. III (Nonesuch edn, 1938)

Encyclopédie des chemins de fer et des machines à vapeur, Paris, 1844

Faith, Nicholas, *Mayday* (Boxtree, London, 1998)

Faith, Nicholas, *Black Box* (Boxtree, London, 1996)

Green, Philip, *Britain's Greatest Railway Mystery* (Context Books, Farnham 1978)

Hall, Stanley, *Railway Detectives, the 150-year Saga of the Railway Inspectorate* (Ian Allan, Shepperton, 1990)

Harrington, Ralph, 'The Railway Accident: Trains, Trauma and

Technological Crisis in 19th-century Britain', in *Traumatic Pasts: History and Trauma in the Modern Age* (eds. Mark Micale and Paul Lerner, Cambridge University Press, Cambridge, 2001)

Legg, Stuart, *The Railway Book* (Fourth Estate, London, 1988)

McKenna, Frank, *The Railway Workers* (Faber & Faber, London, 1980)

Nichols, Roy Franklin, *Franklin Pierce* (University of Philadelphia Press, Philadelphia, 1931)

Rayner, Peter, *On and Off the Rails* (Novelangle, Stratford-on-Avon, 1997)

Sandstrom, Gosta, *The History of Tunnelling* (London, 1963)

Schivelbusch, Wolfgang, *The Industrialization of Time and Space in the 19th Century* (Oxford University Press, Oxford, 1986)

Simmons, Jack, *The Victorian Railway* (Thames & Hudson, London, 1991)

Smith, David L., *Tales of the Glasgow & South Western Railway* (Context Books, Farnham 1977)

Tomalin, Clare, *The Invisible Woman* (Viking, London, 1990)

Index

Index